Girls on the Brink

Girls on the Brink

Helping Our Daughters Thrive in an Era of Increased
Anxiety, Depression, and Social Media

Donna Jackson Nakazawa

HARMONY

BOOKS • NEW YORK

Published in the United States by Harmony Books, an imprint of Random House, a division of Penguin Random House LLC, New York.
HarmonyBooks.com
RandomHouseBooks.com

Harmony Books is a registered trademark, and the Circle colophon is a trademark of Penguin Random House LLC.

Library of Congress Cataloging-in-Publication Data
Names: Nakazawa, Donna Jackson, author. Title: Girls on the brink / Donna Jackson Nakazawa. Description: First edition. | New York : Harmony Books, [2022] | Includes bibliographical references.
Identifiers: LCCN 2021054151 (print) | LCCN 2021054152 (ebook) | ISBN 9780593233078 (hardcover) | ISBN 9780593233085 (ebook)
Subjects: LCSH: Girls—Psychology. | Teenage girls—Psychology. | Daughters. | Parent and child.
Classification: LCC HQ777 .N35 2022 (print) | LCC HQ777 (ebook) | DDC 305.23082—dc23/eng/20211108
LC record available at https://lccn.loc.gov/2021054151
LC ebook record available at https://lccn.loc.gov/2021054152

ISBN 978-0-593-23307-8
Ebook ISBN 978-0-593-23308-5

Printed in the United States of America

Book design by Andrea Lau
Jacket design by Irene Ng
Jacket photograph by DEEPOL/plainpicture

10 9 8 7 6 5 4 3 2 1

First Edition

For my daughter, Claire, and my son, Christian, and for all girls and boys and their parents, mentors, and teachers, everywhere

Contents

INTRODUCTION   xi

PART ONE
Growing Up Female

CHAPTER ONE   Our Girls Are Not Okay—Why Are So Many of Our Daughters Struggling?   3

CHAPTER TWO   Is This a Toxic Era for Girls?—Yes, and It's Worse than You Thought   20

CHAPTER THREE   The Missing Years—We've Stolen Girls' Safe "In-Between Years"   36

PART TWO
The New Science of Why Our Girls Are Struggling

CHAPTER FOUR   Two Windows in Time When Early Stress Shapes a Child's Development   47

CHAPTER FIVE   The Power of Social Safety—Why Feeling Under Threat and Unsafe Affects Girls in Unique Ways   59

CHAPTER SIX   When the Pump Gets Primed—What Happens When Girls Are Stressed Out and Estrogen Hits the System?   74

CHAPTER SEVEN   Too Much Too Soon—The Impact of Early Puberty on Girls' Well-Being   86

CHAPTER EIGHT   How the Hazards of Growing Up Female in Our Society Shape Girls' Brains over Time   94

PART THREE
The Antidotes

CHAPTER NINE   The Building Blocks of Good Parent-Child
Connection and the Importance of Family
Resilience   117

ANTIDOTE 1
Get in Sync—Understand the Connections Between Your Stress,
Your Trauma, and What You Are Communicating to Your Child
at Every Age   119

ANTIDOTE 2
Observe Your Reactions in Parent-Child Interactions and Dial
Back on Evaluating Your Daughter   124

ANTIDOTE 3
When Your Daughter Turns to You, Make It a Good Experience
for Her   131

CHAPTER TEN   Make Her Home Her Safe Space   139

ANTIDOTE 4
When Hard Things Happen (and They Will), Be Prepared to Respond
in Healthy, Supportive Ways, Even When Your Daughter Shares
Hard-to-Hear Information   141

ANTIDOTE 5
Power Up on Joy (Especially) in Difficult Times   151

ANTIDOTE 6
Don't Solve All Her Problems for Her—Leave Room for
"a Little Wobble"   153

ANTIDOTE 7
Wonder Aloud Together to Help Build Resilience to Stress   158

ANTIDOTE 8
Go Slow on Development—Keep the Biological Brakes Engaged   162

ANTIDOTE 9
Create Routine, Ritual, and Structure—Including a Family Media Plan 166

CHAPTER ELEVEN Bring in What the Wider Community Can
                    Provide   174

ANTIDOTE 10
*Engage the Power of Benefactors, Mentors, and Avatars to
Help a Girl Feel She Matters*   177

ANTIDOTE 11
Help Her Find "a Sense of Something Bigger"   190

ANTIDOTE 12
*Take the Pressure Off Your Parent-Child Relationship and
Get Some Professional Help*   193

CHAPTER TWELVE Ready Her to Stand on Her Own   204

ANTIDOTE 13
Encourage a Sense of Mastery   205

ANTIDOTE 14
Help Her Develop a Voice of Resistance   209

ANTIDOTE 15
Have Her Write It Down to Break the Cycle of Negative Self-Talk   216

CONCLUSION   224

APPENDIX A: Growing Up Female, by the Numbers   233

APPENDIX B: Resources and Further Reading   239

APPENDIX C: The Antidotes at a Glance   243

ACKNOWLEDGMENTS   245

NOTES   249

INDEX   289

INTRODUCTION

A GOOD LITMUS TEST for the health of any society is how well it treats its girls and how well its girls are faring. When we look at the mental health of American girls today, one thing becomes clear: We as a society are failing pretty miserably. Depression has long been more prevalent in girls than in boys, but rates of depression in girls have now reached epidemic proportions. One out of four adolescent girls reports suffering from symptoms of major depression compared with fewer than one in ten boys. Girls and young women are twice as likely as boys and young men to suffer from anxiety. In 2021, the Centers for Disease Control and Prevention reported that suicide attempts had recently increased 51 percent among girls compared with 4 percent among boys. These statistics cannot be explained by higher rates of awareness or diagnosis. They are real, and they are scary to every parent of every daughter and to anyone who cares about young women.

Even as rates of depression and anxiety in girls rise, the reasons behind this downturn in adolescent female health have been difficult to comprehend. Why does this disparity between girls' and boys' mental health emerge as girls enter puberty? And why is this trend worsening now? In the pages to come, I follow the discoveries of leading researchers who, in the face of today's crisis among girls, have pivoted to answering these two questions. Not only do their findings tell us that we are raising girls in an era whose problems are different from those of previous generations, but they also offer us a new scientific understanding of how mounting adversities affect girls' bodies and brains in surprising and unique ways. In the face of today's ongoing toxic stressors, these negative effects can begin to manifest at a biological level in distinctly different ways as boys and girls enter puberty and come of age. This, coupled with the stress that accompanies simply growing up female in our society, is a more important driver of today's depression and anxiety epidemic among girls than anyone previously realized.

WHEN I FIRST began to report on these scientific findings, I wondered if it was wise to try to view what lay behind today's teen girl mental health crisis through a biological lens. Even as it became clear that something was happening to girls due to the environment in which they lived and that it affected them during puberty in ways distinct from boys, the question of whether sex differences played a role was not a room I was eager to enter. I feared even opening the door to the discussion, lest it be misused or misinterpreted in ways that harmed girls—wrongly implying that female biology was somehow weak, or that girls themselves were somehow to blame.

Nothing could be further from the truth. Let me say it clearly: The female body and brain are more susceptible to being adversely affected by chronic stress *only* when the source of that stress remains unaddressed and unmitigated. Indeed, in a healthy environment, one that fosters girls' well-being, girls can possess distinct *advantages* in navigating adversity. Such an environment would include a healthy, strong relationship with parents and other adults; the experience of a deep psychological sense of safety in the world; and feeling seen and valued in society.

Adolescence is a time unlike any other, full of unimaginable promise—a golden period marked by learning and possibility and growth. As hormones rush in and begin to create visible physical changes, the brains of teens become especially ripe, agile, and flexible, open to new opportunities and experiences and to learning new approaches to self-awareness, coping, and connection that can prepare teens to navigate even highly complex challenges. And yet adolescence is also a precipice. Each young person stands at its brink, poised either to falter or to stride forward and thrive as they cross into young adulthood. So much depends on the emotional, social, and environmental terrain in which they come of age.

This may be truer for girls. As you will see in the pages that follow, the aspects of the female stress-threat response that make the female body susceptible to the biophysical ill effects of adversity and toxic environments as a girl comes into puberty are also what make the female adolescent brain remarkably flexible and responsive to positive shifts in a girl's lived experience. But a supportive environment that provides strong scaffolding for a girl's healthy development is not created merely through the absence of trial and adversity or by buffering children and teens from every form of toxic stress (even if such a thing were wise, or possible). A neuroprotective environment is one in which the conditions that foster a sense of being safely seen, deeply connected, and valued have been set in place by parents and other family members, mentors, and community. Each of these neuroprotective spheres of influence lies nestled inside the next, larger sphere, as with a series of Matryoshka dolls, each painted wooden doll held inside the next. If we are to grow strong girls, each neuroprotective sphere must pass the litmus test of whether girls feel secure and connected within it. Ultimately, this is what ensures that each girl, represented by the smallest figure at the center, feels safe within herself.

There are myriad ways we can harness the tremendous power of this science to promote new layers of resilience in girls. If we can identify the toxic chronic stressors a girl faces, reduce what stress we can, and provide adequate support in the face of adversity, we can create a different coming-of-age environment for girls, one that will yield a very different outcome. Indeed, we now understand the core factors that, when bundled together, are neurobiologically protective both in preventing mental health concerns in girls and in helping those girls who are already struggling.

Just as today's change in girls' health is not due to any single variation in their environment, protecting girls against negative shifts in the female brain and immune health likewise has many moving parts. The right interactions and interventions that help girls feel safe can promote a cascade of powerful changes at the biophysical level—acting as a cellular antidote to our culturally complicated, toxic era and setting the stage for new possibilities for flourishing. Over time, bundling together small micro changes can alter a girl's life and emotional trajectory.

In many ways, I wrote this book because I felt a moral imperative to close the gap between what experts have learned about growing strong girls in an increasingly threat-laden era and what parents need to know.

In addition to talking to research and medical experts, I also follow the stories of three girls whose journeys illustrate why adolescent females do not feel safe in the world we've created for them and how modern stressors are more powerful than we previously thought in shaping every girl's story of who she is and who she can become. I've changed some girls' names and characteristics to disguise their identities, but their experiences are real. Their stories, coupled with the latest insights from science, offer what I hope will be seen as a new and powerful blueprint for how we can raise, and protect the emotional lives of, girls.

The girls I interviewed were very thoughtful about and aware of why they did not feel safe, seen, or valued in the world. Each had endured a very challenging passage into and throughout puberty. Through no fault of their own, these girls learned the hard way. And yet, despite navigating difficult journeys, they each found—with the help of caring others and by bravely searching out answers for themselves—powerful ways to heal. Indeed, the strategies they clung to for learning to thrive are included in part 3 of this book, "The Antidotes."

As you'll read in that section, there are ways to help downshift a girl's stress-threat response, build up her ability to adapt and self-manage in positive ways, and prevent a chronic state of fight, flight, or freeze, even in the face of stressors. This, in turn, can help usher in a girl's interior sense of safety and bolster her mental well-being. The fifteen antidotes I lay out in part 3 invite the reader to embrace a new way of thinking about how, when, and where to better promote deep psychological safety and connection for girls across four domains of life experience in which stress can arise—household, environmental, community, and social—while also increasing girls' autonomy and resilience. My hope is that these antidotes will enable parents to help their daughters avoid having to muddle through or struggle quite so much—and, indeed, enable them to flourish. I hope, too, that these antidotes will help teachers, counselors, therapists, mentors, and other adults better support the girls whose lives they touch. The goal is for each of us—in whatever role we play in girls' lives—to help make this difficult and at times precarious passage into adulthood smoother, easier, and therefore more joyful.

PERHAPS TODAY'S GROWING trend of despondency among girls hits home for you because you're worried about a girl you know who is struggling. Or perhaps you've already been on a journey to help a girl you love flourish and thrive but have found yourself unable to uncover the best ways to do so. If that's true for you, you're not alone.

The deeper I delved into this research, the more my own maternal heart propelled me onward. It seems fitting to acknowledge that my foray into investigating the forces confronting today's girls was driven by a love for all girls as well as for my own. For me, the personal has always informed the professional, compelling me to translate emerging science into clear, plain language as best I can. This book is no different. It was written with a journalist's mind and infused with the love of a mother's heart.

I am the mother of a beautiful and, dare I say, remarkable daughter who, like so many girls, struggled throughout adolescence and into her early twenties with mental health concerns—a story that is hers to tell, not mine. Yet, as I write these pages, I cannot stop wondering: If I had known when my daughter was younger, and still free from suffering, what I've now learned, could I have helped her more? Sooner? I cannot know. And yet, understanding this science has helped me know how to help my daughter *now*. Because, for parents, families, and society, it is never too late to better the lives of our daughters and other girls we care about.

The new neuroscience on the biology of female teen flourishing offers all of us who care about the health of girls a new blueprint containing a message of hope, responsibility, and possibility to enhance the lived experiences of girls. It is in that spirit that I offer what I've learned from some of the best minds of our time, and from girls themselves.

Girls on the Brink

PART ONE

Growing Up Female

CHAPTER ONE

Our Girls Are Not Okay

Why Are So Many of Our Daughters Struggling?

Anna Moralis keeps a portrait of her maternal grandmother on her desk in her small Chicago student apartment. Her resemblance to her grandmother is striking—they share large dark eyes, chestnut hair, and a narrow chin. "Just seeing my grandmother smiling at me helps bring down my anxiety levels," Anna tells me when we meet for the first time. As we talk, Anna leans over a sketchbook and doodles with colored pencils. I wonder if drawing also helps her manage her anxiety.

Anna, who has just turned twenty-one and has a clear sense of herself gained through time and talk therapy, plans to go to law school and focus on social justice. But even when she was young—indeed, by the time she was twelve—she was politically engaged and reflective about the world. "I begged my parents to take me to human rights marches," she tells me. "Everywhere I looked, there was so much social and environmental injustice. Racism, voting rights, terrorism, global warming, climate change, spates of school shootings. On the one hand, I found a lot of confidence by being so engaged; I wrote op-eds for my middle school newspaper and sold candy bars to raise money for kids caught in the Middle East conflict." But immersing herself in larger social issues also made her feel as if "the little things I was going through in my own teenage life couldn't be valid. I had this sense that it was silly for me to be upset about anything happening in my personal life."

Toward the end of middle school, "I became popular for the first time," Anna recalls. "Then social media took over. Social media was terrible for me. I already had a lot of discomfort with my body image. So much of social media is imbued with this constant, pervasive sexism." That year in middle school, "a lot of girls would get together to watch TV shows like *Pretty Little Liars,* in which perfect-looking twentysomethings played perfect-looking sixteen-year-olds. They had *Victoria's Secret Fashion Show*–viewing parties and posted pictures of themselves on Snapchat trying to look sexually mature and model perfect. That wasn't good for me or for my self-image."

When Anna turned fourteen and entered high school, the social scene grew far more challenging. "The friends I'd had in middle school dropped me. They said I was 'too nice' and my concern for social justice was 'fake'; that I was trying to get attention. I couldn't make new friends because my magnet school was so tiny." Anna's precocious self-awareness became a double-edged sword. As her peers made fun of her, she began to turn her capacity for observation and reflection against herself. "I had this sense that if I were skinnier or prettier or happier or less serious, I'd be included in the things everyone posted about on Snapchat and Finsta," she says, referring to the private accounts teens use to share inside jokes and gossip with a restricted group of peers. "Maybe I'd even have a boyfriend. I assumed there was something missing in me and *that* was the reason I was missing out."

Using the language for self-reflection that comes with therapy, Anna sees, looking back, how "the role models imposed by the world around me for how to be female were bombarding me from screens, phones, computers, TV, which everyone my age was on six or seven hours a day.

The screen version of the feminine ideal overshadowed real life. I never got to choose how *I* wanted to be as a female teen."

Anna's mother, a physician with the U.S. Army Medical Corps, was stationed overseas. "I felt very alone. I told myself, *Oh, so what if I don't have friends? It's not that bad; it could be worse.* I wasn't suffering from atrocities—there was no war or school shooting or flood or fire on my own doorstep—so how could my own sadness be valid? But inside, my depression snowballed. I didn't understand what I was so sad and fearful about. We didn't even have the pandemic! It was more like a pandemic of a growing feeling of unsafety about everything, everywhere I turned."

Anna began restricting her meals to tiny portions. These periods were followed by binge eating. "When I was fourteen, I gained fifteen pounds. My mom came home on leave, and one day while my parents and I were driving, I was sitting in the back seat and they said, 'Anna, you've gained weight. We're worried about it. We wanted to talk to you about eating less and signing up for an exercise class.' They didn't seem to notice that I was also no longer my bubbly self. . . . On the one hand, my parents supported who I was on the inside—they told me I was a really good writer and would be an amazing novelist one day—but I was also living in this larger, toxic soup of damaging, gendered messages about being female, and that led me to process everything I heard them say in a toxic way, especially when it came to messages about my body: *You are less than if you are fat. If you are fat, even the people who love you aren't going to accept you for who you are.*" This added to Anna's "pervasive sense of invalidation, of not feeling seen for who I was and what I was going through." And that contributed to a "vicious cycle of eating and purging."

Academic stress, meanwhile, snowballed. "I was in a competitive magnet school. I'd be at school seven hours a day, totally stressed because I knew I had to do well to get the accolades of top grades and college acceptances, and totally bored by the endless work teachers assigned. When I was fifteen, sixteen, and seventeen, I spent every free minute doing activities or homework until midnight. I'd spend all weekend doing more homework. Even though my school talked about valuing 'learning' over awards, that was just not true. It was all about getting the accolades."

Anna's mother took a second tour overseas. Anna was at home with her dad and her elder sister and brother. Her sister, several years her senior, went off to college. "Suddenly, I was the only girl in my house. I often felt that when there were family arguments, I was somehow the one who'd said or done something wrong. My dad could be very patronizing. And that would lead to explosive clashes between us. He'd say something condescending, and I'd slam my door and stay in my room. It was always made out to be my fault; I was always the one who got the blame for all this ridiculous, constant anger simmering in our household, and [I] had to apologize. My brother clammed up. My dad got so fed up with single parenting, he completely disengaged. I started going out and drinking a lot with this one friend I had. I started eating a ton. When I think back to that time, I can see I felt this overwhelming sense of female powerlessness, coupled with a sense of just being abandoned. I had no female mentors, and my family felt ruptured. We'd always had this very loving family when I was a kid—but suddenly, that was gone. My mom and I would talk on Skype a lot, but there was no one I could turn to to help me process life as a teenage girl in a pretty fucked-up world."

Throughout the rest of high school, Anna put forth the appearance that all was okay—that she was okay. She was eighteen when she left for college, carefully concealing her mounting sense of melancholy and unease. It was then that things fell apart. It was as if she had buried all her fears and sorrow and sense of dejection in some bottomless black hole inside her, and now the hole had become so large that it had swallowed her, too, until she could no longer find herself within it.

Anna was a few months into her freshman year when her anxiety and depression came to a head. "I alternated wildly between binge-eating and eating almost nothing for days. I began to have these repetitive, anxious, obsessive, depressive thoughts I couldn't get away from in my own head." Alone, without outside support from others, and lacking coping skills for managing the stress she was experiencing, Anna began to look for solace in all the wrong places. "I chose all the worst ways to try to validate myself, which played perfectly into the ways in which women in our society are led to expect to be treated. I hooked up with guys who treated me like shit while hoping one of them would find me attractive and interesting enough to date."

She felt she had to put forth a constrained version of herself to the world, one that meshed with the teenage female ideal. To Anna, it seemed that the girls in her friend group were better able to fit their psyches more easily and neatly into that ideal, immersing themselves, amid the rigors of academic life, in the shallower concerns of parties, hooking up, selfies, and TikTok.

Little things—stressful moments Anna would normally have been able to shake off—took on more magnitude for her. "I got a B-minus on a history paper, and it felt like the end of the world. I started throwing up all the time from nerves. I threw up in the hallway of the history department after seeing my professor. It was humiliating. I started to obsess over things friends said to me, and [I] couldn't stop worrying that they were making fun of me when I wasn't around."

That winter, when Anna came home for the long holiday break, she tried to make small talk with her parents, but she found it hard. She made halfhearted efforts at fake cheeriness and tried to remain civil. She stayed in her room a lot. She cried at seemingly small things, like losing a favorite pencil. One afternoon, her mother and father sat her down. They told her they didn't want her to return to academic life until she saw a therapist. Anna was as furious as she was miserable. "That entire holiday I was caustic with everyone. I guzzled all this wine and said really rude things to everyone except for my grandmother, who just kept hugging me. Inside, I just felt unseen and invalidated and completely invisible to my family."

Anna gazes out her window for a moment, then turns back toward me with a soft smile, as if she has, since those days, found compassion for that younger teenage self. "I think what I really wanted, what I really needed, was to connect with *someone* and feel connected to myself."

A Growing Despair Among Girls

Anna is certainly not alone in her feelings of isolation and self-loathing, and to a certain degree, some of what she describes might arguably be considered garden-variety growing pains. But for Anna and many other girls today, there is something more than normal teen angst and adolescent social anxiety at play here. An increasing number of girls report feeling overwhelmed by a pervasive sense of anxiety and depression in the face of mounting stressors as they journey from their preteen years into young adulthood. Indeed, as you read Anna's story, perhaps a girl comes to mind whom you deeply care for (your daughter, niece, student, or a friend's daughter) whose passage from childhood to young adulthood seems marked by a worrisome degree of emotional distress or a sense of understandable fragility in an increasingly challenging coming-of-age landscape.

Our girls are simply not okay. Depression is occurring more often in girls today than in the past, and it's presenting earlier than it did just two decades ago—often by ages twelve or thirteen. Higher diagnosis rates alone don't account for this troubling spike. Indeed, when researchers assess mental health in young people, they don't rely on diagnoses. Because many teens who experience mental health symptoms are not diagnosed, national data on mental health problems in teens relies on other criteria: Researchers screen teens to find out if they've faced emotional or behavioral concerns that have been so significant they've disrupted their normal daily life, lasted for twelve months or longer, and/or required counseling. Recent studies that rely on these metrics show that, by age seventeen, more than a third of girls report having experienced at least one "major depressive episode" over the past year of their lives, marked by feelings of "worthlessness and guilt." This isn't just some transient angst: A major depressive episode is defined as a period of weeks (often longer) during which a person experiences persistent sadness and hopelessness, fatigue, changes in sleeping habits, loss of interest in activities, or lingering thoughts of suicide.

Every year, the gap between the rates at which girls and boys suffer from depression and anxiety persists—and between 2018 and 2019, that gap widened by 14 percent. Between 2016 and 2020, girls were, on average, 48 percent more likely to have a depression diagnosis and a 43 percent higher rate of anxiety disorders compared with boys of the same ages. The sense of day-to-day well-being that girls experience also differs from that of boys: Nearly 50 percent of young adult females report as many as ten days of "poor mental health" during the past month, compared with 28 percent of young adult males.[*]

I want to be clear: Boys today are struggling, too. Of course they are. Anxiety disorders in boys can often manifest as behavioral problems or

---

[*]   For the purposes of this book, I focus on biological differences between what are called cisgender women and cisgender men (i.e., those who identify with the gender assigned to them at birth), though, throughout the book, I use the simpler *biological sex differences.* When I use the term *sex,* I refer, as biologists do, to genetic and hormonal differences between cisgender females and males. When I use the term *gender,* I refer to the common roles that have been ascribed to people living as female or male in our society, also known as *gender roles,* which impact an individual's concept of themselves. I use the terms *girl, woman,* and *female* (along with the corresponding male terms) to refer *both* to sex differences and to gender roles, often interchangeably. However, this should not be construed to imply that sex and gender roles cannot shift, be fluid, or change for individuals, or to invalidate the gender identity or lived experience of transgender and nonbinary people, which I respect and recognize. Research on biological differences between cisgender men and cisgender women is itself a growing and important area of study, and I hope this research becomes more inclusive of transgender and nonbinary individuals and how they fit into this framework.

attention issues and be misdiagnosed or missed altogether. Boys facing depression are also more likely to commit suicide compared with girls. But the challenges boys and girls face often have distinct root causes, and it would be a disservice to our children to ignore this.

Moreover, recent suicide trends also point to a growing epidemic of despair among girls. The gap between suicide rates in girls and boys is narrowing: The rate at which preteen and teen girls take their own lives has tripled over the past twenty years, including in girls ages ten to fourteen. In 2021, suicide attempts increased 51 percent among adolescent girls compared with 4 percent among boys.

Statistics even hint at when this surge in girls' growing distress first began to escalate—even as it flew under the radar for too long. When we dig deeper into the data, we see a startling subtrend: Today's precipitously rising rates of anxiety and depression are observed only in those under the age of twenty-five. According to a 2019 study in the *Journal of Abnormal Psychology,* although rates of experiencing a major depressive episode in the last year increased 52 percent among all adolescents ages twelve to seventeen and 63 percent among young adults eighteen to twenty-five, this trend did not exist in young people ages twenty-six and older. Feelings of hopelessness, restlessness, worthlessness, and suicidal thoughts were also significantly higher for those under twenty-five, compared with those twenty-six and older. This increase in major depressive disorders and emotional distress was far more prevalent in girls and young women compared with boys and young men of the same ages. Taken together, study authors say this suggests "a generational shift in mood disorders and suicide-related outcomes."*

This downward turn in girls' well-being, which existed long before the COVID-19 pandemic, became more abysmal after prolonged pandemic-related stress. According to University of Michigan researchers, nearly half of parents say they noticed that their teenager's mental

---

*   In 2022 terms, that would apply to young women ages twenty-*eight* and younger.

health worsened during the pandemic. Roughly one-third of girls displayed new or worsening signs of depression or anxiety compared with fewer than one in five boys. Emergency room visits for teen mental health crises rose 31 percent during 2020, the year pandemic lockdowns began, compared with 2019, and this increase, too, was far steeper among girls.

VERY RECENTLY, SCIENTISTS and public health researchers have started to unpack the "why" behind this concerning phenomenon. The authors of the *Journal of Abnormal Psychology* study cite "cultural trends" since the mid-2000s as precipitating this downward trend in female teen mental health. In additional analyses, researchers even pinpointed the specific year that teen girls' mental health first began to drastically worsen: 2012. And yet it is only since 2016—when the National Institutes of Health asked that sex differences be factored into the design and reporting of preclinical research—that scientists began to more deeply consider male and female sex differences in the biological underpinnings for how, when, and why depression and anxiety develop in response to adversity and stress.*

Their eye-opening findings offer us a much clearer explanation for why our girls are suffering so deeply, while also giving us a hopeful new

---

* For decades, lab research used male animals almost exclusively in experiments involving the brain. Preclinical research in neuroscience begins in animal studies. Later, findings are extrapolated to and explored in human clinical trials. In 2016, the National Institutes of Health asked that sex differences be factored into the research design and reporting of animal studies. Prior to that, regardless of what aspect of mental health was being studied under the microscope (how stress affects the brain; how the brain changes in depression, anxiety, or PTSD; or the way in which the brain and immune system interface in mental health disorders), the study of female biology was rarely included in animal studies or preclinical research. Thus, research findings and assumptions were skewed by the fact that they originated in male animal research models.

foothold into better understanding the complexity of today's coming-of-age experience for girls. In simple terms, this science tells us that chronic stressors affect the female brain very differently from the male brain and that although these changes begin early on in development, they most often start to manifest during puberty, in often harmful ways. At its essence, this science shows us what happens when girls are beset by myriad stressors, how these adversities manifest in the way girls feel and in their psychological well-being, and why these stressors are more powerful in shaping every girl's story than we previously realized.

> *Science tells us that chronic stressors affect the female*
> *brain very differently from the male brain and that*
> *although these changes begin early on in development,*
> *they most often start to manifest during puberty,*
> *in often harmful ways.*

The Four Domains of Childhood Stress

Stress is a simple word that most of us utter every day of our lives, but it is also a catchall term, and hence, a confusing one. When we use the word *stress,* what exactly are we talking about? Most of what we know about the way stress and adversity can shape children's well-being emerges from a body of research known as the Adverse Childhood Experiences (ACE) Study. ACE literature consists of more than two thousand well-replicated studies conducted over the past twenty-five years that have demonstrated that exposure to different types of childhood adversity before the age of eighteen raises the likelihood of a child's developing mental or physical health disorders in adulthood.

These *stressors,* or sources of stress, are found in four broad domains. The first of these are *household stressors,* the kind of adversity a child faces in their own home. These might include growing up with a parent or caregiver who suffers from a mental health disorder, who is an alcoholic or has a substance use disorder, or who has a chronic medical illness; experiencing parental separation or divorce; losing a parent before reaching adulthood or being separated from a parent. It also includes poor treatment at the hands of a parent or primary caregiver, such as being chronically criticized or put down; physical neglect, such as not being taken to the doctor when ill; emotional neglect, such as feeling that your family doesn't have your back or care about you, witnessing violence in the home, or being bullied by siblings; and physical and sexual abuse.

The second domain of childhood stressors and adversities is *environmental*. These encompass natural disasters and fallout from the climate crisis, such as hurricanes, earthquakes, wildfires, and mud slides; the stress imposed by the COVID-19 pandemic; and exposure to toxins, infections, and pollution.

Childhood traumas also occur in the broad domain of one's *community*: growing up with the threat of racism; facing discrimination, poverty, or community violence; going to substandard schools; lacking adequate housing; and being exposed to or even having to prepare for the possibility of school shootings.

Finally, there are the *social stressors.* These are the emotional or interpersonal stressors children traditionally meet in social milieus, amid cliques at school or in their neighborhood. However, as children and teens live more of their lives online, on social media—navigating the liking and disliking, the critiquing, and the ever-present threat of being left out or made fun of—chronic stress in this domain has become more acute and a new and pressing source of concern.

When we take a step back and view the adversity found in these four domains of children's and teens' lives, we can see they share several common denominators. They are chronic and unpredictable; one never knows when they might recur. They imbue in a child a feeling that they are in some way under threat, which interrupts their basic sense that they are safe in the world. This stress may be felt on an emotional level, as a sense of fear, anxiety, shame, worry, loneliness, or creeping dread. Or it might be felt on a physiological level, as an underlying tension a child might not even be aware she carries in her body. Or it might be felt more overtly as panic, manifesting in an elevated heart rate, butterflies in the stomach, the feeling of one's heart being caught in one's chest. All these sensations of unsafeness can plunge a child into a low-grade or acute state of "fight, flight, or freeze," in which the body and brain prepare to defend against the perceived threat, run from it, or freeze in place to escape notice. Over time, this elevated sense of uncertainty as to what lies around the next corner promotes a rise in inflammatory chemicals in the body, which in turn can trigger changes to the immune system and the architecture of the developing brain.

MOST OF THESE stressors affect boys and girls alike. All children and teens have now experienced a deadly public health emergency, and many lost family members to the pandemic. According to a 2021 CDC study in *The Lancet,* by the summer of 2021, for every two adults who died due to COVID-19, one child was left without a parent or other caregiver, such as a grandparent who lived with them.

Pandemic worries stack up on top of other growing chronic stressors, including school and other mass shootings. A Pew Research study recently found that nearly 60 percent of students report fearing that their school will be the next target in the endless line of school shootings. Kids as young as six regularly participate in active-shooter drills against potential armed intruders.

At the same time, this generation faces the real-time consequences of climate change like no other generation before it. Our children are growing up in communities that are flooding or being hit by record-breaking numbers of mud slides and hurricanes, suffering unprecedented heat and droughts, or burning down amid wildfires. Or they're witnessing these events 24/7 on media platforms. They're also watching external forces divide communities and generate growing political discord and rage and witnessing horrific racial injustices, including violence against Black and Asian American people, police misconduct, and massive refugee crises occurring all over the globe. Add to this the fact that 17 million children in the United States go to bed hungry and that 2.5 million children don't have a bed to call their own. It's no wonder Columbia University professors now teach a course called The History of the End of the World.

These kinds of life-or-death stressors would normally be shouldered, and dealt with, by the adults in their lives. Only, the adults haven't done a very good job at coming together to address them. Kids don't feel safe because they know they *aren't* safe. They are facing an array of existential threats for which we, the adults, have offered no good solutions. Despite being scared about what kind of future they can hope to have, children are also expected to achieve more, earlier, in academic settings; contemplate the college process while they are still practically kids; and discern their identity often while growing up with hovering, overinvolved parents or overstretched parents working multiple jobs. And they grapple with all this while knowing that not too far along in their future, they will have to tackle looming career and economic uncertainty for themselves.

WHEN WE CONSIDER the array of adversities today's children face, it might seem that certain types of chronic toxic stress are more potent than others. But this turns out to be mostly not true—*all* forms of chronic adversity can affect a child's brain and biology. Neuroscientists at the University of Colorado have demonstrated that the nervous system can respond to emotional stress "as if it were cellular damage." Emotional and biological stressors work along the same brain pathways, leading to the release of inflammatory factors that, if left unchecked, slowly begin to affect lifelong health. But emotional adversity becomes traumatic only if a child experiences that stressor as being in some way harmful to them or threatening to their psychological or physical safety in the world.

This concept can be difficult to wrap our minds around because we've been taught to think of our mental health as being separate from our physical health. But our well-being is created first and foremost (including from our earliest stages of life) from our ongoing, felt sense of safety. It is not "I think, therefore I am." Really, it is "I think and *feel*, and therefore I am."

A child's brain and body are always receiving and interpreting cues from their environment. From the moment you begin life in your mother's womb and throughout your childhood and teenage years, your brain is a meaning-making machine. It is always engaged in a complicated interactive dance with every nuance of your environment. All your senses—smell, touch, taste, sight, hearing—send your brain messages about whether you are safe or not safe. It is your brain's number one job to constantly be on the lookout for, assess, and prep you and your body for new incoming threats. At the same time, your brain is always chatting with your body's immune system in a 24/7 conversation, deciding whether subtle messages you're receiving from the world around you signal imminent danger.

Toward this end and throughout childhood, the body and brain begin storing away stressful or traumatic experiences—in effect, making note of them for future reference. And in this brain-environment dance, chronic stress in childhood and the teenage years acts as a kind of master instructor, if you will, training the nervous system, immune system, and brain in ways that lay the foundation for how your brain and body will respond to stressful experiences for the rest of your life. This is why an ACE score of two or higher is considered significant in terms of influencing a child's future physical and mental well-being.[*]

---

[*]   A word here on ACE scores. The original ACE questionnaire developed by Kaiser

The Gender Divide

When we turn to neuroscientists who are investigating why escalating levels of stress are affecting girls' health in such distinct and harmful ways, we learn that much of the answer lies in new understandings of what happens when girls approach puberty and of how the developing brain makes sense of toxic stressors. Indeed, it is during puberty that, for females, a history of chronic personal and environmental stressors begins to manifest in psychological costs.

To begin with, this is largely thanks to the influx of sex hormones—namely, estrogen. In the right circumstances, estrogen can be enormously protective, but in the face of too many accumulating stressors, it can amplify the effects of stress on the developing female brain. This, in turn, can switch on genes associated with the later development of mental health disorders.

One of the biggest ideas here, however, is this: Our evolutionary biology (the way our bodies and brains evolved since the time we were hunter-gatherers) has a great deal to do with these differences in how modern stressors affect female teen health. The reason that experiencing chronic, toxic stress while growing up female becomes so problematic is rooted in our evolutionary history, when traumatic experiences could mean death—much more often than they do in modern life. Day in and day out, deeply biological evolutionary responses are being triggered by the all-too-modern conditions of being a teenage girl in a world flooded

---

Permanente researcher Vincent Felitti, M.D., and CDC epidemiologist Robert Anda, M.D., published in 1998, asked adults about ten types of childhood experiences, such as physical or emotional abuse or neglect by a caregiver, sexual abuse, and other types of dysfunction in the home. But these ten adverse childhood experiences are not the only kinds children face. Millions of children experience discrimination, poverty, racism, sexism, and environmental and social stressors. Thus, when I refer to the ACE score in these pages, I'm referring to scores based on this original ACE questionnaire. However, community, environmental, and social stressors also deeply affect child and adult well-being in harmful ways.

with a growing array of potent challenges, many of which are novel to our times. These, in turn, stack up on top of the traditional hurdles young humans have always faced as they come of age and the unique adversities a child may face in her home life.

At its crux, this is a story about the legacy of our evolution as humans and how we were shaped by real, mortal dangers. The dangers of today manifest in different ways, but they nevertheless have a powerful effect, putting girls especially at risk. Simply stated, our brains, our hormones, are mired in our evolutionary past.

> *Day in and day out, deeply biological*
> *evolutionary responses are being triggered by the*
> *all-too-modern conditions of being a teenage girl in a*
> *world flooded with a growing array of potent*
> *challenges, many of which are novel to our times.*

Finally, and most important, there is a great deal about the experience of growing up female today that is deeply detrimental to girls, and this new toxicity, made ubiquitous and worsened by the advent of social media (which we will explore in depth in chapter 2), is contributing to the way girls are suffering mental health crises in alarming numbers.

Struggling as a female adolescent is nothing new, of course. Great novels, from *Little Women* to *A Tree Grows in Brooklyn*, recount the angst-filled quest to find one's identity during these years of life. And the question of why girls show significantly higher rates of anxiety and depression in adolescence is a long-standing one. For decades, psychologists have sought to untangle what does and does not contribute to the healthy development of the inner lives of girls. In 1994, psychologist Mary Pipher, Ph.D., first published her classic book on raising girls, *Reviving Ophelia*, the title of which refers to a teenage character in Shakespeare's *Hamlet* who despairs over her love for Hamlet and familial expectations; she ultimately drowns herself. And yet, since Pipher's clarion call to protect and nurture the inner selves of adolescent girls a quarter century ago, and many large-scale efforts to address this concerning trend, our national epidemic of female adolescent depression and anxiety has only continued to increase. Moreover, today's generation of girls is clearly in a particular kind of pain that is qualitatively and quantitatively different from that of previous generations.

Children across every society and era have faced adversity, but there are factors that make our times particularly and insidiously destructive. For parents raising children in times of historical trauma, like war, a child's need for a safe haven might seem clear. For those of us raising daughters today, though, it can be difficult to know whether and when a girl's experiences might derail her mental health. Times have changed. The problems girls face now are entirely different from those of the past, and we need to change our techniques and approaches to raising strong girls if we are to help them flourish and thrive.

Today, science tells us why we have not yet succeeded in "reviving Ophelia." Myriad toxic, societal, and environmental stressors, taken in combination, have become neurobiologically detrimental to a generation of young women as they move through puberty and into adulthood. Our modern adolescent female crisis in well-being is not just a psychological phenomenon; it is a biological one.

CHAPTER TWO

Is This a Toxic Era for Girls?

Yes, and It's Worse than You Thought

WHEN JULIA ABERNATHY turned eleven, she developed "really quickly," her tomboy body shifting from "boyish lines into big curves." Julia describes those preteen years as we walk around the college town where she's finishing her sophomore year.

"I was a very active kid, climbing trees, running around with my brother, making forts under the dining room table. Then—overnight—I had these *boobs*," Julia says, her gravelly voice making her sound older than her twenty years. "To me, my boobs were like two fat bags growing on my chest. I wanted to ignore them and get on with living my life, but they were all anyone else saw. Everyone began treating me differently. My parents are great; they've helped me through really difficult years in ways that have made a huge difference. But looking back, [I see] they were learning as they went. They said things that were the opposite of what I needed to hear. My dad's friends would be at our house and say stuff like, 'Oh, Julia is so beautiful. My God, she looks like a grown woman already!' They'd be staring at my body, and no one would step in to say, 'Hey, cut it out. She's eleven!' Or my mom would joke, 'My God, Julia turned sixteen overnight!'

"I started wearing oversize button-down shirts to hide my body, so older guys wouldn't stare at me," Julia recalls. "I just wanted to climb trees and bake cakes, but so many of my memories of my preteen years are of me warding off passes from older guys who'd lean in close and give me these lingering stares or say things like 'You have the greatest tits!' Just walking down the street, past a construction site, even when I was with my family—guys would shout, 'Here comes trouble!' and 'Better lock her up now!' And I'd think, *How am I trouble, exactly?* It infuriated me and embarrassed me at the same time that it made me realize I wasn't really safe if this was how men saw me from twenty feet away."

Julia turned twelve in 2013, in the midst of the smartphones-for-middle-schoolers boom. "I didn't like Facebook and Insta and Snapchat, but you had to do it if you wanted friends," she recalls. "Once, a friend posted a cleavage shot, so I posted a cleavage shot. I felt scummy right away. I remember saying to myself, *You're being an idiot right now,* and I took it down. I tried to post upbeat photos and captions, to keep up appearances. It was a way to try to stay part of the in crowd. But the showcasing of everyone's best, most beautiful self was very hurtful. So much of social media has to do with girls' bodies . . . girls posing provocatively in group selfies at a party with the camera held at a certain angle so they look skinnier, etcetera, etcetera." Julia groans audibly with the twenty-twenty vision of one now eight years older. "Social media is like open season for evaluating girls' body shapes—our skin, our faces, our hair. By the time you are ten or eleven, you catch on that the more a girl is on social media, and the more she postures herself to appear grown up and sexually developed, the more social power she holds. I was already a very insecure teen. On the one hand, I'd feel like I had to ante up; but on the other hand, I felt this rage, like, *I don't want to be part of this, this is so completely fake and wrong and competitive and not who I want to be.*"

An arc of spraying water from a lawn sprinkler catches us unaware as we walk along the street; the light shower rains in quicksilver droplets, here and then gone. Julia laughs as we step quickly out of it, and for a moment, in her smile, I see the open face of the eleven-year-old she once was.

By age thirteen, she had learned to live with the nonstop litany of "Oh, Julia has big tits!" and "Julia is really hot!" as she walked down her school's hallways. As high school began, "even though I felt I was really smart, I didn't have the chance to be seen as smart, because of all of these other things that were happening. I was categorized as being 'into boys' when, really, boys were into me—and not even *me*, but my *body*." One day that year, she recalls, "this senior boy stuck his tongue down my throat and put his hand up my shirt during lunch. A teacher saw us and just told us to go to class. I didn't feel seen by anyone. I started to feel, *Well, if a guy doesn't want to leer over me, am I worth anything?* Like, *Okay, if I'm being seen as this sexual object, and no one sees me as one of the smart kids, then all I am is this object.* I didn't get a chance to choose my own way of being feminine—that was chosen by people and events around me. That shaped how I saw myself and my place in the world for a long time.

"My school was just your average public school, so we had to do a lot of extra things if we wanted to get into a good college," Julia goes on. "My grades had fallen. So I had to work harder—retaking and retaking the SATs, bringing up grades, landing internships. I was completely stressed out all the time. I started to want to stay home from school." At school, she says, it was like the collegiate Hunger Games: one hundred kids competing for the same slots at name schools. Parents rushed their kids from club meetings to team sports to tutoring. "Nothing felt real or authentic to me anymore.

"I didn't like myself as a person, and I thought, *Okay, fine. I'm going to have sex with older guys; maybe* they *will understand me. If this is how everyone sees me, why not lean into it?*" Maybe, Julia thought, hooking up with older guys would offer her that "sense of freedom I was missing." That, she says, "turned out to be a *huge* mistake. I felt so alone and angry. A part of me was, on one hand, secretly enraged by the injustices of being female—how we as females are hypersexualized and dismissed, from being discounted by teachers, to constant mansplaining from boys and men, to the fact that a woman can't win as president." But, at the same time, "I also felt like I was powerless to do anything about any of it, including in my own life. Leaning into being seen as sexually powerful seemed like the only road to my freedom." That initial hope to find freedom by dating older guys didn't linger long. "That year, I'd find myself sobbing uncontrollably at school or at home, or I'd just shut down and go completely quiet and act as if everything was fine," she recalls. "A part of me was just hoping someone would notice: 'Hey, something is going on with Julia.' All I could think about was how much I hated myself. I started having panic attacks. My heart would start racing, and I'd get very lightheaded and pass out. Occasionally, I would hear a voice that wasn't there, telling me how stupid I was. I started to feel like I wanted to die."

When she was fifteen, she began cutting herself. "My parents found out I was cutting. They were upset, and looking back, I don't blame them at all. But at the time, I didn't understand I needed help, so my parents' efforts turned into a game of cat and mouse. I'd try to find ways to escape from under their control, and they'd respond by intruding into my life more. They put software on my phone and my computer. So I bought a second phone off another kid and used it secretly. I didn't want to talk to my parents—though, in retrospect, I realize I *did* want to talk to them but didn't feel I *could*. I never went to my mom to ask her advice, unless things got out of control. One older guy threatened to leak nudes of me, so I went to my mom, and she called the police. Now that I've had years of therapy, combined with the other work I've done to get to the good place where I am now—not to mention the efforts others ended up making on my behalf—I realize, looking back, that I wanted to be left alone because I wanted to die. I didn't want to have to think about my mom and dad or how upset they would be, so I just kept telling myself, *I've got this!* when clearly I didn't."

Julia's parents, who were growing increasingly concerned, took her to family therapy. "I didn't speak one word the entire time," Julia recalls. "I just wanted it to be over. When I was alone, I started to mess around with choking myself with belts. No one knew." One day, at the end of her sophomore year of high school, when she was fifteen, she drank bleach. "My memory of that time is very spotty. I'd been dating another crummy guy and had a crummy breakup. I remember feeling embarrassed because, to everyone else at the time, it seemed like I'd tried to take my life and ended up in the ER, and then in a psychiatric ward for ten days, over a boy. But that wasn't it. I wanted to break up with *myself.*"

Unwitting Guinea Pigs in a Social Experiment

Adults who work with young people on a daily basis—like Robin Cogan, R.N., a school nurse in Camden City, New Jersey, and a Johnson & Johnson fellow who teaches at the School of Nursing at Rutgers—are increasingly concerned about the emotional health and inner lives of our girls. Cogan is the leader of today's school nurse movement to assess and protect young people's health, and she has participated in congressional press conferences to sound warning bells about the myriad traumas and mental health concerns facing America's youth.

"If you were a fly on the wall in the life of a school nurse, even before COVID-19, you'd have seen that cots in our infirmaries were full of kids exhibiting symptoms of anxiety, depression, and somatic physical symptoms brought on by stress," Cogan tells me. "There is a generational epidemic of anxiousness which we have never seen before; kids and teens are facing things they just didn't deal with ten years ago. We spend thirty-five percent of our day addressing mental health and stress-related issues. These stressors are mind-blowing and worrisome in their newness, number, and constancy." Research backs up Cogan's concerns: In 2017, thirty-two hospitals reported that the percentage of teens being hospitalized for suicidal thoughts or actions had doubled over the past decade. Moreover, she adds, girls are clearly suffering in greater numbers. "It's clear to those of us who work with children that even as girls and boys face the same pressures, rates of anxiety and depression are skyrocketing more among girls." This remains true even as more young people are referred for counseling. (Though it is also true that too few children and teens who would benefit from therapy ever receive it.)

Today, given the COVID-19 crisis, teens' rates of anxiety, depression, and eating disorders have only worsened. The pandemic has poured gasoline on an existing fire. But there is one toxic influence that has been around far longer than the virus, one that Cogan believes has caused this generation of girls to fare very differently from the girls who came through her school just ten or fifteen years ago. And it is a major contributor to so many school infirmary cots' being filled with adolescent girls.

"Every day, as school nurses, we observe, observe, observe. We see that even very young girls, from the ages of seven or eight years old, are trying to navigate the signals they receive on social media about who and how they should be, look, and behave, which are inherently sexist. By the age of eight, this question of how to be the right kind of female is already pervading their minds as girls."

IN SEPTEMBER 2021, *The Wall Street Journal* ran a now-famous series called the Facebook Files, which exposed internal documents showing that Facebook (recently renamed Meta, which owns Instagram) has known for years that Instagram can be toxic to girls' mental health. In one internal report, Facebook's own researchers warned executives that among girls who felt bad about their bodies, 32 percent said "Instagram made them feel worse." "We make body issues worse for 1 in 3 teen girls," researchers concluded. Forty percent of teens said feelings of being "unattractive" began when they started using Instagram. About a quarter of teens who reported feeling "not good enough" said that feeling, too, began on Instagram. Many felt the app had undermined their confidence in their friendships. Other data shows that the majority of children start using social media apps between ages eight and thirteen— even though users are supposed to be at least thirteen to have an account. Teens regularly reported wanting to spend less time on Instagram, but they also reported lacking the self-control to do so. Other controlled studies—which compare girls who frequent social media to those who don't—paint a clearer picture: the more time a teenage girl spends on social media platforms, the more likely she is to develop depressive symptoms, poor body image, and lower self-esteem, and this association between social media use and depression is far stronger for girls compared with boys. It's possible, of course, that some girls turn to social media because they're already feeling anxious or depressed, and they seek a way to connect to their peers. It may also be that some teens are more vulnerable to these adverse effects. The research is limited, but what we do know is cause for concern.

According to Jean Twenge, Ph.D.—author of the book *iGen* and professor of psychology at San Diego State University—adolescent girls today spend twice as much time on smartphones, and on social media, than boys. Girls also spend more time texting and scrolling on digital platforms. But even among girls and boys who are equally heavy users of social media, the same amount of time spent on digital media is more strongly associated with lower well-being among girls. Twenge argues that social media induces "feelings of upward social comparison," or the feeling that you do not compare favorably with others—a belief that exacerbates greater body image concerns for girls and appears to be especially harmful to their psychological health.

Twenge is one of the researchers who, along with New York University psychologist Jonathan Haidt, Ph.D., found that 2012 was the year when rates of teenage depression, loneliness, and suicide began to rise sharply in girls. They investigated why this turning point in female mental health occurred and believe that much of the reason for this lies in the fact that in 2009, Facebook added a Like button and Twitter added a Retweet button. By 2012, these features had turned each social media platform into "an outrage machine that made life online far uglier, faster, more polarized and more likely to incite performative shaming." Users' feeds gained followers based on engagement—meaning how well a post could trigger big, overwhelming emotions. Twenty twelve was also the year social media use became ubiquitous among adolescents. Instagram grew significantly in popularity, inviting young women to "compare and despair" as they scrolled through posts showing faces, bodies, and lives reedited to depict images of perfection rather than reality, writes Twenge. This "had particularly strong effects on girls and young women." It is as if, around 2012, a poison entered the water and girls' minds began to sip that water daily.

Studies looking at brain scans underscore the ill effects that being evaluated has on brain health. At UCLA's Brain Mapping Center, researchers examined what happens in the teen brain when kids scroll through social media posts and images that have a high number of "likes." When teens see popular photos, the reward system in the brain—which includes an area known as the nucleus accumbens—becomes "especially active." (This is similar to what happens in our brains when we nibble on chocolate or think about winning the lottery.) The brain's reward system is especially malleable during adolescence. Over time, perusing what's "liked" on social media (including posts that show other teens engaging in risky behaviors like smoking or drinking) can affect a teen's ability to differentiate between healthy and unhealthy choices. This, in turn, can alter their capacity for decision making and self-control, turning off what researchers call the "be careful" filter. Other research shows the more an individual engages in behaviors that activate the brain's reward system, the more the brain anticipates future rewards, and the more you want to engage in that behavior again, even if it's harmful.

We have less insight into how teens are affected physiologically by feeling personally excluded or disliked on social media. We do know that feeling socially excluded in adolescence, in general, is associated with an array of future health problems: when kids feel left out, they're more likely to develop metabolic syndrome, heart issues, and obesity by middle age. Similarly, being excluded—or observing others being excluded vicariously—activates areas of the brain associated with experiencing physical pain.

As they scroll on their phones, girls are also more likely to be inundated with images that edit out or erase other girls' imperfections and flaws, and are more likely to feel they have to join influencer beauty trends and fashion standards. Consider the 2020 Instagram fad on encouraging girls to pose with "Barbie Feet": Stand on your tippy toes, elongate your legs, and flex your thigh muscles so it looks as if you're wearing high heels without any shoes, like a Barbie doll. Or consider the Victoria's Secret Fashion Show craze of super-thin, super-busty models strutting in their underwear wearing angel's wings.* At the same time, girls are far more likely to post images of themselves (body, clothes, hair) and receive critical, negative, and/or sexist messages in response, compared with boys. Girls also get messages from two directions: critiques from other girls about whether they fit in or are popular enough and voyeuristic remarks from boys commenting on their looks or rating them. This is rarely the case for boys.

---

*   Between 1995 and 2018, models who walked the runway in the Victoria's Secret Fashion Show got thinner, though their hip-waist ratio remained the same, a 2020 study found. Due to public pushback, Victoria's Secret discontinued its lingerie fashion shows in 2021—evidence that consumers can collectively effect change.

Robin Cogan believes that the very early encroachment of social media and the way in which girls are highly sexualized and critiqued about their bodies from a very young age have become even more problematic in recent years, not just because of smartphones, but also because of the increasing prevalence of Apple Watches (or cheaper versions of such): "Grade school and middle school kids constantly use Instagram and other, more secret apps on their wrists," Cogan says. "They are communicating through visuals all day—photos, videos, TikTok. And we know that pictures are processed sixty thousand times faster by the brain than words." This, in turn, Cogan believes, is leading to "girls being bombarded with thousands of images [telling them] to be perfect, impossible expectations for what they should look like, and a constant communal judging and oversexualizing of their female body at a crucially vulnerable and formative age."

Images, especially, evoke a strong physical reaction and inspire other children to mimic and mirror those behaviors. "If a girl is scrolling online and sees dozens or hundreds of images of other girls posing seductively at the age of nine, she is more likely to do the same," says Cogan. "If children see videos of other children engaging in self-harm behaviors, they are more likely to do the same."

To echo an idea first put forth by novelist Iris Murdoch, humans are the only creatures who create pictures of themselves and then "come to resemble the picture." If this is true, then today's culture has created a social media–made image that reflects back to girls what it means to be—and how they should be—female. Girls growing up today are creating identities from their phones and digital media, assigning personal, physical, and emotional value to themselves based on how they appear in photos and whether they are liked, tagged, and followed.

Every platform is a little different: compare and despair on Instagram, where the focus is on appearance, beauty, and lifestyle; perform your heart out on TikTok for likes, laughs, or thrills; filter or shapeshift your face on Snapchat; and compete to be the wittiest or most opinionated on Twitter. The line between experience and performance becomes blurred.

As humans, we constantly evaluate ourselves by seeing how well we stack up to others, gauging our own level of attractiveness, intelligence, social status, and success. Research shows that as much as 10 percent of our thoughts involve comparing ourselves to those around us. And the more time we spend trying to determine our social worth in this way, the more likely we are to feel dissatisfied and distressed about our lives. Photos on social media are shared and liked as if they tell a truth about someone else's amazing life, or face, or body, but more often, they offer up a very convincing lie or, at best, a momentary, curated glimpse against the backdrop of a longer, harder, and more complex lived experience. This world of façades exacts a cost: Youth who dwell on thoughts about how well their body compares with others are more likely, for example, to have symptoms of disordered eating. How can your daughter's interior sense of self thrive if it's inundated with lies and illusions? Again, you as a parent may be doing everything right to help your daughter flourish. But even a well-loved girl's sense of who she is and of her strength, worth, and power will diminish over time amid an avalanche of sexist messaging.

In addition to eroding self-esteem through negative social comparison, time spent on social media can detract from face-to-face relationships. As Twenge puts it, "Electronically mediated social interactions are like empty calories. Just imagine what teenagers' health would be like today if we had taken 50 percent of the most nutritious food out of their diets in 2012 and replaced those calories with sugar." And yet, social media interactions give the brain the impression that one is engaging in meaningful social togetherness. (To rework a quote from philosopher Theodor Adorno, social media "endlessly cheats its consumers out of what it endlessly promises.") The brain also gets tricked into believing that the sense of not being good enough, instilled via thousands of images and skewed messaging, is real and meaningful. And all the while the comments roll in—the good, the bad, and the ugly.

For an increasingly large swath of girls, a smartphone or Apple Watch at the age of eight, nine, ten, or eleven seems to be a gateway to their being influenced by a girl-poisoning culture. This is really a millennia-old tale in which a patriarchal view of the feminine ideal influences whether a girl feels accepted or rejected as she crosses the threshold from puberty into teenagerhood. And yet, being accepted often comes with the price tag of her being sexually objectified. Even as it is true that girls enjoy more choices, freedoms, and opportunities today than ever before—and there is more online awareness via movements like MeToo and TimesUp—at the same time, social media has cranked up the volume of misogynistic voices and views. Think of how the social media machine descended on Greta Thunberg, Hillary Clinton, Taylor Swift (who shared in a documentary that she often starved herself before concerts to the point of nearly passing out), Britney Spears, tennis players Serena Williams and Naomi Osaka, and so many before and since, when they weren't quiet or compliant (aka feminine) enough.

Even a well-loved girl's sense of who she is
and of her strength, worth, and power will diminish
over time amid an avalanche of sexist messaging.

Girls must grapple with the clear message that, as they get older, they're going into a world laced with gender inequities and sexual harassment. In September 2021, the two leading headlines on Twitter were "Blogger Disappears on Her Trip with Boyfriend" and "Gymnasts Slam FBI, Olympics, for Ignoring Reports of Sexual Abuse for Years." In March 2021, the headlines changed, but the stories were similar: Seven women were shot and killed in Georgia in a racist, misogynist, hate-spurred spree. A policeman in the United Kingdom murdered a woman while she was walking home. These are bookended by stories of powerful men abusing younger women—from morning TV host Matt Lauer, financier Jeffrey Epstein, Fox News network's Roger Ailes, TV star Bill Cosby, to movie mogul Harvey Weinstein. You can simply insert the name of the latest male predator and complete the sentence with how he groomed, coerced, harassed, or forced less powerful, younger females or teen girls to perform sex acts.

This is the reality. How can girls feel safe coming of age in a world in which so many prominent men have used their power to harm girls like them? At the same time, these threats are amplified by social media clickbait algorithms that elicit fear and outrage, so that viewers feel they, too, are in some way under attack, even when they scroll from the safety of their sofas. The reality is terrible. The Twittersphere portrayal of it, replete with vitriolic comments and discord, not only mirrors legitimate concerns, it magnifies threat. This is what girls marinate in every day on social media.

During the past fifteen years, as we have seen, the rates of depression and suicide among girls and teen girls have skyrocketed. Yet, again, the cohort of young women just ten years older (who were born before 1994, and who, in the year 2022, are age twenty-eight or older) does not show this same increase in mental health concerns. As the famous neurologist Oliver Sacks once wrote, perhaps as a word of warning, "younger people, for the most part, who have grown up in our social-media era, have no personal memory of how things were before, and no immunity to the seductions of digital life. What we are seeing—and bringing on ourselves—resembles a neurological catastrophe on a gigantic scale." And girls seem to be at the epicenter of this catastrophe.

REGARDLESS OF THE positive messages they may receive from their family of origin or from teachers about their potential, girls are constantly encountering more destructive messages from the outside world about what we as human beings consider acceptable or are willing to normalize when it comes to the treatment and equality of women. Even as some social media sites have started to push back and speak up about fat shaming and a healthy body image, these messages on health and wellness (from parents, schools, and online platforms) can't always compete with the unrelentingly sexist cultural vibe.

The era of MeToo and TimesUp has brought into stark focus the conflicting messages facing girls: to measure up to an ideal of effortless physical female perfection in behavior and appearance while staying vigilant in the face of sexual harassment and safe in a male-dominated society; and to be beautiful and desirable while also guarding against sexual abuse. This dilemma puts girls in a state of biological implausibility. How can you walk the tightrope of being both attractive and safe while living an independent, fearless day-to-day life in a society that values the first for women so much more than the latter?

And often, from an early age onward, girls like Julia and Anna lack the kind of wider community connectedness and close relationships with older female role models who can buffer them from the avalanche of toxic sexist messaging society constantly serves up. None of this is new, of course. What *is* new is our understanding that being inundated with this conflicted messaging may be (as we will see in part 2 of this book) affecting a generation of girls at a neurobiological level in ways we're just beginning to grasp.

Many sociologists feel that receiving so many confusing mixed messages (messages that shift based on who is doing the messaging and that sometimes contradict one another) is introducing a kind of cognitive dissonance, which is itself a stressor. Consider just one example: The National Academies of Sciences, Engineering, and Medicine reports that even though women make up more than half of medical school classes, "up to half of female medical students are sexually harassed during their training." Indeed, "[g]ender discrimination is so prevalent in the field that there are currently ongoing lawsuits against major institutions," including the Mount Sinai Health System, the Oregon Health and

Science University, and Tulane. (Meanwhile, the pay gap between male and female doctors remains considerable: female physicians are paid, on average, 25 percent less than their male peers.) We tell girls they can be anything, but as they work to become who they want to be, they also can't help but see that male harassment and unfair treatment may await them and that being good at something doesn't make them safe while doing it.

The juxtaposition of, on the one hand, being told that you have the freedom and safety to be anything you want to be and, on the other, of coming of age in a society in which there are clearly negative consequences to being female is a chronic unpredictable toxic stressor—and one more lens through which we can examine why this generation of girls feels high anxiety. Moreover, this idea that the world is full of endless and exciting opportunities for girls requires them to be able to imagine the strong, capable women they will become in some far-off, distant future. Meanwhile, if, in daily life, they are repeatedly exposed to themes that normalize being objectified under the male gaze, that messaging will slowly exert more influence over their self-view than will imagining their future, empowered selves.

Again, other times in our shared history have, of course, imposed trauma on young people; take world wars. How could twenty-first-century stressors come anywhere close to being as taxing? We don't have all the answers, but when comparing past stressors to today's, we have to bear in mind that cataclysmic world events like World War II or even 9/11 happened to an entirely different generation, one without all the added stressors of today's world converging simultaneously. It isn't just about *what* is happening; it's also about the cumulative effect of *all* that is happening.

Another difference may be this: endless critique-laden comments on social media make everything feel more up close and personal and societally dysfunctional at the same time. As Surgeon General Vivek Murthy, M.D., writes in his 2021 report, *Protecting Youth Mental Health,* social media tools "pit us against each other . . . and undermine the safe and supportive environments young people need and deserve." During past eras of great national distress (world wars or the Great Depression) there often existed an idea of communal togetherness amid the heartache and loss. Fear and grief seemed to be shared. But we don't really come together as a society anymore. In today's world, on media platforms, opinions are given the same airtime and weight as well-honed expertise and knowledge. Online platforms intentionally drive divisiveness between opposing "sides" just as they turn up the volume on criticizing girls and women if they look or behave the "wrong" way. Digital media isn't just a potent rapid delivery system for the poisoning of girls' brains; it's also a powerful delivery system for feeling personally blamed or shamed.

As the media critic Emily Nussbaum wrote in a tweet referring to the treatment of singer Britney Spears by the media, "It's not some ancient story of misogynist horror—and in certain ways, things seem worse now, because of social media. Every feed is a tabloid; every phone is a paparazzo." Moreover, "a lot has flattened out across the internet, where no one ends up specifically responsible."

We talk about "time being up," but the reality is that the times in which we live are uniquely harmful for girls. Meanwhile, every girl holds a toxic and often misogynistic message delivery device right in the palm of her hand.

CHAPTER THREE

The Missing Years

We've Stolen Girls' Safe "In-Between Years"

I N A SMALL waiting room in Pikesville, Maryland, a teenage girl and her mom sit waiting, while another mother waits for her daughter to come out of Amy Karlen, Ph.D.'s, therapy room. Behind them, framed photographs of folks going about their daily lives in urban Baltimore hang as if in an art exhibit; Karlen is not just a well-respected female adolescent psychotherapist in the state of Maryland; she's also a photographer whose artwork has been exhibited locally.

The door of Karlen's office opens, revealing two big comfy chairs and a sofa. She comes into the waiting room. A teenage girl enters behind her, grinning and looking toward her mother. It doesn't take long to figure out why. Karlen breaks into song, belting out, "Happy birthday to you, / Happy birthday to you . . ." She seems to be aware, in a good-natured way, that she is extremely off-key. She braves her way through the familiar chorus, as everyone looks toward the young girl's mother, who has put her checkbook down, confusion on her face.

"Happy birthday!" the mother and daughter who are sitting together call out.

I join in with the felicitations—I'm here to chat with Karlen for twenty minutes or so, before her next appointment begins, and I am not known for my singing—but who can resist joining in a round of the Happy Birthday song when there are only six people gathered in a small room?

"But it's not my birthday!" the serenaded mother says.

Karlen gives a knowing, reassuring smile. "Charlotte and I were just talking about how hard it can be sometimes to do simple things when we feel anxious," she says. "I'd confided to her that I'm tone-deaf. I can't sing at all. The idea of singing anything in public makes me sweat. So Charlotte made me a deal: If I came out here and serenaded the waiting room, she would work on doing some of the things that she finds it hard to do when she feels anxious, too."

Charlotte and her mother leave on a light note, and the waiting mother-daughter pair explain that they're there to drop off intake paperwork they've filled out. A moment later, everything is quiet, and I follow Karlen into her office.

Karlen, who serves on the board of the Maryland chapter of the Association of Family and Conciliation Courts, has worked with thousands of girls and young women over the span of her thirty-five years in practice. I'm curious to see if she can offer me a more boots-on-the-ground perspective about the perfect storm of factors that seems to be affecting our girls today.

She begins by zeroing in on the fact that, for many of today's girls, childhood has been cut radically short, not just by early exposure to social media, but on many other levels. "In a society where we believe the chances of our children succeeding are increasingly diminishing, the way we raise our kids has become affected. For girls in particular, this has led to a loss of what was once an extended period of safe passage into late childhood, when girls used to get to enjoy exploring the world, playing in a more carefree manner, learning about safe social bonding, and emotionally maturing, all while enjoying the protection of their family and community. Over the past fifteen to twenty years, we've stolen away that crucial transitional period of identity formation between childhood and adolescence from girls."

For instance, Karlen explains, "fifth and sixth grade[s] used to be a time when girls were free to gravitate to other girls who shared their interests and who[m] they enjoyed hanging out with on the playground or after school. Girls came through those in-between years of nine to thirteen or so immersed in the camaraderie of genuine friendships without the pressure to invest in so many structured and competitive activities." That easy, innocent bonding period was, says Karlen, "a cornerstone of childhood and served as a crucial learning phase during which girls safely explored how to negotiate differences in friendships, how to be a caring friend, and enjoyed a less intense period in which they could explore the world."

Today, during those same in-between years, girls find instead that they are often categorized by other girls on a competitive, hierarchal, performance-oriented level: Who is getting attention—in social cliques, with boys, on social media, in sports, in terms of physical sexual maturity, appearance, and achievement? "That provokes excessive anxiety at a much younger age," Karlen tells me. Suddenly, we've introduced to a set of threats and rewards in terms of how one is viewed or accepted at a vulnerable stage in both identity and physical development, years before girls' brains are equipped to deflect that kind of competition and criticism and put it into context. At the same time, she explains, "there is a more tenuous distinction in the media or on social media between being a girl and being a woman: Girls are frequently sexualized almost as women. And vice versa: Women are sexualized as prepubescent girls. Which means that one of the first introductions girls get to being female, as they begin to form their own identity as a woman, centers on the most threatening and least genuine component of being female— being seen as a sexual object." As Karlen talks, I think of how her observations closely mirror Julia Abernathy's experiences and sense of a lost childhood.

Karlen's phone has pinged quite a few times since we sat down. She picks it up and quickly texts someone back. "An eighth-grader who is struggling a lot today," she tells me before putting her phone away. "We often see this early emergence of sexuality and objectification impacts on female-to-female friendships as well," she continues. "The 'mean girl' and 'queen bee' aspects of girls' interactions are perpetuated by the insecurity that accompanies being thrust into a role they are not developmentally ready for."

As kids transition from grade school to middle school, they also move from schools full of familiar friend groups into more alien settings, among kids they may not know. Shifting trends in education, which impose more mature expectations, behaviors, and accomplishments on children at younger ages, also bring on more stress. For instance, kindergarten, which used to be a time of play, is when today's kids learn much of what used to be learned in first grade. Standardized testing, active-shooter drills, budget cuts, and the COVID-19 pandemic have overshadowed or eradicated playtime, recess, leisurely lunch hours, PE class, dance, art, and music. Middle school has emerged as the new high school, as the coming pressure of the college process creeps earlier and earlier into the child experience.

"This consuming preoccupation with ensuring our children's success has led to a parental mindset that early achievements and accomplishments will ensure positive outcomes," says Karlen. For example, when educating their children, parents gravitate toward schools that promise to have their kids reading in preschool or kindergarten, "ignoring studies that tell us that reading at such an early age has a complex and unclear correlation with reading outcomes." These earlier time lines for achieving academic benchmarks interfere with normal, healthy stages of development.

By middle school, many students begin to echo their parents' concerns about their futures and achievement. "In clinical practice, we see an ever-mounting number of students—and girls in particular—who present with anxiety disorders along with a perfectionistic drive. The rallying cry of 'everything counts' turns middle schools into an arena where adolescents feel heightened pressure to perform and achieve. In therapy, adolescents often voice a belief that accelerated placements and victory on the sports field will land them not only in the dream college, but ultimately, in the dream life." Yet, simultaneously, kids "are cracking under the heat and pressure. And ironically, students who have somehow dodged these pressures are sometimes referred for therapy because parents or educators are concerned about their motivation."

We've raised our expectations for children and teens to unrealistic and unsustainable levels without making space for them to just be kids. Rates of perfectionism have increased in children over the past several decades: Youth today cite putting pressure on themselves to achieve more than did previous generations. A recent report on adolescent wellness from the Robert Wood Johnson Foundation underscores this: Three in ten teens today report problems with perfectionism. Perfectionism, in turn, is associated with a greater likelihood of developing anxiety disorders and depression. Researchers believe the top environmental forces disrupting adolescent wellness include this increased pressure to excel as well as the impact of poverty, trauma, discrimination, or social media.

The Starling Effect

This competitive atmosphere extends out of the classroom, permeating family and community life, too.

Across evolutionary time, our kids have come of age within the context of a community, which conferred considerable safety even though the environment around them contained multiple dangers. But in our current child-raising environment, it often appears as if everyone were out for their own child, trading favors (or cash, as in the 2019 college admissions scandal involving celebrities and select schools) to get their kids into the right schools, rooting for their own kids from the sidelines at the expense of the well-being of *all* the kids in the community. No matter how many brownies parents might bake for their child's team or classroom birthday party, we live in a "my kid first," "anti-tribe" era.

Some sociologists call this "the starling effect." Male starlings compete for the best nests with other birds, such as bluebirds and woodpeckers, and they can be tricky and aggressive when they set out to create an ideal nesting place for their babies. Adult starlings have been known to peck holes in other birds' eggs, remove building material from nests, kill babies that have already hatched, and even build their nest right on top of an existing bird's nest, burying and destroying the other bird's eggs or hatchlings. Once starlings have gotten rid of the competition for resources, they fluff up their own nest and raise their babies in style.

It's a harsh example, but it serves our purposes as an analogy for the "my kid first" environment that is taking a psychic toll on today's teens. Rather than feel safer because Mom and Dad are willing to do anything for them, kids seeing their parents focus so much on their success can lead to the inevitable conclusion that, sure, Mom and Dad might be on your side, but, it then logically follows, other parents in the "tribe" may be waiting for you to mess up so *their* kid can score that goal, win that prize, get that college acceptance letter, earn the best grade. The way in which we approach child-rearing has radically changed, too; we don't rely on shared, communal structures for childcare; school days are longer and more regimented, and every family is its own island, each of whose inhabitants hopes *their* offspring will get the best and be the best at everything. This kind of familial isolationism is changing the society we live in and adding to the stress burden on teens during a critical developmental window—at exactly the time when they need added re-assurance that the community-at-large has their back, before they go off into the world on their own.

"This dual messaging feels irreconcilable for teens," Karlen tells me. "While, on the one hand, teamwork and collaboration are emphasized as effective learning strategies, on the other hand, parents reinforce the view that our current world is a place with limited resources for those on the move to success. The underlying message becomes 'Never forget: The competition is fierce.'" Alternately, some parents may stress that they only want their teens to try their best, "while simultaneously cor-ralling resources to ensure achievement," she adds. "How can children and teens discern the real message, or not feel that everything is riding on the heels of their feats? All kids realize, on some level, that they are competing within the 'village' that is also supposed to support them. Anxiety permeates, and for some, this results in attaining their goals, often at a cost. For others, it contributes to resentment, opposition, withdrawal, anxiety, or depression."

Put these trends together, says Karlen, and "we've stolen away those years during which girls were once free to learn what safe, genuine bonding in relationships feels like and, instead, we've replaced it with a period marked by competition, threat-and-reward judgments, and oversexualization." All this put girls in a chronic hyper-alert state during a critical time in their development, in which (as we shall see in chapter 4) genes for depression and anxiety are being activated or not activated. "The crucial period of late childhood during which girls used to be free to learn what safely flocking together felt like has simply evaporated."

Familial isolationism is changing the society we live in and adding to the stress burden on teens during a critical developmental window—at exactly the time when they need added reassurance that the community-at-large has their back, before they go off into the world on their own.

Other cultural shifts play into this loss of childhood. Earlier in our history as a young country, communities and neighborhoods often drew together based on aspects of their culture, whatever that culture might be amid the larger American melting pot. That sense of community offered an expansive sense of safety, of being known by lots of adults; children came of age amid a larger flock. Today, we tend to rely on having a good enough nuclear family to ensure that children feel that the people around them have their best interest at heart. But the nuclear family, while the most powerful and important thing in a child's life, may not be sufficient to help calibrate a child's nervous system as they encounter challenges throughout their day. If girls (like Julia and Anna) come into puberty and face myriad new stressors and adversities, many of which are unique to being female, and simultaneously feel there is no one or nowhere to safely flock to, it can affect their lifelong mental health and the tenor of their future.

And, says Karlen, "parents and schools often don't realize they are promoting this expectation of early maturity by reinforcing societal messaging that values certain 'Wow!' characteristics in girls." Parents may not notice how comments that place an emphasis on their daughter's being compassionate toward friends (rather than addressing her own needs and emotions) or about their daughter's developing breasts send the message that maturing quickly is more desirable than the normal time line of childhood.

IT'S AN OLD DISEASE—sexism, violence against women, a lack of female power—but with social media, a lack of community, and increased pressures in all areas of teen life, we may very possibly have made the illness temporarily worse.

When we start to unpack the emerging science, we can see that girls' rising rates of mental and physical health issues are caused not by any single recent change in their environments, but by a perfect storm of escalating factors, many of which have been unwittingly set in place by us, the adults who love them. These growing toxic environmental stressors can negatively affect the bodies and brains of both girls and boys in concerning ways. But females are often hit harder. Still, the question remains: Why?

PART TWO

The New Science of Why Our Girls Are Struggling

CHAPTER FOUR

Two Windows in Time
When Early Stress Shapes
a Child's Development

Neuroscientist Tracy Bale, Ph.D., is troubled by the growing rate at which American girls are suffering from anxiety and depression. Before Bale came to the University of Maryland School of Medicine to direct its Center for Epigenetic Research in Child Health and Brain Development, she served as codirector of UPenn's Center for the Study of Sex and Gender in Behavioral Health. During her tenure at both these institutions, Bale has been studying the role of childhood stress as a risk factor for adolescent mental health disorders and how chronic stressors at different stages of development (from conception through the teen years) affect females and males differently.

Bale, who also serves as president of the International Brain Research Organization, has a reputation for getting things done and for graduating good scientists, which means she is both patient and a stellar teacher of complex concepts. This is fortunate, because when she and I sit down together for the first time at a low-key Baltimore eatery, what we delve into—the core scaffolding for understanding the biological underpinnings of the generational shift we are seeing in girls' health—gets a tad complex.

What Bale has found, she tells me, leaning forward as she speaks, is that "females and males undergo very different timing windows of vulnerability during development, and during these distinct, crucial windows, chronic stressors and adversity are more likely to impact their well-being." These stressors, as we've seen, can include a range of adversities or trauma in childhood: stressors in home life, environmental crises and pandemics, community stress such as poverty or violence, and emotional stressors in social relationships or social interactions. Although it may seem a little confusing, because it also uses the term *environmental,* researchers such as Bale refer to all of these myriad stressors that can affect a developing child's health as *environmental insults.*

Our society is increasingly laden with environmental insults for all adolescents, of course. But to better understand why the female teenage body and brain can, over time, become more vulnerable, we have to go to the very beginning of every child's story, all the way back to the womb.

How Early Adversity in a Child's Life Can Affect Who They Become

After you were conceived, and as you grew in utero, you were protected by your mother's womb. Around you grew a complex cluster of your own cells tangled with your mother's: the placenta. The placenta serves as a sort of filter to lessen the blow of anything harmful headed your way from the world surrounding you as a mother-baby duo. "Almost anything that might be deleterious to your developing body and brain—chemicals your mother might breathe in while walking across a newly fertilized lawn; elevated stress hormones in the face of emotional stress; infections; the ramifications of your mother's diet—are all, at least to some degree, buffered by the placenta, though perhaps not entirely," Bale explains. "The question with any such environmental insult is: How well is the fetus protected from harm?" This is why, when physicians decide if a medication is safe to take during pregnancy, the first consideration is whether data have shown that it crosses the placenta.

In addition to acting as a screen against as many toxins and stress-related hormones and chemicals as possible, the placenta also acts as a kind of superconductor of information. "The placenta sends the brain trillions of messages that signal, even as you're cocooned in your mother's womb, what kind of world you will soon be coming into, so that your nervous system, immune system, and brain will be primed in a way that will best mesh with whatever awaits you," Bale explains. That's because the question that the brain cares most about during gestational development is: What's next? Will you be born into a world that is safe or unsafe? What exactly do your brain and body need to get ready for?

From the womb onward, and throughout childhood and adolescence, stressors influence the behavior of our genes. This is a relatively new idea. Until very recently, modern genetic science assumed that most of our genes were fixed, just like our hair, skin, and eye color. Fixed, inherited genes were seen as like a builder's rough plans for a future house—in this case, for the architecture of a child's developing body and mind and for the adult she or he might one day become. Genes were blamed or praised for many of the characteristics others may have observed in a child while he or she was growing up. Hence the saying used when, for example, the son whose father bellowed at him throughout his childhood begins to bellow at his own kids, "The apple doesn't fall far from the tree."

But over the past few decades, a growing field of newer research into how genes work has overturned this thinking. Just as we (our body and brain) are engaged in a constant, intricate dance with the environment around us, so are our genes. And the way in which our genes behave is shaped by minute influences. This process is called gene expression, or epigenetics. It is a 24/7 cellular machination that turns our experiences, and our biography, into our biology.

Almost all the cells in your body contain your genes, but only a small percentage of those genes become activated over the course of your life. Different genes can be switched on at different times: some during development in the womb, others during childhood, some during puberty or the teen years, others during adulthood. Some genes are active all the time. Some never turn on. Yes, you inherit your genome, but the package of genes you inherit is perhaps less important than which genes become operational. Environmental influences, both good and bad, determine which genes are set in motion in the body and will be expressed across an individual's life span. Will you develop your mother's knack for math? Your father's talent as a pianist? Your mother's generalized anxiety disorder? Your father's arthritis?

The genes that influence these tendencies can vary in the degree to which they turn on, much the way a dimmer switch can determine how faint or bright the light from a chandelier becomes in a room. Different influences and events in your life can crank the dimmer switch to full wattage or keep it switched off altogether, so that a particular gene stays dark across your lifetime. We hope, as we raise our children, to create a sense of safety, love, and security that helps keep that dimmer switch dialed *down* when it comes to negative genes that lurk in our gene pool and dialed *up* when it comes to activating the good ones.

ALTHOUGH THE PROCESS of gene expression happens throughout our lives, there are two timing windows during which genes are far more vulnerable to shifting in both negative and positive ways: during fetal development and, again, during puberty. During the first period of heightened vulnerability to stress, precisely how well the placenta protects the fetus from any environmental insults depends on the baby's sex. Bale breaks this down: "Just as females have two X chromosomes, so does the female placenta. Just as males have both an X and Y chromosome, so does the male placenta." During fetal development, the placenta's X chromosomes confer a protective role; they create a stronger buffer zone between the mother's world and the baby's than Y chromosomes. Why? X chromosomes carry X-linked genes, "which serve as regulators, or molecular brakes, during development, which helps to keep the female fetus from being as deeply affected by every environmental stressor the mother encounters." Bale offers up this simple analogy: This doubly strong female braking system is like having a car with a well-built chassis; your body won't register every bump, jolt, or pothole during a long road trip. The developing male fetus, for its part, has fewer molecular regulators.

"Having fewer molecular regulators is like having a car with touchy brakes and a chassis that makes you feel every pothole and turn," says Bale. When you get out of that car after a long drive on bumpy roads, you'll probably find that your back aches and you feel a little shaken and stirred. What this means, Bale explains, is that "the female placenta is better able to protect against external stressors and keep harmful stimuli from ever reaching the developing female brain, whereas the developing brain of the male fetus is more at risk. This is why similar environmental insults affect boys more in utero, before birth, compared to girls."

Bale has demonstrated in animal models that when a pregnant mother is exposed to emotional, physical, and immunological stressors, the male fetus and brain will show "thousands of epigenetic changes in response to those stressors, and the female fetus will show almost none." This is the case for humans, too. "That's why male babies tend to be more vulnerable during pregnancy, in ways which show up at birth, and why we see so many more boys in neonatal intensive care units, or NICUs, than girls. When girls are in the NICU at birth, girls [also] recover and go home faster and sooner than boys." It is also why even though more boys are born than girls, the death rate among males is higher, so that by age ten, the male-to-female ratio evens out to be fifty-fifty.

And yet, although girls enjoy this brief, early layer of protection during gestation, after the cord is cut, that benefit begins to disappear. Just a decade or so down the road, girls lose any and all advantage over boys and become far more vulnerable to the adverse effects of the stressors in their lives. The female advantage becomes a double-edged sword, one that flips just as puberty sets in.

DURING THE YEARS that Anna Moralis and Julia Abernathy crossed the threshold into teenagerhood, and throughout their adolescences, their psyches were being shaped by events not only in their day-to-day lives, but in each girl's past, from the womb onward. And from the moment Anna and Julia entered puberty, all the cumulative stressors each had ever faced began to have a more powerful impact on her well-being. For it is at this moment that the female brain becomes more vulnerable in the face of outside stressors compared with the male brain. Suddenly, environmental insults have a bigger biophysical effect on girls' developing brains and immune systems. And that is, in large part, because the female immune system becomes newly dominated by the influx of female hormones, including estrogen.

A girl who has been chronically stressed before puberty may not show signs of the effects of that adversity until puberty begins. For, it is only then, when estrogen comes in, that underlying inflammatory processes that have been set in place due to chronic stress begin to manifest in the brain. Sometime between the ages of seven and thirteen, a girl's brain releases a signaling hormone that it sends to the pituitary gland, a pea-shaped endocrine organ that sits just under the brain. The pituitary gland sends a few more signaling hormones into the bloodstream that tell the body to set all the wheels in motion and begin the process of puberty. In girls, these hormones travel to the ovaries, stimulating them to begin producing estrogen, the primary hormone that causes a girl's body and brain to mature and change in ways that will eventually prepare her for pregnancy and motherhood. Puberty begins with a similar process in boys, a little later along the developmental time line, starting around age twelve, when the brain signals the testes to start producing testosterone.

When the process of puberty begins for girls, it's a bit like releasing the handle brakes on a bike. Bike and rider take off toward their destination with purpose: to travel from pubescence into becoming an adult woman, with adult levels of female hormones. At first, bike and rider travel at a leisurely pace. But as a girl passes through the early stages of puberty, and estrogen ramps up, the pedals, wheels, and gears begin to move faster.

As our hypothetical bike riding speeds up, estrogen influences every cell in the body from head to toe, enhancing communication among all the systems and organs, including the brain—where the process of puberty first began. In the brain, estrogen massages, soothes, and protects neurons and boosts blood flow, helping to regulate emotions and mood state, enhance cognition and memory, and sharpen clarity of mind.

As we all know—for we were all once teens, too—for both girls and boys, emotions can be intense during this process, moving quickly from low to high to low again in record time, as never-before-felt infusion-like rushes of emotions flood body and mind. The thrum of sexual excitement, the black dog of loneliness or despair—everything feels bigger (confusion, anger, sadness, elation), and teens often have little clue as to why.

Beneath the surface of these shifting emotions, hormones are hard at work. "Once the brain kick-starts this process of puberty, the job of estrogen, as it comes on board, is to oversee the maturation of all the systems and organs of the body," Bale explains. This includes enhancing "the growth of neural connections in the brain, so that all the different areas of the brain talk to each other and work in sync."

This master orchestration—chaotic as it may seem to the teen going through it, or to their confused parent—is purposeful, and that purpose is as old as time. And this is where we move from a basic Biology 101 lesson on puberty into asking the bigger question: Why is it that girls are suddenly, at the onset of puberty, more affected by outside social, societal, and environmental stressors, compared with boys?

"Ultimately, the primary role of hormones, including estrogen, is to also make sure that your brain and body are geared toward the same goal: future procreation," says Bale. And in order to do that—to prepare you, as a female, to procreate and become a mother on a biological level—"your brain first needs to take into account and evaluate all of the stressors and hardship in your environment. This includes factoring in all of the experiences of adversity and trauma you've ever faced in your life, right up to that point."

It's a bit like a computer system calculating the odds for a board game based on where on the board a player's piece sits now, and on the past moves that have taken place. By assessing these odds, your brain is trying to figure out how to prepare you for whatever future threats may be waiting for you and your children. The goal is to "reduce risk for you and your future offspring, so that you can safely carry a child, and [to] keep you and your baby free from any potential harm headed your way."

It makes sense, then, that during this sensitive window, past and present adverse experiences and toxic social-environmental influences get wired into how the brain becomes programmed and how it will work. Bale offers up another helpful analogy. Imagine that the female brain is a house, that estrogen-driven puberty is a period of its major remodeling and rebuilding, and that external stressors are a sweeping thunderstorm: "Imagine you've lived in the same house for a while," says Bale. "You're about to undergo a renovation. You decide to redo the interior walls, the electrical wiring, and basic plumbing. Suddenly, a big thunderstorm sweeps through the area, flooding the house. Lightning strikes the electrical panel. As you begin to remodel the house after the storm has passed, the pipes, electrical system, floors, and interior will have undergone some lingering damage." Puberty is the stormy period during which past and present environmental insults begin to manifest in the remodeling changes made to the architecture of the brain.

Then, based on the information the brain and body have absorbed, the brain that was once so wide open and loosey-goosey during puberty begins to tighten up again. It's a different brain, based on whatever intel it has received along the way.*

The decisions the brain makes in terms of how safe a girl growing up feels or does not feel based on past and current stressors are instrumental to determining how well the brain will wire up for lifelong mental health and well-being. When Anna Moralis faced myriad stressors during middle school and high school—being separated from her mother for long periods of time, feeling that she "was somehow the one who'd said or done something wrong" during arguments with her father in a way that led to an intense "sense of abandonment," sensing that her family life had "ruptured," being bombarded from girlhood on by social media and screen images of a feminine ideal imbued with "pervasive sexism" that made her feel ashamed of her own appearance, being ostracized by other girls who saw her as too serious-minded, and coming of age in a world rocked by the devastating and deadly effects of climate

---

* Puberty is a time of intense pruning in the brain. But when children have faced chronic adversity or trauma and/or have experienced an insufficient sense of safety with primary caregivers, immune cells in the brain called microglia can become primed by the immune system to over-prune synapses. When estrogen comes rushing in, and the brain begins to remodel as part of normal development, this neural pruning process can become set on overdrive, leading to a loss of needed synapses. At the same time, the cortex area of the brain, which is associated with the ability to think and reflect on one's own experiences and the world, is undergoing significant maturation. When girls relive and reinterpret past and present experiences in unhealthy ways, this new intellectual firepower for thinking and making sense of experiences can get turned inward. This is made worse by the onslaught of social media and images in media that signal to girls a skewed idea of who and what they should be.

change, school shootings, pervasive racism, and "so much social and environmental injustice"—her brain was taking in all that intel day after day, year after year. Anna's brain factored in all these stressors as it calculated exactly what kind of world Anna would need to contend with as she crossed the threshold into puberty and her reproductive years.

When Julia Abernathy, at the age of eleven, faced the stress of having her breasts be "all anyone else saw," of marinating in comments like "Better lock her up now," of having older boys push her up against lockers and fondle her breasts, and of being ignored for her academic promise while hoping someone would notice that "something is going on with Julia," her brain was factoring in how unseen, unsafe, and alone she was.

On the one hand, Anna and Julia grew up as girls enjoying all the advantages of twenty-first-century life. On the other hand, the way in which each girl's brain was shaped by her growing inherent sense of unsafety in our world was rooted in the oldest and most basic tenets of sex differences and neurobiology.

This pubescent brain-estrogen-stress interaction, Bale explains, is a significant part of why girls are impacted by mental health disorders at twice the rate of boys. And "it is why the biggest window for the development of depression, anxiety, bipolar disorder is during adolescence." Early stress can lead to epigenetic changes in specific genes that help oversee the stress response, including genes that can set the inflammatory stress response on high. This ramped-up immune response to stress can, in turn, increase the risk of mental health disorders.

Research suggests that some of these epigenetic shifts in response to stress occur in sex-specific ways, affecting girls more than boys. Researchers at Johns Hopkins and Harvard medical schools tested saliva in seventy-five people over the course of thirty days while simultaneously tracking their levels of cortisol, the hormone involved in mediating our response to stress. Using cortisol as an indicator of overall stress levels, researchers compared those levels to two other factors. They tested participants' blood samples to see if there were shifts in a particular gene associated with increased vulnerability to stress, known as FKBP5, and whether epigenetic changes to this gene could also be correlated with increased cortisol-indicated stress levels in people's lives. At the same time, they tracked how the test subjects felt—were they feeling anxious, depressed? They found that when levels of nighttime cortisol rose, the FKBP5 gene also underwent epigenetic changes, indicating an increased overall vulnerability to stressors. These two biological changes were, not surprisingly, associated with increased symptoms of depression and anxiety. However, this link among cortisol stress levels, epigenetic shifts in genes that increase susceptibility to stress over the long term, and increased feelings of despair was found only in women, including teenage girls.

Our nervous system is always poised to detect danger in our environment. This process of detecting threats, which leads to a cascade of neurotransmitters and hormones that prepare us for fight, flight, or freeze, is as primitive and inescapable as it is automatic: It's our source code as humans. We don't have all the answers yet on how sex hormones moderate the way in which stress at critical junctures in childhood gets stored and wreaks havoc at puberty; this is science in motion. Hormones other than estrogen are likely to be involved, and more research is emerging. But what is clear is this: Our psyches and the way we think and feel are shaped by our biological response to all the stressors we've experienced in both the past and the present, and this 24/7 shaping appears to be more fine-tuned by the nuances of our daily environment in females.

"If you routinely felt a sense of unsafety growing up because of myriad circumstances around you, all of that gets integrated into how your brain becomes wired up during this period of estrogen-driven integration," Bale explains. She underscores, however, that this is not necessarily always a negative. "Just as girls' brains are more intricately intertwined with negative stimuli in their environment, they are also deeply influenced by positive stimuli."

Our psyches and the way we think and feel are shaped by our biological response to all the stressors we've experienced in both the past and the present, and this 24/7 shaping appears to be more fine-tuned by the nuances of our daily environment in females.

Females start out with a biologically determined advantage. If we can understand what environmental interactions between birth and puberty disrupt this benefit, and what kinds of interventions protect female flourishing, we can rewrite girls' stories as they come of age so that they regain this innate biological resiliency.

CHAPTER FIVE

The Power of Social Safety

Why Feeling Under Threat and Unsafe Affects Girls in Unique Ways

NOT LONG BEFORE the COVID-19 pandemic altered life as we knew it, Deleicea Greene had just been crowned the 2019 Youth Poet Laureate of Baltimore. Her onstage performances of slam poetry in spoken-word contests up and down the East Coast came after she had spent much of her childhood writing poetry and secreting the pages under her pillow.

"By the time I was ten, I was already feeling really depressed and anxious and alone," Deleicea tells me when we meet in person at a small outdoor coffee shop. At first, Deleicea appears to have a cheerful, hopeful demeanor. But after we settle into our wobbly chairs at our small table, it's clear that, behind her round wire-rimmed glasses, her warm brown eyes signal something tangibly sad.

It's difficult for her to make sense of her childhood, she tells me. "Now that I'm twenty-one, I ask myself, *Hey, didn't anybody notice I was so sad?* Someone should have taken me to see a school counselor or a therapist. No one did." Born in Baltimore City, Deleicea was six when she and her mother moved to the city's outskirts. "My mom didn't want me to get involved in some of the habits that she saw girls in the city picking up; she didn't want me caught up in the wrong things." Deleicea recognizes this as a brave move for a single mom. But there was a downside. When she started at her new grade school, she says, "the bullying began."

"I was bullied all throughout elementary school because I was chubby," she tells me. "This one boy started calling me Jelly Doughnut, and another boy called me Big Mac. I'd try to make friends with other new kids when they came to our school, but then they'd hear me getting called these names, and they'd leave me out, too." The small irony, Deleicea says, is that "my mom didn't have the money for us to eat out; I'd never had a Big Mac or a jelly doughnut." As she got older, being ostracized hurt even more because as kids started to socialize and have sleepovers and parties, "I was one hundred percent excluded."

All this impacted her school performance. "I wasn't the best student. I'd get all As and Bs and then a D in math. My mom would say, 'It's so easy to get on honor roll in elementary school; why aren't you on it?'" But part of the reason Deleicea struggled was that after school, when she needed help with homework, there was no one to turn to. "My mom has a learning disability, so I had to read all of her mail for her and help with paying our bills. I'd go home from school and take care of those things for her. And then I'd go to my room and try to do my homework, but I didn't know where to turn to get help. I felt so sad and alone all the time. There was just no one. I started to think about suicide a lot." At school, the bullying worsened. So did Deleicea's sense that she was both socially and academically inept. "We were all in the same classes, and then one day, we were all separated into gifted and nongifted, and I wasn't in any of the gifted classes."

Then her mother met a new boyfriend, who moved in with them. "It wasn't bad in the beginning," Deleicea continues. "The first year was almost normal. My mom gave him a lot more attention than she gave me, but that wasn't that big a change for me. Then he started to cheat on her, and by that point she was financially dependent on him." Deleicea hesitates as if the rest of this story was painful for her to relay. "There were a lot of times when my mom was sobbing, and they'd be yelling and screaming and cussing each other out." Around the same time, she was being bullied by an older girl who "kept calling me the B-word." She told her mother about it, expecting her to come to her defense, but her mother told her, "Hey, I hear what you're saying, but sticks and stones won't break your bones, so suck it up. Can't you see what I'm going through here?" Any degree of closeness they'd once shared dissipated. "My mom just stopped having my back. I realize now that I was just really neglected."

Then her mother's relationship with her boyfriend "got really bad." One evening when Deleicea was ten, her mother began screaming from the kitchen. "I was getting ready to take a bath. I heard them yelling. I went out into the hallway, and he was chasing her from the kitchen into the bedroom with a hammer in his hand. I ran after them, but he'd locked the bedroom door behind him." Deleicea knew her mom kept a tiny key above the doorjamb; she jumped up to get it and then opened the door. "He was on top of my mom, and he had the hammer raised over her head, and she screamed, 'No! Deleicea is here!' and he stopped." Deleicea's eyes are watering as she continues. "I had to call the police, file the report. A few months later, we had to go to court, and I had to testify." Deleicea and her mother never saw the boyfriend after that day. "I always felt like my role in life was to take care of my mother, as if she were the child. That was all I knew. But even as I was protecting her, I also felt more alone than ever."

At thirteen, Deleicea began self-harming. "I didn't like how I looked. I didn't like my life. I didn't like my body. I didn't like myself. I started cutting myself. It was this hatred toward myself, and I didn't know what to do with it." She began to feel physically sick and fatigued, too. "For me, depression felt like having no energy and no motivation. I didn't do anything except go to school and get through the hours. I was the parent. . . . I didn't have anything other than taking care of [my mother] in my life. I just lay in bed all the time, feeling too fatigued to do anything. But at the same time, I was filled with this restlessness and anxiety. Being alone with my own mind was painful."

By the end of junior high, Deleicea recalls, "I hated school taking up such a large portion of my life. I'd started to make a few friends by then, and they were ambitious. They started talking about wanting to go to college. I wondered why I wasn't ambitious like them." In hindsight, she realizes, "many of my friends had also faced a lot of trauma. They'd been told all their lives, by parents or teachers, that they would never amount to anything, or they'd been verbally abused. And that made them want to fight back against that and prove themselves. For me, it was different. It was more like I grew up giving all of my energy away to someone else and never having anything left for me. I didn't think I could do anything or be good at anything. While everyone around me was gearing up to figure out what they wanted to be when they grew up, I could barely get out of bed. I'd been neglected so long that I'd learned how to neglect myself."

The Importance of Feeling Safe Is Baked into Our Genes

To better understand Deleicea Greene's story—and, indeed, the story of every girl—and to grasp the toll that feeling unsafe and excluded can exact on a girl's body and brain, we have to step back in history to a long-ago era in human evolution. Back in hunter-gatherer times, humans faced the ever-present perils of predators and warring tribes. Unless you were vigilant and constantly attuned to even minute signals of danger afoot, you died young. But beneath this basic survival instinct was a deeper biological imperative: to survive through puberty unscathed in order to mate and procreate and have your genes carry on in your children and beyond. This was true for males and females, of course, but for females, the stakes were higher. Not only do females give birth, but mothers provide breast milk and maternal warmth—resources that are crucial for the survival and healthy development of babies. Females had to stay alive long enough not just to safely reproduce and bear children but also to feed, nurture, and protect them throughout the perilous years of childhood. This required watchfulness and resourcefulness.

But, of course, a female's ability to pick up on even minute threats that might put her children in peril didn't mean just being alert to immediate or obvious physical dangers. It also required staying highly attuned to social cues and emotional threats inside her tribe. For females in many human societies, being able to find enough food and shelter to support an infant and young child depended on a lot of cooperation and collaboration within her tribe. Thousands of years ago, when humans were hunter-gatherers, facing social threats was a physically dangerous proposition. If you were left out or made fun of by members of your tribe, you might also find yourself left behind while a group went out digging up tubers or harvesting fruit; or you might be the last person to get your serving of meat when an animal was roasted on the communal fire. Not only would you have a harder time getting pregnant and successfully raising an infant, but you would also be more vulnerable to disease. So would your offspring. If a predator were nearby, you might not hear the call of alarm because you wouldn't be near the heart of the tribe, and you could more easily be attacked. In some instances, you might even be completely ostracized or abandoned without food, shelter, or the tribe's protection.

Once left outside the tribe, you would be exposed to the elements, predators, and other hostile tribes—which would make you many times more likely to be wounded and, as a result, at the mercy of infectious pathogens. Given the cascade of ill effects that could follow from even a small social slight or being gossiped about, it made sense, anthropologically, that when one faced even moderate signs of being ostracized, one would begin to mentally fear being excluded altogether. One's body, too, would begin to prepare for the worst—which would lead to a heightened stress response. This amplified stress response would, in turn, rev up your immune system to get ready to do battle, increasing levels of inflammation in the body. It makes good sense: If you were facing the dangerous proposition of surviving life on your own, your body and brain would have to prepare you. Not only was your life at stake, but so was the life of your children.

For this reason, George Slavich, Ph.D., professor in the Department of Psychiatry and Biobehavioral Sciences at the University of California, Los Angeles, and other scientists believe that females evolved, generally speaking, to have a greater sensitivity to perceive and detect threats, thus ensuring their own survival and that of their offspring. Slavich, who is also the director of UCLA's Laboratory for Stress Assessment and Research, refers to this link between experiencing a pervasive underlying sense of unsafety (which may be felt only at an unconscious level) and a prolonged physiological inflammatory stress response as the Social Safety Theory.

"Our perceptions of the events and conditions around us deeply influence our most basic internal biological processes, moment by moment," Slavich explains. "These biological processes include our immune system and inflammation within the body." And "just as we know that developing and maintaining strong social-emotional bonds and feeling safe and seen and known within relationships is a fundamental aspect of human happiness, experiencing emotional threats to our sense of social safety and to our connection with others raises our risk for both mental and physical health problems."

If your being left out, not being part of the "in crowd," or being harassed meant you might end up being further isolated or even abandoned by the tribe, which could mean being harmed or wounded, your immune system had to prepare way in advance, at the very first sign of your being socially excluded. Over thousands of years, our human immune system has evolved so that, in the face of social threats, it begins to prep us for the possibility of ensuing injury or infection, as it would with physical stressors.

Moreover, because feeling emotionally or socially unsafe may have been predictive of imminent harm, we have also become highly adept across evolutionary time at being able to imagine the mere possibility of being excluded in social situations. Among our ancestors, those who possessed the best Spidey sense (what we might think of as an especially keen ability to sense potential danger, as epitomized by the comic-book superhero Spider-Man) and who could pick up the possibility of being dissed before it even happened would have been far more likely to survive in the tribe.

And females, who had to give birth and protect their young, very likely had the best Spidey sense of all, because they had to live another day to have more babies and keep safe the ones they'd already brought into the world. Those females whose genetic makeup made them exquisitely attuned to potential threats in the world around them, Slavich explains, "gained an enormous advantage: They survived, and so did their progeny." But having this survival antennae also came with a price tag: a greater propensity for one's immune system to go from on alert to overdrive.

Slavich explains it this way. Abundant research has shown us that "just the hint of social threat or adversity, whether it's feeling evaluated by peers, social conflicts, or feeling rejected, pricks up components of the immune system that ramp up inflammation." This heightened immune response is critical for our survival when we face an actual physical threat, such as a mugger in a parking lot at night. But this same response is also being activated by modern-day social threats that can't really harm us. Being made fun of by the in clique at middle school? Worrying, *Does so-and-so not like me?* Imagining you might be excluded from an upcoming party that friends are posting about on social media? Feeling your parents are tone-deaf to your emotional distress? None of this is going to lead to your being physically wounded. None will lead to your being in danger from marauding tribes or strangers. And yet, to the human brain, it feels as if it could. In other words, if girls are mean to you at school, it may trigger underlying neurobiological shifts that signal your body that the troop or tribe may be about to abandon you in the wild.

And although nasty girls and frenemies have always been around, social media now amplifies those threats into everyday surround sound. This places girls back on the dark hamster wheel of ruminating—often at night, alone in the dark, with no adult to turn to.

"After all, the brain has been around for a *lot* longer than social media or even our current social structure," Slavich explains. And when the brain tells the immune system to stay in overdrive, this leads to persistent increases in inflammation, which drive anxiety, depression, fatigue, chronic pain symptoms, and autoimmune conditions. Not surprisingly, neuroimaging studies of young adolescents show that experiencing interpersonal stress and social rejection is among the strongest predictor for depression. Teens who experience just a brief episode of social rejection show changes in neural networks on brain scans and an increase in depressive symptoms over the course of the following year.

When we think of someone like Deleicea Greene, who was bullied from grade school and into high school, those effects become even more magnified. Deleicea faced the challenges of being bullied, violence in her house, and neglect—all against the backdrop of historical trauma among Black Americans, structural racism, poverty, and discrimination. She faced adversity in her home, her community, and at the hands of a racist society.* The director of the National Institute of Mental

---

* As researchers unpack the relationship between social threats, the inflammatory stress response, and girls' mental health, it's important to take an intersectional perspective and underscore that Black and Indigenous girls of color (BIPOC girls) experience the additional unsafety that comes with growing up amid discrimination and racism. Racism—whether overt or structural—signals danger, a threat to one's survival, which can engender biophysical changes that profoundly affect well-being. As Wanjiku F. M. Njoroge, M.D., a child and adolescent psychiatrist at Children's Hospital of Philadelphia, writes in a 2021 review in *Current Psychiatry Reports*, systemic, structural, and internalized racism—including inequalities

Health, Joshua Gordon, M.D., Ph.D., recently reported that suicide is now "the second leading cause of death" in Black children ages ten to fourteen and the third leading cause of death in ages fifteen to nineteen. Even among children twelve and younger, Black children are "more likely to die by suicide than their white peers." Other research shows that during the past decade, the suicide rate among Black girls increased at twice the rate as that among Black boys.

OR TAKE ANNA MORALIS. As Anna moved through puberty into early adolescence, her stress-threat response likely stayed activated day in and day out. She faced escalating academic stress and was deeply affected by social and environmental injustices happening in the world around her, from school shootings to climate change to racial injustice. When middle school friends began to form new cliques that excluded her, when girls posted about socializing without her on social media, and when hypersexualized images of girls trying to look like adult female models permeated social media—all at a time when Anna felt a lot of insecurity about her self-worth and developing body—her Spidey sense that she was being socially excluded or critiqued by her "tribe" was repeatedly triggered.

We might switch out some of the details and say the same about Julia Abernathy. Julia's interior warning system was also highly attuned. Somewhere inside her, she recognized both the terrible wrongness and danger of being harassed by older boys and men while being discounted

---

in school access and health care—"shape the health status of [BIPOC] youth." Although Njoroge and her co-authors urge us to "distinguish the various outcomes these multiple forms of racism have on the health of minoritized youth," researchers at the Medical University of South Carolina recently concluded that current models of early childhood adversity have "largely neglected the multifaceted influence of racism on mental health outcomes." This is something that needs to change.

for her intellect and the ongoing hardship of coming of age in a society that denies women agency while simultaneously sexually objectifying them.

At the same time, each of these girls lacked the robust social connection and positive experiences (an overarching emotional safety net) they needed during this critical developmental window to buffer the effects of the social and environmental stressors bombarding her. For Deleicea, Anna, and Julia, their stress-threat responses never had a chance to turn off. Their nervous systems never had a chance to relax or reset.

In chapter 4, we delved into how unmitigated stressors can have a powerful effect on a girl's development due to the onboarding of estrogen. What this research tells us is that in this stress-estrogen dynamic there is one type of stress that has a particularly potent effect on female well-being: social stress. This is largely thanks to evolutionary mechanisms that have led to females becoming more alert to social threats in the environment. And this means that when girls meet up with social threats, it makes the estrogen-stress interaction all the more damaging.

The Power to Bounce Back from Ruminating

But an activated stress-threat response in the face of social stressors is just one half of the story, says Slavich. "It's not just how strongly your brain and immune system respond when a social threat appears to be present. It also matters how quickly you are able to bounce back from worrying about potential social slights and move on, without ruminating about what might have happened." For children, of course, this means it matters that they have a trusted adult to turn to, someone who can help them bounce back and with whom they feel safe, seen, valued, and known. Being able to feel safe with and connected to caregivers and adults is the single most important ingredient in a child's physical and mental health and in the health of the adult she or he will become.

"This social threat response is most beneficial when it turns on quickly to alert you to something bad and then turns back off again when the stressor has passed," Slavich explains. The problem is that "the human brain is able to symbolically imagine threats happening in the past, present, and future, even when they are not actually happening in real time right in front of us. Just imagining that something bad is happening tells your brain that a hyperimmune response is necessary, which activates the stress response and your immune system." In other words, the mind-body connection is as sensitive to what is imagined as it is to what is real. If, after each perceived threat has passed, this threat response stays activated, that's problematic.

Ongoing rumination (replaying every bad social interaction or anticipating more social-emotional stressors in the future) creates a potent inflammatory hit. "The longer the period of time from [our] feeling under threat to getting to that recovery stage and feeling a sense of intrinsic safety and well-being again, the more the stress response shifts into a lingering state that can damage one's health." (And, indeed, in part 3 of this book, we'll delve into all the ways we can dial down this stress response.)

Humans, as far as we know, are unique in their creative ability to symbolically imagine the motives and actions of others. And while it can help us to be able to think through other people's thoughts and intentions—this function enables us both to imagine and cocreate together and to have empathy, or to put ourselves in other people's shoes—it also means that, as humans, we tend to spend hours imagining other people's potential bad intentions, replaying conversations or comments, ruminating about what we could or should have done differently, all the while trying to predict future events that may or may not occur and preparing for how to handle them if they do.

Even as you plan to achieve a preferred positive outcome regarding a socially or emotionally hurtful or worrisome situation, says Slavich (such as preparing for a meeting with a difficult boss), "you can be experiencing the collateral damage of an elevated threat response in the absence of a real and present threat, because during all those moments of planning, there is nothing actually bad happening right in front of you."

In each of these scenarios, the threat response stays fired up for naught.

The Link Among Social Threats, Inflammation, and Depression

It is this chronic vigilance in the face of potential threats that researchers believe plays a role in the teen female mental health crisis we face today. Neuroscientists at Temple University have shown that, beginning in puberty, females are more likely, compared with males, to go into a state of high alert in the face of social stress—such as bullying or other high-stress interactions. Girls are also more likely to pump out increased production of stress-related inflammatory chemicals (as measured through simple blood tests) when they enter a high-stress state. Other data tell us that individuals with heightened levels of inflammatory stress factors are more likely to suffer from depression and anxiety. In fact, elevated levels of physical inflammation in the body often precede symptoms and diagnosis of depression and anxiety by years. To wit, children who at age ten show elevated levels of inflammatory factors have a significantly increased chance of developing depression by the time they turn eighteen. Furthermore, females with higher inflammatory factors are three times more likely to develop depression within four years, relative to those with lower levels of inflammation.

In 2021, Duke University researchers showed that experiencing stressful events in childhood is associated with having higher levels of physical inflammation years later, at age forty-five (the age cap for their study). Moreover, when individuals who faced adversity growing up encountered stressors in their adult lives, they developed higher levels of inflammation in response to that stress compared with those who faced similar stressors in adult life but who had not also faced adversity in childhood.

Elevated rates of inflammatory stress factors are also closely correlated with changes in neural connectivity (as evidenced on brain scans) in crucial areas of the brain that are associated with depression and anxiety. Simply stated, emotional responses can spike our physiological stress-threat response to shift in ways that can lead to neural changes in the brain associated with depression and anxiety disorders.

We also know that the effects of childhood adversity dramatically influence an individual's vulnerability to developing depression and bipolar disease. In a 2020 meta-analysis of the literature, psychiatrists at Dell Medical School at the University of Texas, Austin, found that early childhood adversity was statistically "the single biggest contributor"—more than any single gene—to the risk of individuals' later developing a psychiatric disorder. Early life adversities such as those that Deleicea navigated were also linked to recurring episodes of depression or bipolar disorder and an increased risk of suicidal ideation. The study authors write that the reason for this includes changes in levels of inflammatory factors that "contribute to disease vulnerability and a more pernicious disease course."

Adverse childhood experiences (ACES) also have a greater impact on female mental health than male mental health. Ten percent of men who experience two or more types of childhood adversity later develop major depression. But more than twice that number, 25 percent, of women who've experienced two or more categories of ACEs go on to develop major depression later in life. Similarly, whereas 8 percent of men who have a history of three or more types of adversity develop an anxiety disorder in adulthood, nearly three times that number, or 22 percent, of women who faced three or more categories of adversity will do so.

The fact that we emotionally respond to social threats like being left out or criticized on digital platforms as if the threat were the same as our being snubbed by fellow members of our ancient tribe, or even injured, is what evolutionary biologists refer to as a classic "evolutionary mismatch." The horror of feeling left out triggers a harmful biophysical response even though these feelings are unrealistic in response to the actual situation of, say, simply being made fun of on Finsta or TikTok.

THE SOCIAL SAFETY THEORY tells us that our molecular makeup is extremely permeable to social-environmental influences, especially negative ones—and for girls, this is especially so. And it helps us to understand why social media can be so damaging to the developing immune systems and brains in children and teens. We know that the human immune system evolved across evolutionary time to respond to social threats as if they were threats of impending physical harm.

If you're getting, on the one hand, the constant message that, with one false step, you'll be cast out of the girl tribe and, on the other hand, that girls and women in general aren't safe in a sexist world, then you won't feel safe on any level. You're not entirely safe among your peers. And as a girl, you're certainly not safe on your own in our larger world. The stress-threat response never switches off.

Throughout anthropological (i.e., human) history, social-emotional environmental threats were more likely to be life-threatening, but they were not a constant. Now, in the digital age, the immune system is responding to dozens or hundreds of likes, dislikes, and comments (which signal acceptance or rejection) every minute.

Put all this science together, and it suggests that teenage girls' immune systems respond more vehemently to negative stimuli in the world on a biophysical level. And this happens during a critical timing window in neurodevelopment, during which the genes that will determine symptoms and disorders across the lifespan turn off or on. This tells us that today's spike in chronic mental and physical health disorders among girls is a biologically rooted phenomenon: We have created a social-environmental landscape that may be altering the female stress-immune response in ways that turn on genes that derail thriving.

Experiencing a sense of safety is not binary, of course. It's not as if you feel either safe or unsafe. One's sense of safety exists on a continuum. Moreover, what might promote a feeling of inherent threat in one person might not do so in another, depending on the degree and quantity of adversities a child or teen has faced, their inherited resilience or genetic predisposition for disease, and whether they have the support they need to help put their stressors in context and process what they are experiencing. Stress is made toxic because a child or teen is experiencing that stressor as harmful or threatening to them both when and after it occurs, without relief. The fact that girls today are suffering as they are tells us that on the continuum of feeling safe, girls feel on some deep and abiding level that they are not safe in the world that we adults have created for them.

Today's spike in chronic mental and physical health disorders among girls is a biologically rooted phenomenon: We have created a social-environmental landscape that may be altering the female stress-immune response in ways that turn on genes that derail thriving.

CHAPTER SIX

When the Pump Gets Primed

What Happens When Girls Are
Stressed Out and Estrogen Hits the System?

O N THE FIRST day of high school, Deleicea Greene was running behind schedule. She was in a rare hurry: For the first time, there was something happening at school that had captured her heart and imagination. Her ninth-grade English teacher, Mr. O'Leary, was hosting a poetry club. Deleicea dug out a few poems she'd been keeping in notebooks and was late getting to Mr. O'Leary's classroom. The boy who'd been bullying her for nearly a decade was also there, but Deleicea was busy "thinking about my poetry, not about my tormentors." A well-known slam poet named Jacob Mayberry, who worked at the school assisting disabled children and serving as a poetry club advisor, was there, too.

"We all had to read one poem. It was the first time I'd ever seen anything like that in my life," Deleicea tells me. "I had this feeling, like, here I am for the first time, about to finally do something I love. Say something I care about. Say something I really wanted to say. I read my poem, called 'Battle Scars.' It was about cutting myself." It was not the bravest thing Deleicea had ever done—she had already testified in court against the man who'd physically abused her mother, and she'd been taking care of her mom's finances, bills, and herself for as long as she could recall—but it was a defining moment for her all the same.

After she read her poem aloud, the room went silent. "I looked up, and Mr. O'Leary and Jacob were both looking at me. As if they really saw me and wanted to see me." Then Jacob asked, "How old are you, Deleicea?" She was fourteen.

For the next few years, Deleicea felt both relief and hope. "Poetry became my life. I stopped cutting myself. I made friends. I started to get my act together so that I could get into college." She applied to a small liberal arts college and received a scholarship.

Things seemed to be on the upswing. But once Deleicea got onto her college campus, when she was eighteen, things fell apart. "I was on my own for the first time, trying to handle all of my classes, without any support," she says. She'd signed up for six courses that interested her, and because she was the first generation in her family to go to college, no one, not even her academic advisors, stepped in to tell her it was two classes too many for one term. She started falling behind and stopped going to class. No one on campus seemed to notice. She was so stressed by the thought of flunking out and letting everyone down that she stopped eating. Every time she went home, her mother, who was worried, sent her back to school with groceries. Deleicea didn't touch them. "The depression and anxiety were so acute, I lost thirty pounds in one semester. My depression made me not want to be in my dorm room, where everyone was doing their work or socializing like normal college kids. The anxiety made me so restless I couldn't sit down, I couldn't focus. I thought I could handle my course work and class load, but it was too much, and I didn't know who to talk to about it." Deleicea spent whole afternoons walking alone through the streets of her small college town. "I wandered around trying to shush these thoughts about killing myself. I kept thinking, *I don't matter, my existence is so insignificant.* I considered walking into busy traffic. I had this overwhelming feeling of aloneness."

Soon thereafter, "I flunked out of college. When I got home, I was beside myself; I started cutting myself again. The suicidal ideation came back, and it was intense." Deleicea's depression and anxiety began to manifest in her physical health in more worrisome ways. "I was so exhausted and tired; it was like I was living with the flu all the time." One day, she was driving home from seeing a friend and totaled the car. She walked away with minor visible injuries, but the scars she carried inside were deeper than anyone could see.

NOW TWENTY-TWO, Deleicea looks back and sees how the stressors of her childhood manifested in her experiences as a young woman. She lets out one of her signature sighs, which seems a counterweight to her wide-open, hopeful face, before wrapping up her story: "Since no one had ever stood up for me, and I had always been the parent in the house, I had no way of recognizing that I needed advice. I didn't know how to reach out so that someone would step in." As Deleicea got older, the stress of systemic racial injustices also began to weigh heavily on her. It wasn't just in college that she felt her struggles went unnoticed by everyone around her. "In middle school, even though I went to a Black school, I had mostly white teachers. Once a teacher yelled at me for having 'attitude' when I was just being quiet because I was so sad. It's hard to know, looking back, whether my lack of self-worth was because of my depression or just being ignored by the whole system." After finding her voice in her poetry club in high school, "I started to take a closer look at the history of Black people in this country and how we've been treated. And that's when I began to use poetry as a tool for social justice."

The Past Lives On in the Body

By adolescence, Deleicea's stress response had already been primed in childhood to be on high alert by events in her home life as well as her experiences growing up in a society riddled with individual and systemic forms of racism. The added stressors she encountered in college pushed her back to the brink, into physical exhaustion and depression that seemed too burdensome to bear.

There is a saying in the trauma science world that it takes hundreds of times of being safely soothed by a parent for a child to learn how to soothe their own nervous system. For Deleicea Greene, who, conservatively speaking, could be said to have had a very high level of early childhood adversity, this adage proved all too apt. No one successfully modeled for her how to cope or ask for help when she was overwhelmed. Over and over again, there just wasn't anyone for Deleicea to turn to.

Twenty-five years of literature on adverse childhood experiences tells us that toxic stress in childhood doesn't give kids grit or make them stronger or tougher. It reduces their well-being for life. And the way that it does this is by slowly shifting the nervous system to a high-alert response and breaking down the immune system. Over time, this affects not just the body but also the brain, in harmful ways that can alter a child's promise across a lifetime. Powerful forces early in life can, without intervention, slowly shape who each child becomes. This understanding profoundly changes the way we think about stories like Deleicea's and how and why the kinds of stressors she so bravely faced in childhood began to affect her so deeply in young adulthood.

The Estrogen Connection

To better understand how to connect the dots among femaleness, early childhood adversity, puberty, and mental health, we have to dig a little deeper into how estrogen powers up the female immune system.

No one is better equipped to talk about the intersection of sex differences, estrogen, and health than immunologist DeLisa Fairweather, Ph.D., who serves as director of translational research (i.e., research that applies laboratory discoveries to human clinical trials) and associate professor of medicine and immunology at the Mayo Clinic's Florida research campus, in Jacksonville. Fairweather studies sex differences in human disease and, specifically, how males and females differ in terms of the ways in which environmental exposures trigger inflammatory processes that precipitate mental and physical health disorders. Fairweather is also the author of a seminal body of work in the field of adverse childhood experiences. She has found that for each category of toxic childhood stress a female faces prior to the age of eighteen, the likelihood that she will later develop a serious autoimmune disease (such as lupus, rheumatoid arthritis, or multiple sclerosis) in adulthood increases by 20 percent, compared with males, whose rate of developing autoimmune disease increases by half that, or 10 percent, when they face the same number of ACEs growing up.*

Fairweather and I connect over Zoom. On the day we speak, we are well into the COVID-19 pandemic. She and I have met before, when her lab was housed at Johns Hopkins's Bloomberg School of Public Health. I recall her robust energy and how, back then, she loved to sketch on whiteboards while explaining her research. Today, Queen palm fronds sway behind her outside the window of her makeshift home office.

I ask Fairweather what she thinks about the link between today's social-environmental landscape and today's troubled teen girl generation. For her, the resonant mystery isn't whether the continued declining well-being of the American female adolescent is real; it is, she underscores. Her concern is why we as a society don't seem to be acknowledging that this troubling new trend is a biological as well as a psychosocial phenomenon. "If you look at what's happening to girls as purely a psychological phenomenon—which is how it's portrayed by the media, educators, and therapists—you're missing what's happening on a fundamental, cellular level," she explains. "When we look deeper at the

---

*   Fairweather is also cofounder of the Mayo Clinic's center for studying hypermobile Ehlers-Danlos syndrome (hEDS), a connective tissue disorder that affects joint hypermobility and can lead to painful joints; it affects primarily young women.

mechanisms of what is really going on in the female adolescent body, it becomes clear that girls' escalating rates of mental health and inflammatory disorders are a biological response to navigating an overwhelming set of nonstop societal and environmental stressors, which are signaling to this generation of girls that they are under threat. These stressors are coming at girls in ways that augment the biological pathways that trigger prolonged inflammation, which, over time, can flip the switch on genes that play a role in mental and physical health disorders."

Mounting social-environmental stressors are leading to increased rates of mental health disorders in boys, too, Fairweather reminds me. But there are two important distinctions. For one, "girls face additional social and emotional threats just by virtue of *being* female in our society." For another, evolutionary sex differences in how hormonal and immune pathways intersect mean that social threats often exact a higher biological cost for girls. With this double whammy, a high load of chronic, toxic stress becomes, over time, especially damaging to girls' bodies and brains. "Taken together, chronic unmitigated stress, the onset of female hormones at puberty, and pervasive cultural sexist messaging create a perfect biopsychosocial storm that can change the female brain and immune system."

She sums it up thusly: "At the same time that we've introduced so many social-emotional demands and emotional pressures on girls, these stressors are now entering girls' lives earlier and earlier. We also know that social media is amplifying all of these danger signals. It's a toxic cocktail of social influences that can rev up the function of the immune system in harmful ways right at a critical juncture in development."

When you take all this together, it's almost as if, says Fairweather, "we need a new planet for girls."

> *"Taken together, chronic unmitigated stress, the onset of female hormones at puberty, and pervasive cultural sexist messaging create a perfect biopsychosocial storm that can change the female brain and immune system."*

So why is it that estrogen, which is enormously protective to females early on in life, in the womb, can later increase female vulnerability to disease? Fairweather explains: "Estrogen should be highly protective and help regulate the immune response. It's a regulatory hormone and, normally, very beneficial." This is why, during gestation, females carry the survival advantage they do. During puberty, when estrogen rushes on board, it ushers in a more vehement stress-immune response. After all, the female immune system is poised, at all times, to protect the female's ability to one day carry another life, especially in the face of any potential outside threats.

In the right circumstances, this added immune boost can be good; it helps protect the body against potential infection. But when girls in today's world are exposed to unrelenting chronic stressors or feel they are in some way constantly under threat, and the stress response never has a chance to turn off, estrogen can stop being protective, Fairweather explains. Suddenly, "it's like a code switch. In the face of too much stress, estrogen can begin to exacerbate the stress-immune response and make things worse, amplifying the impact of all of the past and present toxic stressors that girls have ever been exposed to. Over time, we begin to see that this leads to heightened inflammation and changes in girls' brain and immune health." To be clear, estrogen isn't the cause of the problem. It is only in the face of unrelenting toxic stress that we see these shifts occur.

It makes very little difference if these stressors are social-emotionally or physically toxic. "We have increasingly good evidence that the human brain doesn't distinguish very well between being hit with emotional trauma versus chemical toxins," Fairweather explains. "Toxic social signals play out on the same networks in the brain as toxic biological signals."

Once again, this is science in motion. We are still figuring out the underlying sociobiology of how trauma and adversity during critical developmental periods promote inflammation in body and brain, precipitating epigenetic changes and mental health concerns. There is still a lot to piece together— not just in terms of male-female sex differences, but also in how these findings shed new light on the well-being of other groups of young people, like BIPOC youth, who grow up beneath the crushing shadow of bias or discrimination. Socioeconomic deprivation— growing up in poverty, as Deleicea did—is also associated with higher levels of physical inflammation in adulthood. When the brain clocks that there is scarcity (a lack of the resources needed for basic survival), the immune system signals its arsenal of cells to step up inflammation, which in turn affects cellular health in both body and brain.* Consider, too, youth who identify as LGBTQ. A recent survey of 35,000 LGBTQ youth found that 75 percent reported experiencing discrimination in daily life, and this stress took a high toll on their physical and mental health: Forty-two percent of LGBTQ youth had considered attempting suicide over the previous year.† There is a lot we don't know about the stress-hormones-puberty interaction in different groups who grow up facing hate and discrimination.

IN TERMS OF male-female sex differences, we do know that estrogen is context dependent. In the right circumstances, it offers us many advantages as females. Estrogen is part of the reason that females, despite being physically smaller than men and having smaller organs, can nev-

---

*   Epigenetic shifts occur, too. FKBP5, the same gene we discussed in chapter 4, becomes altered in females who face chronic psychological distress in ways that increase stress vulnerability by generating more inflammation over time.

†   Two important reminders of the synergistic effects of gender, the brain-immune response, and adversity. Acknowledging the emerging research on sex differences and the brain shouldn't be misconstrued as promoting a view of gender as binary or as ignoring the experience of youth who face a deep sense of unsafety in our culture due to their gender identity or sexual orientation. We also don't know what differences emerge in transgender youth who go through transitions. We just do not have these answers; that research hasn't yet been done.

ertheless do everything a human male does (pump oxygen, think fast, be awake sixteen hours a day) while also having the added, necessary fuel to carry a child to term. Women can do so much more with less because of hormones. If we are stressed, or catch the flu, or get a vaccine, estrogen helps us launch a much more robust defense. This big-punch immune response also means that when our immune system pricks up to do battle against a foreign invader, or in the face of ongoing emotional stressors, we produce more inflammatory proteins, called cytokines, and more fighter immune proteins, known as antibodies, which set out to neutralize whatever outside threat might be attacking the body. This is probably why, during the COVID-19 pandemic, the fatality rate for women was less than that for men. (That said, "post-COVID," or "long-hauler," syndrome has been much higher in women of reproductive age, another example of estrogen tipping the immune system into overdrive.)

In normal circumstances, this battalion of inflammatory cytokines and antibodies behaves like a protective joint force. But if, over time, emotional stressors continue to signal the nervous system that you aren't really safe, and the nervous system keeps pumping out those stress chemicals, this prolonged physiological reaction signals the immune system to continually churn out inflammatory cytokines and antibodies.

And this is one of the means by which chronic emotional and societal stress can, just like physical stressors, lead to physical illness. It's a bit like a car factory assembly line running at double capacity, but without a factory manager on site to oversee the quality of the cars rolling off the line. If you ramp up the number of cars you manufacture without making modifications to accommodate the increase, that higher rate of production will cause congestion, mayhem, and confusion on the factory floor—and will also affect the quality of the cars. This is similar to the way in which producing too high a level of inflammatory cytokines can cause problems in the body. Too lengthy a cytokine response can disrupt multiple bodily systems and organs, leading to heightened, prolonged inflammation in body and brain.

Antibodies also have a good and a bad side. Under the right circumstances, antibodies are powerful fighter proteins: When we are beset by infectious pathogens, antibodies rush forth to attach themselves to the invaders, so that other parts of the immune system can rid our body of them and remove them from our vicinity. But when the body is overwhelmed by toxic stressors, the immune system becomes more prone to make mistakes here, too. To go back to our car manufacturing analogy, a higher number of cars will roll off the line as lemons. In the human body, these "lemon" antibodies are referred to as "rogue autoantibodies" because they can mistakenly attack the body's own tissue or organs, causing autoimmune diseases such as rheumatoid arthritis, multiple sclerosis, and hyperthyroidism—which, respectively, afflict women at three, four, and ten times the rate of men.

Normally, says Fairweather, steroid hormones known as glucocorticoids (or GCs, for short) help regulate antibody production. In our car factory analogy, these are the factory managers. But when females face chronic ongoing stressors, these production managers become less able over time to suppress rogue autoantibodies, even as estrogen keeps signaling the body to pump out more of them. This means that more "lemon" antibodies get produced, even as the immune system's control mechanism starts to fail.

This is part of the reason that, during puberty and adolescence (as estrogen ramps up), if a girl faces an array of chronic stressors and environmental insults, it can overwhelm the female immune response and cause the stress response to get stuck in the on position, leading to an overproliferation of both cytokines and rogue autoantibodies. Regulatory steroid hormones, GCs, have abandoned their task, setting the stage for increased inflammation.

And as we've seen, a growing body of research shows that inflammation (the body's response to chronic stressors) is also one of the primary pathways by which genes for mental health disorders get switched on. (Remember what we've learned thus far about epigenetics and the fact that your genes are always dancing with your environment.)

Research shows us exactly how this can play out in girls today. In one 2020 study, researchers gave twenty-four young adult women who'd experienced childhood adversity and thirty-three young women without a history of adversity a twenty-eight-item questionnaire about stressors they faced in childhood. Both groups of young women also underwent a stress test. During the stress test—a classic one used in research models called the Montreal Imaging Stress Task—the women were asked to solve difficult math problems on a computer screen without being given adequate time. While they solved problems, they were also given negative feedback both online and in person by an evaluator who critiqued their efforts. At the same time, both groups of young women underwent fMRI scans of areas of the brain associated with depression. Researchers also tested the young women's blood levels of cortisol to measure levels of stress-induced inflammatory factors.[*]

Brain scans showed that, in response to the experiment's stressors, those who faced early trauma showed significantly increased activation in areas of the brain associated with depression. They also had much higher levels of stress-induced cortisol compared with the young women who didn't have a history of adversity.

What this tells us, in simple terms, is this: Girls who face chronic childhood stressors have a lower set point at which the stress response gets flipped on. This lower threshold means that hurtful or toxic interpersonal interactions may raise their levels of cortisol and affect brain networks more quickly. Over time, this heightened stress response can cause epigenetic changes that increase the chances that a girl will de-

---

[*] For more on exactly why hormonal changes can affect girls' brains differently from boys', please see the notes at the end of this book.

velop depression or anxiety as she grows up. But this underlying vulnerability might not be apparent to parents or teachers. It may show up as sensitivity or fragility or, to use today's vernacular, being easily triggered.

THIS IS ALL a little daunting to contemplate. I know it is for me. I, too, am the mother of a daughter. I don't present this research to amplify fear, but rather as a clarion call to change the landscape in which girls come of age. (My concerns about how overwhelming and worrisome this science can seem are why part 3 of this book is devoted to fifteen antidotes that will help dial down the stress-threat response and help ensure that girls thrive.) Never forget, under the right conditions, the brain is remarkably plastic. Indeed, the robust aspects of the female stress response that can make girls more susceptible to biological changes in the face of adversity are also what afford girls, under the right conditions, enormous possibilities for change and transformation. Because that which makes one more vulnerable to the ill effects of negative environments on a cellular level is also what makes one more responsive to the healthful effects of positive environments. Under the right conditions, this upside to female biology can emerge as a kind of adolescent epigenetic superpower. This is the great hope and promise of epigenetics.

Indeed, there is so much promise in this research. Fairweather puts it this way: "From prepuberty onward, girls are the canaries in the coal mine for the world we live in." Yet knowing this is ultimately empowering for families and communities. "Every single thing we do to help girls makes a difference; when we begin to remove even small layers of stressors in girls' lives and add in protective approaches, their bodies stop getting these danger signals that harm the brain and immune system. We must be more proactive as a society in keeping this code switch from ever being turned on in the first place or, if it's being switched on, intervene to turn it off again."

CHAPTER SEVEN

Too Much Too Soon

The Impact of Early Puberty on Girls' Well-Being

S INCE THE BEGINNING of time, life has been inherently stressful for females, who have held less power in patriarchal societies and have traditionally been more physically vulnerable than boys. Threats against girls and women have long abounded. Girls today certainly hold more power than females did when humans roamed as hunter-gatherers, or during the Middle Ages, or even in the 1950s, a repressive era in terms of female roles. So, why are girls' brains and bodies suddenly so at risk now compared with other eras in history? Why do so many girls find themselves standing on a precipice today and in danger of a free fall?

Part of the reason lies, of course, in the constellation of stressors unique to modern life that we've explored, including the amplification of toxic, gendered messaging via social media; the loss of freedom, emotional safety, and play in late childhood; the increased early pressure to perform and succeed; and the general chaotic state of the world, from school shootings to climate change. But that's not the whole picture. If we look at this generation of girls' increasing rates of mental and physical illness as metaphor—to borrow from writer Susan Sontag—we have to ask: What else lies behind this disease that's making girls like Julia, Deleicea, and Anna unwell? What else contributes to this injury?

Puberty Is Happening Earlier

At the University of Maryland School of Medicine, neuroscientist Margaret McCarthy, Ph.D., who serves as the James and Carolyn Frenkil Endowed Dean's Professor, is largely regarded as one of the scientific mothers of the study of sex differences in early brain development. McCarthy—who goes by Peg—outlines for me what she believes is one of the most crucial factors driving today's troubled female teen phenomenon. It has to do with the timing of puberty versus adolescence. Puberty is a developmental stage. Adolescence, however, refers to a specific age range.* "Puberty is happening earlier and earlier for girls," McCarthy explains. "Puberty used to occur later in adolescence, and now it has advanced to younger and younger ages, so that it often occurs early, *before* adolescence." And that's a problem, because this means that "puberty is happening before the developing female brain is ready to be remodeled in response to what's going on in the environment around it."

In our anthropological history, females went through a prolonged period of childhood, starting between the ages of six or seven and ending around thirteen or fourteen. During this period, if they were in a protective society, they freely explored the world and learned a lot about safe social bonding with other females their own age. This extended developmental phase, during which they were able to become more emotionally mature all the while knowing they had a safe place under the protection of the larger tribe, occurred before they went through prepuberty and puberty—and before the brain began to remodel itself.

"Early adolescence was supposed to be well under way *before* the

---

*   Because puberty is now occurring earlier in girls, there is a movement to consider the onset of adolescence as occurring at age ten.

onset of puberty and before girls became sexually active—but now it appears that, in some cases, this sequence is happening in reverse, particularly for those girls who go through puberty before the age of twelve or so," says McCarthy. At the same time, the timing of adolescence (the period between childhood and young adulthood) has stayed the same. Puberty, however, is occurring earlier, on average, on the developmental time line. "Which means that that crucial period of safe developmental maturity has been lost for these girls. Now, suddenly, hormones come in too early, during a very sensitive time, and begin to revamp everything before the brain is developmentally ready to go through that rewiring process."

Like all good science communicators, McCarthy suggests a metaphor to help bring this science home. Imagine that you're in a valley redolent with rich soil and covered with beautiful saplings and mature trees. You're about to climb up the mountain to reach a mountain pass. If heavy rain falls while you're still down in the valley or low on the mountain trail, you might be caught in high floodwater and harmed, as trees are uprooted and mudslides forever alter the landscape. But if you are already higher up on your mountain trek and entering the passes that have been carved out of rock, even though rain may pour down, drenching everything, you are safer than you would be lower down in the flood at the bottom of the valley. "Estrogen should come in as you get up to that last mountain pass, when the trail is already well defined," says McCarthy. But for many girls today, estrogen is coming in when they are still low down in the valley terrain. It's too soon, and the ground is too easily altered by adverse conditions. And that "is analogous to the way in which we see too many changes happening too early in the brain's neural connections and how they wire up in the brain."

"When hormones come in at the wrong time, and there is a plethora of environmental stressors, the hormonal system does what it's supposed to do to integrate the systems of the body and wire up the brain—

only now it's doing it during an early, critical period in brain development, when this integration of toxic stressors into brain remodeling wasn't supposed to be happening," she explains. "The brain remodeling that used to happen when girls were older, and more mature, is now happening during a time when the brain shouldn't be getting remodeled. The brain may be opening up at the wrong time."

This matters in terms of setting the stage for a healthy brain and mental health throughout a girl's life. During this process of remodeling, the last area of the brain to mature is the prefrontal cortex, which helps us analyze our thoughts and impulses, control our emotions, and engage in good decision making. As this area of the brain matures, it hooks up with other key areas of the brain, making crucial synaptic connections. The process takes years. This is why a trauma or chronic stressor that occurred when a child was four or six or ten might not show up in terms of mental health symptoms for years, long after the stressor occurred. When brain remodeling happens while the prefrontal cortex is engaged in this crucial rewiring process, it can interfere with the creation of strong, necessary neural connections. Faulty connections in this area of the brain can play a role in mental health disorders like depression and bipolar disorder.

> *"The brain remodeling that used to happen when girls were older, and more mature, is now happening during a time when the brain shouldn't be getting remodeled. The brain may be opening up at the wrong time."*

Early puberty, and the hormonal changes that puberty ushers in, is one more contributing factor for why girls are more harmfully affected by adverse childhood experiences and toxic stress in ways that make them more susceptible to depression.

Research by a team of female neuroscientists at Emory, Harvard, and the Broad Institute, known as the Grady Trauma Project, a large-scale study of 12,000 individuals, brings this fact home. For fifteen years, the Grady Trauma Project has examined the impacts of stress and trauma on behavioral health outcomes in a high-risk, highly trauma-exposed predominately Black population in Atlanta, Georgia. The researchers' hope is to understand why girls and women are more at risk for stress and trauma-related adverse health outcomes, including neuropsychiatric disorders and immune dysfunction. One area of study has been to examine whether the age at which a trauma or adversity occurred was associated with higher levels of emotional dysregulation (meaning experiencing more mood fluctuations and having a greater difficulty regulating one's emotional reactions and responses when encountering stressors) later in life. The neuroscientists at the Grady Trauma Project found that women who had faced early adversity demonstrated higher levels of emotional distress by middle age, in general, compared with men, and that those women who were first exposed to childhood adversity, maltreatment, or interpersonal violence during their middle childhood years (specifically, ages six to ten) demonstrated higher emotional dysregulation scores by middle age compared with those first exposed to adversity later in childhood.

Why Is Puberty Coming on So Early?

This leads to a new volley of questions, of course: Why are girls entering puberty at such an early age? Scientists don't have all the answers yet, but they do have hypotheses. To begin with, a growing body of research suggests that facing early adversity can itself advance puberty. In one study, researchers at the University of Pennsylvania showed that exposure to adverse childhood experiences is associated with the earlier development of permanent molars, a sign of accelerated physical development. "The idea of a stressful environment advancing puberty makes some evolutionary sense," says McCarthy. "The developing brain is getting the message *I'd better hurry up and reproduce, because I may not live very long.*"

Girls today also have a higher body mass, in general, due to shifts in our modern diet. Researchers at the University of Washington believe there may be a relationship between high body fat (which plays a role in producing and regulating hormones), or obesity, and the earlier onset of menstruation and puberty in girls. This shouldn't be read as body shaming, however—body fat is far from the entire story. And we know, of course, that other problems arise if a girl's body mass is too low.

Another recent societal shift may also play a role in early puberty in girls, though it remains hypothetical, given that there is no ethical way to test this theory. With the advent of 24/7 media on phones, computers, and TV screens, kids are exposed to scenes rife with sexual innuendo and interactions at earlier ages and for more time. The theory is that this visual and auditory signaling that "sex is in the air" may also play a role in alerting the brain that the wheels of puberty should be set in motion, releasing the brakes on the reproductive system and signaling puberty to begin. In other words, when girls are exposed to a hypersexualized adult environment, and they mirror that in their behavior, puberty may be happening earlier in order to match a girl's environment. "People are used to the idea that the brain controls behavior," says McCarthy, "but behavior can also influence the brain. In the case of young girls who are playacting, it is plausible that the brain responds by promoting hormones that initiate puberty."

All these factors may intertwine to affect female development. Environmental shifts lead to hormonal shifts. Hormonal shifts influence the earlier onset of puberty.

I SPEAK WITH Julia Abernathy by phone and share the broad brushstrokes of recent research on the brain and what leading scientists have to say about the stressors facing girls today. I'm curious if these findings, which help explain the complexity and depth of many young women's emotional wounds, offer additional insight into her own early experiences. "Completely," she agrees. "When I hit puberty at eleven, the narrative of my life changed overnight." Julia's voice grows louder, as if she were angry in retrospect. "Inside, I still felt like an eleven-year-old kid because I *was* just a kid. I felt something big was being stolen from me. I had to live with this pervasive, creepy sense that men saw me as this *thing* that they wanted to be with sexually."

At the same time, Julia adds, "it wasn't as if I consciously thought, *Oh, this is harming me.* It's only now that I see how harmful it was to be sexualized that way and pressured to play that role of the hypersexualized female around boys and men years before my brain could cope with that shit." Even knowing this research, Julia still carries a sense of guilt over the fact that she "unwittingly bought into the idea that being hypersexualized by men would somehow carve out a pathway to personal power and freedom, when it really just obliterated my ability to figure out what I wanted or needed. I feel like I never got to have the space to see where my creativity and imagination might have taken me, or figure out the world, or even explore my own sexuality in my *own* way until much later on, and after . . . well, a hell of a lot of suffering. It took a long time and a lot of work to create a new story around my own empowerment."

When we think of the science on how early chronic stress engenders changes in areas of the brain that are instrumental in forming our sense of self and of our place in the world and in our perception and interpretation of our experiences, Julia is spot-on: the early adversity she faced due to her gender interrupted her ability to see where her creativity and intellect might take her.

When Julia describes, in retrospect, how detrimental it was to her development as a preteen and teenage girl to have been sexualized as a child, and her pervasive sense that something was being stolen from her, her instincts are also right on target. Something was being stolen from Julia, not just emotionally, but on a cellular level: a period of time in which she could still feel secure to explore the world and find out more about who she was and who she wanted to be, allowing time for her brain to mature and integrate in optimal ways. Julia entered puberty before her brain had safely remodeled itself. And all that trauma of not being seen for who she really was, coupled with the chronic repeated stress of being ill used by men, became—until she sought and received the help and support system she needed—a part of the "intel" upon which her brain reorganized itself.

CHAPTER EIGHT

How the Hazards of Growing Up Female in Our Society Shape Girls' Brains over Time

JULIA ABERNATHY IS home on break from college, lounging on her bed, which sits between two sunny paned windows, wearing old sweatpants and an oversize white T-shirt. A string of soft white Christmas lights twinkle in small arcs behind her. On one wall is a poster from *The Last Airbender,* an anime fantasy series about a group of children who set out to save the world from darkening forces by mastering the elements of air, earth, fire, and water. Julia has her computer in her lap as we catch up over Zoom. It's a few days after the end of her college term, and she seems understandably exhausted. She has just declared her major, computer engineering, and she tells me she is one of only a few females in the program.

"I've been dealing with the fact that the male entitlement in computer engineering is out of this world," she says. "Guys make all these insulting comments like, 'Oh, do you need help?' while they stare over my shoulder and watch what I'm doing. It's always a guy who does this, never a woman. They flirt with me by telling me about their internships. One guy said, 'I'm in an internship with the CIA; I can help you with your coding.' I had to tell him, 'Did I ask you? Have I ever asked you at any point for help?' And then, of course, they are like, 'What the heck are you getting so upset about? Why are you so sensitive?'"

Julia picks up a statue of a Buddha that sits on her bedstand. Her chipped rust-red nail polish is the same color as the wooden figure. "I am learning how to stand up for myself, but it is a work in progress." She puts the statue back and resettles herself among her pile of pillows. I ask her if she's hanging out with any of her friends from high school. "That's tied up in another story," she says. "My friends from high school and I just aren't close anymore. And I think that is because of the things I went through in high school. Which just reinforces the sense of shame I've always carried about my teen years."

She pauses for a long moment, and I wait for her to say whatever it is she seems to want to tell me. Her voice is a little unsure as she begins. "A year or two after my suicide attempt, when I was seventeen, I was raped. I'd been at a party where everyone was drinking a lot. I drank a lot. This older dude, who was at least thirty, said he would help me walk to my Uber. I was pretty close to passing out and was fumbling with my Uber app to call a ride. Then he offered to drive me home instead. A part of me thought, *I don't really know if this is safe.* But I'd seen him around before. I more or less mumbled, 'Sure, okay.' He drove me in the wrong direction, and I was like, 'Where are you going?' He drove me to a dark spot and just kept grabbing me. He locked the door. At some point I passed out during part of it, and then, next thing I knew, I was on the side of the road, naked. He'd inserted something in me. I remember huddling on the side of the road, telling myself over and over, *Oh, this is all that I'm good for, so it must be my fault that this happened to me.*" She had her phone and texted a friend, who arrived with spare clothes and dropped her off at her home.

Julia didn't tell her parents. "I told myself it was because I didn't want them to know I was drunk. But it was really because I felt so guilty, like it was my fault because of the choices *I'd* made. A series of miscalculations on *my* part led to it happening. I felt like I'd walked right into it. I told a few close friends, and they were shocked, but it was kind of like, 'Well, what did you expect was going to happen when you got in that dude's car?' I thought someone would comfort me, or ask me if I was okay, or suggest I go to the police, but no one did. And I didn't really know how to ask for help from the adults in my life at that point. There was another girl in my school who was raped, at sixteen. She didn't tell her parents, either. For me, I just felt like I was used goods. I was embarrassed. More than anything else, I felt completely alone." She takes in a deep, slow breath. "A lot of me is still wrapped up in that trauma and the things that happened with guys when I was an adolescent. All through high school, I think I felt like, *Hey, even if I tell a guy no or don't want something to happen, it's still going to happen anyway, so deal with it.* It has taken me a long time, and a ton of therapy and other work, to find my way back to choosing what I want for me."

As a teen girl, before you have a chance to form your identity as a female sexual being, you've already been put into one of a few buckets by everyone around you, Julia tells me. "You're either not attractive enough or desirable by some bogus male code, so poor, left-out you. Or guys decide you are sexy, by some bogus code of objectification that has nothing to do with who you are inside, and will work that edge and try to manipulate you. But if, at any point along the way, you're misused or coerced or traumatized by guys who are stronger or older, well, you're bad."

Today, at college, she feels this same frustration. "When I ask male computer engineers to stop condescending to me, they can't really understand where my annoyance is coming from. Their mansplaining touches into that place a lot of young women have where we are just sick and tired of being seen and judged and categorized in one bogus way or another."

As a student, Julia is picking up on the general frustration women feel over being unfairly judged in professional life. Her comments make me think of the words of Rebecca Traister, author of *Good and Mad: The Revolutionary Power of Women's Anger*, who wrote, with ample irony (on the topic of how girls are expected to behave in the face of male critiques and mansplaining), "Take the diminution and injustice and don't get mad about it; if you get mad, you will get punished for it, and then you will be expected to fix it, to make sure everyone is comfortable again."

Think of Paxton Smith, the eighteen-year-old valedictorian who in 2021 ditched her prepared graduation speech and instead used her three minutes to talk about Texas's restrictive new abortion law, which bans abortions after six weeks of pregnancy (before most women know they are pregnant), even if the pregnancy is the result of rape or incest. Smith spoke out on behalf of all women, saying a "decision that will affect the rest of their lives" had been "made by a stranger." She went on: "I have dreams and hopes and ambitions. Every girl graduating today does. We have spent our entire lives working toward our future, and without our input and without our consent, our control over that future has been stripped away from us. I am terrified that if my contraceptives fail, I am terrified that if I am raped, then my hopes and aspirations and dreams and efforts for my future will no longer matter." As she spoke, says Smith, a woman at the side of the stage "aggressively" signaled that her microphone be cut off. Later, her high school said it would review their protocols for future student speeches. (A girl doesn't have to live in Texas to feel the threat of restrictive laws about women's bodies and choices. You can be a girl growing up in Anywhere, USA, and still feel the stress and implied threat that comes with listening to others—most of whom are powerful men—debate what control you should have over your own body and determine your fate, including whether you can access an abortion after being raped, or at all.)

Or consider the words of then-eighteen-year-old Grammy winner

Billie Eilish, who was lambasted across media platforms for wearing loose, comfortable clothes while performing onstage: "Would you like me to be smaller? Weaker? Softer? Taller? Would you like me to be quiet? Do my shoulders provoke you? Does my chest? Am I my stomach? My hips? The body I was born with, is it not what you wanted? If what I wear is comfortable, I am not a woman. If I shed the layers, I am a slut. Though you've never seen my body, you still judge it and judge me for it. Why?" Her treatment at the hands of the media and a sexist society resonates with every female whose behavior or body has been pathologized or policed by men's ideas and opinions.

About a month after her rape, Julia says, something in her began to change in a profound way. "I felt I had been beaten down, but a part of me inside knew I had to do whatever was necessary to figure out how to be okay with myself."

JULIA'S STORY IS just one tale of sexual coercion and rape; these scenarios are ubiquitous among girls during their coming-of-age years. Indeed, Anna and Deleicea both shared stories with me about close female friends who had been raped. Parties, college dorm rooms, living rooms—the stage set changes, but the lines of the play do not.

As author Peggy Orenstein writes in her book *Girls and Sex,* "Activists are correct in saying that the only thing that 100 percent of rapes have in common is a rapist. You can shroud women from head to toe, forbid them alcohol, imprison them in their homes—and there will still be rape." (Though to reiterate what should be obvious, what a girl wears or doesn't wear is not what incites rape.) Orenstein underscores the danger of today's "incessant drumbeat of self-objectification: the pressure on young women to reduce their worth to their bodies and to see those bodies as a collection of parts that exist for others' pleasure; to continuously monitor their appearance." At the same time, "when we've defined femininity for [this generation of girls] so narrowly, in such a sexualized, commercialized, heteroeroticized way, where is the space, the vision, the celebration of other ways to be a girl?" In this, Orenstein has perfectly captured Julia's experience growing up female.

Given what we now understand about the cellular machinations of girls' bodies and brains as they come of age, it's not a leap of logic to see how this can, in turn, engender depression, anxiety, and unrelenting despair. But in order to better connect these dots, we also have to look at the broader picture painted by emerging epidemiological data on sex differences, trauma, and mental health.

The High Cost of Growing Up Female in a Sexist Culture

Bob Whitaker, M.D., M.P.H., director of research at the Columbia-Bassett program, a track within Columbia University's Medical School, is the author of the research that tells us, as I cited earlier, that one in four women who've experienced two types of childhood adversity later goes on to develop major depression, compared with one in ten men; and that 22 percent of women who've faced three or more categories of adversity later develop an anxiety disorder, compared with 8 percent of men. Whitaker explains why he thinks women appear to be at greater risk of developing mental health disorders after growing up with adversity. He and his colleagues looked at a nationally representative sample of more than four thousand American adults who were asked questions (related to depression and anxiety) about their current mental health and a range of adverse childhood experiences. They then examined whether the risk of those childhood experiences' leading to later adult mental health problems differed between men and women.

"Exposure to adversity and being female are two distinct risk factors for depression and anxiety in adults," Whitaker says. "And these two risk factors, when taken together, become synergistic—meaning that the risk associated with the combination of these two factors is greater than the sum of the independent risks." For instance, in their national sample, Whitaker and his team found that the risk of developing anxiety in adulthood for males who never had ACEs was 4.7 percent. If you add to this the factor of being female, the risk of developing anxiety rose to 7.2 percent—without even adding any ACEs. For these females, if you add the additional risk of having three or more types of ACEs, then the expected risk of developing anxiety would increase to 10.5 percent. And yet, says Whitaker, "the risk we observed for women with three to five ACEs was 22 percent—more than double the expected number based on adding the separate risks." Similarly, the expected risk of developing depression for women with three to five ACEs was 16.7 percent. Yet the researchers observed that the risk of these women developing depression was actually 27 percent, which was again evidence of a synergistic effect, with the actual risk being far greater than the sum of the separate risks.

I feel my mind flashing back to squinting at the blackboard in statistics class in college, struggling to understand the numbers in front of me. More simply put, I think what this research tells us is this: The same level of adversity does not yield as many cases of depression or anxiety when boys are exposed as compared to when girls are exposed, which means that something else is going on here that accounts for this differential—and this X factor may be growing up female. The fact that the risk is twice greater than the sum of the parts suggests, says Whitaker, that "there is some social and biological process occurring in which these separate risks interact or work together to put girls and women at greater risk of developing depression and anxiety when they are exposed to ACEs."

As we have seen earlier in these pages, to understand what these processes are, we can draw upon what we've learned from other researchers about Social Safety Theory, as well as recent findings in neuroscience and immunology that show that after the onset of puberty, female sex hormones can shift the brain-immune response to stress in ways that up the risk for mental health disorders.

"The data very much hold the possibility that gender is a trauma for girls," says Whitaker. "They don't prove it, but they do tell us that something is going on here and it's not subtle. One of the key possibilities is that because of discrimination, women and girls often experience their gender identity during development in ways that are traumatic. This may be similar to the way many people experience their racial identity—so maybe it should be called genderism. This sort of trauma may interact with other ACEs in a way that makes the impacts more than additive."

And if this is the case, it is crucial to address genderism, because, he believes, "genderism, as a trauma, shapes your identity of self, your social identity, how you see yourself, how you see others, and how you relate to others, which, in turn, creates a biological imprint" that can affect a person for the rest of her life.

OF COURSE, we have to be tremendously careful here as we survey the recent scientific findings on the intersection of stress, biology, and sex differences. Given the historical tendency to ascribe negative attributions to female biology, I fear there is an inherent danger, in my sharing this science, in its being twisted to imply that the female brain is somehow more vulnerable to the world at large than the male brain due to some underlying problem of inferior biology or behavior. Again, nothing could be further from the truth. It bears repeating (and as you will see throughout the third part of this book) that in healthy environments and circumstances, any interior attunement to near or present danger is a strength, a protective mechanism. The female brain is more vulnerable *only* when it encounters unremitting stress. And recognizing this means turning our gaze to the fact that we live in a world that is, and always has been, inherently less safe, and more laden with threats, for girls and women.

In healthy environments and circumstances, any interior
attunement to near or present danger is a strength, a
protective mechanism. The female brain is more vulnerable
only when it encounters unremitting stress.

What this research says—and here I use my own analogy—is that three separate factors (being female, going through puberty, and facing chronic stressors and threats) are synergistic in the same harmful way that environmental conditions often build upon one another. For example, take wildfires: All fires do not burn equally. In one set of circumstances, a wildfire might quickly burn itself out. But if accelerants were used in lighting the flames, an underlying drought exists, or there are high wind conditions, these factors, taken together, become synergistic: The overarching harm done becomes worse than the sum of each of the individual parts.

Michael VanElzakker, Ph.D., a neuroscientist at Harvard Medical School and Massachusetts General Hospital, who studies posttraumatic stress disorder, or PTSD, explains it similarly: We can't ignore the interplay between "sex differences between males and females and the different experiences of adversity and trauma that girls are more likely to encounter in our world." Statistics comparing PTSD in men and women bring this home in stark terms. "Numerous studies show that women in the U.S. have a rate of PTSD of 10 to 12 percent, which is roughly twice that of men, who have a rate of PTSD of 5 to 7 percent. Rates of PTSD in women, in general, are closer to that of male combat veterans; marine veterans of the Iraq war, for instance, have a PTSD rate of 12 percent."

We cannot consider the subtle biological differences between women and men, which may lead to higher rates of depression and anxiety in women, without simultaneously acknowledging the fact that "the types of trauma that are more likely to lead to PTSD are the same types of trauma that are more likely to be experienced by women, often at the hands of men," says VanElzakker. And it is these interpersonal traumas (someone more powerful than you does something to you on purpose that is hurtful), such as the trauma Julia Abernathy experienced, that are also more likely to lead to posttraumatic stress disorder, anxiety disorders, and depression or to exacerbate these disorders in those who already suffer from them.

Women have never enjoyed the sense of safety that men have enjoyed in day-to-day life, and every girl comes of age knowing this—if not by experience, then certainly on some felt level. Even as most men are not sexist, and very few are violent, all women live with the underlying threat of violence and sexual harassment. Even as most men are respectful, girls come of age in a wider culture that is laden with a pervasive, sexist undertone—a culture that sees assault talk as locker-room banter, even at the highest levels of corporate culture and in the person of a recent U.S. president who thought nothing of "grab[bing] 'em by the pussy." Gender messaging is never a nonissue. Girls begin to see from a very early age that the violence in our culture is largely perpetrated by men, and, often, against women; even before they are introduced to social media, they are aware of it to some degree. If they are on social media, they'll see story after story reinforcing this cold truth. Think of the story of twenty-two-year-old Gabby Petito, who disappeared while posting on Instagram about her #vanlife trip with boyfriend Brian Laundrie. Petito was strangled to death; sometime afterward, Laundrie drove her van to his parents' home. He was later found dead. Even though, prior to her murder, callers to 911 had alerted police of having witnessed Laundrie chasing and slapping Petito, when police pulled the couple's van over, they ultimately decided a sobbing Petito was the aggressor. A male police officer seems to commiserate with Laundrie, telling him, "I live with a woman that has anxiety," and "my wife has really, really, bad, bad anxiety," and when she "got put on the medication . . . she wasn't nearly as aggressive or angry . . . ," as if implying Petito is the problem. Investigators ultimately concluded there were no other individuals "other than Brian Laundrie directly involved in the tragic death of

Gabby Petito." Among the many tragedies in this story is the fact that if Laundrie's claims or behavior had been scrutinized, lives might have been saved.

For girls, it is trauma upon trauma: the trauma of growing up female and seeing repeated examples of how unsafe girls are—even with those in positions of authority, who should be protecting them—layered on top of whatever childhood adversity a girl encounters as she comes of age.

How Feeling Unsafe Changes a Girl's Brain

When girls enter puberty and also feel chronically unsafe, what does this look like in the female brain? To answer this question, we first must talk about the link among chronic stress, inflammation, and synaptic pruning in the brain and how these three, together, can lead to changes in the brain that later show up as depression and anxiety. We've already talked about how chronic stressors increase inflammation and disease and how higher levels of physical inflammation are linked to a greater risk of psychiatric disorders in women. We've also seen that children and teens who face adversity are more likely to show changes on brain scans that are associated with depression and anxiety. So, how is it, exactly, that the brain and body are talking to each other? And how is it that a heightened stress-immune response is linked to a loss of synaptic connectivity in the brain?

It is only in the past decade that researchers have solved this mystery by taking a closer look at tiny immune cells called microglia. These cells link our physical and mental health. Microglia function in the brain much the same way that white blood cells function in the body. In healthy, nurturing environments, microglia behave like good doctors, helping neurons to grow and strengthening brain connectivity. But just as our body's immune system can be triggered by chronic stressors to spew out inflammation, when the brain detects a threat (toxic stress, trauma, pathogens, infections), microglia, too, can stir up inflammatory factors that can harm brain health, damaging and pruning away brain synapses that help us think clearly, manage our emotions, respond appropriately to stress, enjoy life, and feel good. Too much pruning (or not enough neural connectivity) can result in depression and anxiety years after a stressor or trauma has passed.

Microglia are constantly in dialogue with the body's immune system, helping to choreograph how the nervous system will respond to the stressors we meet with. This new understanding (that the brain is an intricately sensitive immune organ full of tiny and sometimes hyperactive immune cells that are cross-chatting with immune cells in the body, and that these cells can become hyperactive and can over-prune synapses) provides the biological basis for what we think of as the mind-body connection.

MARIANNE SENEY, PH.D., assistant professor in the Translational Neuroscience Program and Department of Psychiatry at the University of Pittsburgh, has been looking at sex-specific differences in how stress and genetics intersect to trigger changes that lead to depression in the female human brain, as opposed to the male human brain.

Seney underscores the fact that, when it comes to studying these differences, neuroscientists are late to the game. "Until very recently it was assumed that by studying the male brain, we could also understand the female brain and how the female immune system and brain crosstalk," she explains. "But that has turned out not to be the case. As researchers have started looking more closely at the female brain, we have been able to see that the mechanisms by which chronic stress leads to depression and other psychiatric disorders in females is very different than it is in males."

For instance, women with major depressive disorder show more changes to a gene known as DUSP6, which is associated with a greater vulnerability to developing depression in the face of chronic stress. This gene is also correlated with more synaptic pruning of brain circuitry in areas associated with depression. Seney has found—and her research is ongoing—that there are many such sex-specific biological signatures of depression. "We found over a thousand differences in the patterns of genes across the female human brain that shed new light on the interactions between being female, facing stress, and developing mental health disorders. And these differences behave in opposite patterns in women versus men."

When you see the way in which chronic stress affects such a wide range of genes, it's like seeing a world map that shows how climate change affects a wide swath of ecosystems. "How could neuroscientists have missed something so big for so long, even as other areas of research, such as heart disease, have begun to look closely at disease in female models over the past decade?" I ask.

"A main reason that researchers ignored females in the past is that they didn't want those pesky hormones to get in the way," she tells me. "The idea was that if we just study males, the story would be much simpler." And yet "that approach missed an important part of the story, that chronic stress affects men and women differently and that these unique processes in the female brain in response to stress may very well underlie female vulnerability to depression."

WE KNOW THAT chronic stressors can contribute to girls' vulnerability to depression by triggering inflammation, which, as we've seen, can lead to the over-pruning of synaptic connections in the brain. Brain scans show that chronic stress is associated with a greater likelihood of changes to the amygdala, the brain's fear-and-alert system, which triggers a fight-flight-or-freeze response when we perceive threats in the environment; the prefrontal cortex, the decision-making center of the brain; and the hippocampus, which stores memories and helps us make sense of our emotions and experiences so that we can discern whether we're safe or not safe. Together, these areas of the brain help determine how we perceive and interpret the world around us, assess threats, overcome fear, and make sound decisions. In sum, they create our overall sense of well-being.

On brain scans, both girls and boys who've faced emotional forms of childhood adversity and external threats—such as teasing, name-calling (being called stupid or lazy), harsh parental criticism (their family said "hurtful or insulting things" to them), or a lack of emotional nurturance—demonstrate fewer neural connections between the prefrontal cortex and the hippocampus. But girls' brains also show weaker synaptic connectivity between the amygdala and the prefrontal cortex, which helps to regulate how afraid or anxious you feel and whether you will stay caught up in the fight-flight-or-freeze response even after a stressor has passed. Teens who show this pattern in brain connectivity are also more likely to develop anxiety and depression in adolescence.

Adolescents who've experienced chronic early life stress also show disrupted neural activity in what's known as the brain's default mode network, or DMN, which serves as a kind of hub between all the major areas of the brain. The DMN is also what we might think of as the self space. It is the birthplace of our self-related thoughts: our sense of who we are, our ability to reflect on what we've done in the past and what we might do in the future, and the narrative that we create about ourselves for good or for ill. This self-narrative, in turn, affects our ability to feel worthy, practice self-care, or find resiliency throughout our lives. It also plays a role in how well we're able to move our attention from the external world around us and reflect on and evaluate our internal mental state and inner experiences in ways that help the brain enter a state of relaxation. When the core network in the DMN is altered or disrupted, teens are more likely to experience depression and suicidal thoughts. In essence, a teenage girl may lose the capacity to hold on to a healthy, balanced, or realistic view of herself.

Trauma profoundly affects one's sense of self, according to Ruth Lanius, M.D., Ph.D., a leading expert on the function of the DMN in human health, a professor of psychiatry, and director of the PTSD research unit at the University of Western Ontario in Canada. "These disturbances in the DMN are captured eloquently by what patients report to us in clinical settings." People with PTSD often voice this loss of an inherent sense of self with reflections such as, *I don't know myself anymore.* Or, *I'll never be able to experience normal emotions again.* Or, *I feel dead inside.* In the aftermath of trauma, such shifts in one's ability to access a sense of self, Lanius has shown, are reflected, on brain scans, in a substantial reduction in neural connectivity in the DMN when the brain is at rest and when individuals are confronted with trauma-related triggers.

When males and females are under stress, sex differences emerge in this area of the brain, too. In response to stressful interactions that involve possible reward or punishment, females show a greater suppression in areas of the DMN and increased activation in the dorsal attention network, or DAN, an area of the brain that helps us pay close attention to external events with heightened attunement and acuity. This offers one more possible neurobiological explanation for the number of studies that find that, statistically, female teens are more prone to develop anxiety and mood disorders when they repeatedly encounter circumstances involving reward and punishment—such as the likes versus dislikes and the ubiquitous evaluative comments found on social media.

When Deleicea Greene faced bullying throughout grade school and middle school, coupled with neglect at home, she was dealing with two opposing but growing interior mind states. On the one hand, she had to develop a heightened attunement to the possibility of social threats in every interaction with other kids at school. Yet, juxtaposed to that, the neglect she faced at home meant that as she came of age, she developed a suppressed sense of self-identity as well.

Here's an analogy. Think of the DAN and the DMN as each being

one of many radio stations playing in the brain. When the DAN is tuning into social threats in one's surroundings, it's a bit like cranking up
the sound on a station blaring messages like *We could be at risk of harm
here!* Or, *We aren't safe!* At the same time, trauma and neglect turn down
the volume on the station in the brain, the DMN, that puts forth clear,
positive, reassuring messages like *I know who I am and that I matter and
that this doesn't really matter.* These blaring warning messages from the
DAN, combined with a lack of feeling a clear sense of self and identity,
might have been helpful if you were living in hunter-gatherer times and
needed to assess and predict every threat that could lead to death. But in
modern life, when these same brain networks engage in less-than-
optimal ways while you are scrolling through inane comments on social
media or in response to gendered messaging in the world around you,
it's causing pure emotional and, over time, neurobiological harm.

Researchers from the University of Pennsylvania have also demonstrated that after girls hit puberty, the amygdala behaves slightly differently from how it does in boys. Although brain scans of teenage boys
and girls experiencing symptoms of persistent anxiety both show elevated blood flow and activity in the alert and fear networks of the brain
(the amygdala and anterior insula), girls experiencing anxiety show
more activity in the left amygdala compared with boys. The left amygdala becomes highly active when we respond to emotionally stressful
events in the environment by chronically ruminating (dwelling in negative feelings and thoughts about oneself, one's actions or those of others,
and on the sources of problems rather than on their possible solutions)
as opposed to taking action. Studies show that girls are more likely to
respond to environmental stressors and threats by ruminating, which
increases the risk of depression, whereas boys' brains show more activity in areas associated with distraction and action. This may be why
letting go of what-if worries can be so challenging for teenage girls
sometimes; the brain gets stuck on rewind-and-replay-worst-case-
scenario mode, and it's hard to change the channel.

This is all the more problematic when looked at through the lens of the Social Safety Theory because, as we've seen, remaining in a state of rumination (thinking over past interactions, predicting future threats, and existing in a state of anticipatory anxiety) is inherently corrosive. It not only deeply distracts the ruminator from the present moment, but it also keeps that person's interior focus on negative memories and thoughts, the fear-making details, rather than on how to break those thought patterns. This antes up the stress-threat response and primes the body in ways that harm the body and brain over time.

> *Letting go of what-if worries can be so challenging*
> *for teenage girls sometimes; the brain gets stuck on*
> *rewind-and-replay-worst-case-scenario mode,*
> *and it's hard to change the channel.*

Of course, what's happening to girls is only one side of the coin. Researchers are also concerned about the way in which boys' brains are affected by chronic, unpredictable, toxic stressors—which include feeling threatened by narrow, toxic gender messages in a society that forces them into stereotypical boxes. Our culture remains rife with toxic masculinity; it often shames boys for being "unmanly" (i.e., sensitive, gentle, respectful toward women, emotionally expressive, nurturing, apologetic, and accountable when they hurt others) while celebrating them for being "manly" (i.e., aggressive toward women, denigrative of women and their bodies, and valuing "sexual conquests" over connecting with women). For boys, the unspoken, pervasive environmental "threats" they face include the fear of being ostracized or bullied for not being masculine or physically powerful enough. When faced with chronic stress, boys' brains show changes in areas related to anger, attention, and impulse control—the regions associated with behavioral and attention disorders. For both sexes, these gender-related threats, which are based on the messages from society at large, play out in unique biological ways in both body and brain.

And yet, Seney emphasizes, we can also take hope from understanding this complex science. "We've long carried this misconception that if the female brain works differently, or if we observe a vulnerability in how the female brain responds in the face of stress, that must be bad, or it somehow implies that women are more vulnerable in a *negative* way." But, she emphasizes, "we have to get past that ill-conceived notion and recognize and embrace that not only do these sex differences exist, [but that] investigating the key drivers that influence this sex-specific vulnerability to major depressive disorder as a response to stress can help us to better prevent and treat depression in girls and women."

Peg McCarthy agrees. "Understanding that male-female sex differences exist matters for both sexes—the more we know about the female brain in terms of sameness and difference, the better we can help boys and men, too."

To tackle today's teen girl health crisis, we, the grown-ups, must wake up to the fact that we've created a highly stressful coming-of-age environment, identify the most toxic aspects of our cultural landscape, and create new approaches for securing a healthy emotional inner life for all our girls. After all, the female brain is more likely to be negatively affected only when a girl faces unmitigated stress or senses she is under threat. In the face of manageable stressors, a girl's innate Spidey sense serves her well in life, work, and relationships, emerging as her female superpower. And the good news is this: There are ways to nurture and bring forth that superpower strength.

PART THREE

The Antidotes

Where do concerned parents begin in their heartfelt quests to help their daughters? What follows in this section are fifteen principles, or what we might think of as antidotes, that emerged from my conversations with neuroscientists, psychologists, public health experts, and with Anna, Deleicea, and Julia. Many of these are novel to the times in which we live and to the unique problems that confront girls right now. Others are more familiar strategies we've always sensed are essential to girls' well-being—though, up until now, we didn't have the science to back up why they're so crucial to healing the wounds girls carry and bolstering their future resiliency. We don't have to reinvent the wheel or create an entirely new playbook here; we can begin by reprioritizing the doable and build from there, adding strategies as we go.

A number of these insights emerged from girls themselves as they navigated considerable travails where a limited constellation of these protective factors were in place—especially for Anna and Julia. Even so, the handful of preventative, healing approaches available to each was not enough to be 100 percent protective. In many cases, these girls had to proactively seek out and pursue answers on their own, after years of struggling.

The hard truth is, as much as we'd like to Teflon-coat our children against adversity, we're not going to protect them from everything. The world will find them. Genetic predispositions for anxiety or mood disorders may come into play. There is an old saying in genetics: "Genes load the gun, but the environment pulls the trigger." That's too violent an image for my liking, so, to draw on our earlier analogy: Genes are the dimmer switch, and it's the turning of the dial, by forces or hands in the environment, that switches the genes for disease off or on. The hope is that we can— judiciously, lovingly, appropriately—intervene, to the best of our ability, to keep trauma and adversity from switching on genes for future mental and physical health struggles. This makes it all the more essential that, as parents and mentors, we integrate as many of these principles into each girl's life as early and as best we can.

At the same time, these antidotes should not be misconstrued as suggesting that we need to overprotect girls, that if we somehow put them in a bubble until they're twenty, they'll magically be okay. Perhaps it should go without saying, but I'll put this here anyway: Growing strong girls isn't just about helping them better respond to stress or adversity; it's also about how we as adults, and as a society, confront a tacitly sexist culture and reconfigure how we shape the world in which girls come of age.

And as you'll see, many of the principles that follow could just as easily be applied to raising boys. The truth is, if we applied many of them to raising sons, it would not only help boys, but it would also be a part of the solution for helping girls, too. Making things right for our girls means making things right for *all* children. Helping boys ultimately helps girls: How we raise sons impacts the lives of girls and the women they will become.

Still, a number of these antidotes are specifically geared to helping us rethink how we raise girls and the ways in which we understand and respond to their emotions, especially when they feel overwhelmed, angry, or alone—when society so often labels them as sad, mad (be it crazy or angry), or bad—and when our responses to them are gendered in a way that harms their capacity to thrive.

CHAPTER NINE

The Building Blocks of Good Parent-Child Connection and the Importance of Family Resilience

I N A NOW-FAMOUS study known as the Still Face Experiment, developmental psychologist Ed Tronick, Ph.D., who researches infant-parent relationships at the University of Massachusetts, Boston, invites a mother and baby into a room and asks the mother to interact with her daughter and then to stop doing so. Sitting facing her child, the mother engages with her daughter in an animated fashion—and then, abruptly, stops smiling and cooing. Instead, her face becomes utterly "still." At first, her baby looks up questioningly. She coos and smiles at her mother, as if to evoke a similar response. She tries harder, letting out small, happy whoops of excitement as she points at things for her mother to look at, playing a game that mother and child have clearly played before. The baby seems to be saying, *Look at me, smile at me, connect with me, let's play like we usually do!* But, as instructed, her mother doesn't move a facial muscle. The baby begins to cry. Her agitation becomes palpable. She looks back at her mother again. Still no response. She turns away, shrieks, twists and flails in her seat. Only ninety seconds have passed since the experiment began, but as you watch this mother-and-child interaction, or lack thereof, your heart pounds in your chest (or, at least it did for this mother of two). You want to shout at the screen, "Pick up the baby!"

At last, the mother reacts: She picks her daughter up, saying, "It's okay, it's okay," cooing to her in a sing-song tone. Her baby begins to calm down. The few moments of parent-child disconnection have passed. And yet these brief moments during which mother and child fell out of connection tell us a great deal about how babies develop a sense of well-being through their felt sense of engagement with parents and parental love.

The degree to which a parent and child feel in sync with each other on an emotional, physical, and neurobiological level, and in a way that provides a felt sense of safety for the child, is often referred to as parent-child attunement.* In this in-sync state, nonverbal behaviors like eye contact, alignment of heart rate, the release of feel-good hormones like oxytocin, and even brain waves begin to match up between parent and child. When a parent and child are not in sync, or when there is disconnection, this is what Tronick calls a "mismatch" between caregiver and child.

When there is a mismatch, there must be a "repair." Tronick explains it this way: "Parent and child must figure out a way to get reconnected." When a child experiences these moments of repair and "the getting back of connection, she knows she can trust her mother, that she can deal with a negative mismatch experience, that a negative emotion can be changed into a positive one, and that her parent loves her."

Flourishing throughout life starts with parent-child attunement, and this connection starts at the very beginning of life. The first three antidotes share in this theme—to understand how moments of disconnection emerge and why it's crucial to nurture strong, safe, healthy connection mindfully and intentionally with your child so she feels safe

---

* A 2021 policy statement from the American Academy of Pediatrics refers to this state of parent-child attunement more technically, as biobehavioral synchrony.

coming to you with any worry or concern, anytime, no matter the circumstances.

Antidote 1

Get in Sync—Understand the Connections Between Your Stress, Your Trauma, and What You Are Communicating to Your Child at Every Age

When a baby is growing in the womb, the mother's placenta serves as a cellular screening system, buffering the degree to which environmental stressors that surround the mother, including emotional stress and trauma, affect her child's development. After life in the womb, a parent's ability to embody a regulated, present emotional state becomes a similar kind of buffer. A parent's emotional state is the filter through which an infant, child, and later a teen learns to feel and internalize safety. A child's stress response, and their ability to feel safe even in the face of adversity, is formed over time in mirror response to their parent's stress response. And a parent's stress response, of course, is shaped early on in life by *their* parents. This is why healthy parent-child attunement matters so much to child and teen flourishing and is so protective on a neurobiological and immune level.

George Slavich, Ph.D., professor of psychiatry and biobehavioral sciences at UCLA, puts it this way: "One of the primary ways by which children receive signals about how safe they will be in the world as they grow up is by taking in how their parents react and respond to the world."

Babies are exquisitely attuned to the emotional tenor of their caregivers; they pick up on a parent's vocal tension, heart rate, facial expressions, and skin odor long before they can talk. For instance, within moments of their being held by their mother when she's in a state of emotional distress, an infant's heart rate will rise; the baby quickly absorbs their mother's negative psychological residue into their own body. We can see the impact of maternal stress on an infant's neurodevelopment as early as two months of age: Infants of mothers who report high stress show areas of delayed brain development on EEGs compared with infants of mothers who report low stress. Even when parents are arguing while their baby is asleep, the baby's brain can develop a hyperalert response to hearing angry tones.

At the same time, the developing brain is taking in messages from the larger environment: parents' subtle shifts in mood or behavior (as in the Still Face Experiment), belligerent parents, gunshots heard on the street, no food on the table—which can signal a child's nervous system "you're not safe" or "you're under threat." This is, of course, why, as we've seen so clearly, when children face adversity, the brain signals the nervous system to ramp up stress hormones and chemicals in ways that later contribute to depression, anxiety disorders, and health problems. "If a child's brain and body are detecting constant threats, their stress response will develop very differently than it would when feeling a sense of safety," says Slavich. "The crucial question is: Is a child's brain and immune system being tuned to deal with constant threats, or is their brain and immune system being tuned to an environment that is safe and benevolent?"

Recognize and Understand Your Own Trauma Story

We are always shaping ourselves and our story (and the stories of those around us) in moments of communication with those we love. As parents, we hold tremendous power to shape our children through the way we communicate with them; through our words, our gaze, our gestures. The most positive experience a child can enjoy is to feel relationally safe with us, as their parents, in day-to-day family life, regardless of the adversity or trauma a family faces. But, of course, even the best efforts to create a safe emotional home climate and strong family connection can't succeed unless parents are first aware of, and addressing, their own histories of adversity and trauma. If you, as a parent, never felt safely seen or nurtured by your own parents, how can you, in turn, learn to offer this gift to your own child?

Not every mother or father, of course, comes to parenting carrying baggage from their own childhood, but research tells us that the majority does. Two-thirds of adults report having faced at least one category of adverse childhood experiences that involved the behavior or actions of their parents or caregivers in childhood, and 87 percent of those individuals report having faced additional types of adversity at home.* This figure doesn't factor in environmental, community, or social trauma; we don't have good data on these. Whether you as a parent are able to recognize how early adversity affected you, or whether you consider it to have been traumatic, is another matter entirely.

Of course, everyone has confronted some level of adversity in life; we all have some baggage, even if it's only the carry-on variety. Ed Tronick, who developed the Still Face Experiment, suggests that we might view the term *adversity* as including "anything that depletes a caregiver's resources and prevents them from being present to regulate both their own and their infant's psychological state." Substance abuse, marital conflict, parental mental health issues, financial hardship, health crises—"all exert their harmful effects" by depriving the child of healthy moments of "interactive coping through mismatch and repair." It makes sense, then, Tronick posits, that caregivers whose energy for self-regulation "is depleted by [their] dealing with external events such as poverty or community violence, or [by] internal events, such as depres-

---

* For a reminder of the different domains of adverse childhood experiences (ACEs), see chapter 1, "Our Girls Are Not Okay," in particular, the section "The Four Domains of Childhood Stress."

sion or anxiety, may not only fail to buffer the child from stress, but [may] actually transmit the stress of the disruption to the infant. Put another way, a distraught adult cannot calm an upset child and can agitate a calm child." Millions of interactive moments in which an adult helps a child stay calm and self-regulated in the face of adversity, over time, "enables infants to expand their own capacity for coping and resilience, whereas chronic failure of repair diminishes the infants' resources and induces helplessness and fragility."

A relationship with one loving and attuned parent or caregiver is the single most protective factor for any child. This means that, as a parent, if you suffered your own trauma, your first step is to learn how to explore and address your own story of adversity, so that you can build the capacity for self-awareness and emotional self-regulation. For it is your own emotional state that ultimately makes children feel safe and loved. It is what allows a child to truly know, as they grow, that there is at least one person in the world who is utterly crazy about them, who delights in their being, and who will always love them unconditionally.

If you become flooded by overwhelming feelings or are caught up with managing your own emotional distress, you can't really soothe the child who stands in need right in front of you, and parent-child attunement becomes impossible. For many parents, feelings that stem from unresolved trauma sit beneath the surface of family life, like a geyser of unexpressed emotions, spewing bits of steam now and then. Conversely, when you're able to manage your own emotions in the face of stress, your child internalizes this ability to be self-regulated. A teenage girl who is well regulated under high-stress situations has had hundreds of moments in which a safe, loving, connected adult modeled that ability for her.

Moments of disconnection do not mean, by the way, that a parent doesn't deeply love their child; you can adore your child and still not feel self-regulated enough to enter a state of attunement. As Gabor Maté,

M.D., author of *In the Realm of Hungry Ghosts*, writes, this is not a question of parental love, "but of the parent's ability to be present emotionally in such a way that the infant or child feels understood, accepted, and mirrored. Attunement is the real language of love."

Children don't need parents to do everything perfectly when life is stressful; they learn from watching us handle our many human moments of imperfection. But they do need us to do the hard work of learning how to offer up a nonanxious, attuned presence—easier said than done, I know—even when challenges arise.

For years I have taught a writing course for parents, therapists, educators, and others who've experienced childhood adversity and who are searching to understand how the trauma they faced has affected them in adult life, including in their relationships, in family life, and as parents.* In working with thousands of individuals, I've learned that the science on how trauma and adversity affect our well-being, and our stress-reactivity, can feel overwhelming. We've all had our less-than-stellar days as a family, and most (if not all) of us might wish to hit rewind on a few less-than-ideal parenting moments. The science is not meant to scare us, but to wake us up to the fact that the trauma we ourselves faced growing up, if it remains unaddressed, may have set our stress-threat response on high-reactive mode, especially when we encounter the high-stress moments that are inevitable in the cacophony of family life. And this, in turn, can prevent kids from feeling safe, which means we can't provide the kind of love and connection they need to thrive.

---

* This course, Your Healing Narrative: Write-to-Heal with Neural Re-Narrating™, which I taught regularly before the pandemic, and delivered to parents, practitioners, and first responders via universities and hospital groups throughout the pandemic, is now an eight-week online program available to all.

Antidote 2

Observe Your Reactions in Parent–Child Interactions and Dial Back on Evaluating Your Daughter

The knowledge of how their own trauma might unwittingly affect their parenting can weigh heavily on any parent's heart. But you can flip this science to see it differently: as an invitation to dive into the ultimately necessary interior work to address your own narrative of adversity and healing. Sure, this work can be messy—it's not easy to look back at yourself as a child and see how experiences might have shaped your ability to be present or the degree to which you become anxious, irritated, reactive, critical, checked out, or freaked out when events overwhelm you. And yet, this crucial self-exploration will help you arrive, with self-compassion, at a place where, instead of spending so much brain energy managing your own emotions, you learn to self-regulate and pivot to coregulating your child. You simply cannot raise an emotionally resilient daughter without first taking this step. To be clear, trauma healing is a process, and for most parents, the journey continues throughout their lifetime. But over time, the gains for both parent and child can be life-changing.

Rachel Yehuda, Ph.D., professor of psychiatry and neuroscience and director of stress studies at the Mount Sinai School of Medicine in New York, is a leader in understanding how the effects of stress and trauma can create biologic and epigenetic changes. She argues that the knowledge we gain by seeing how our own experiences affects us and by understanding the role that epigenetics plays in this process translates into a form of power. It doesn't "all have to be negative," she says. If we develop an "awareness of what the biologic changes from stress and trauma are meant to do, then I think we can develop a better way of explaining to ourselves what our true capabilities and potentials are." Yehuda generally tells parents who've experienced early adversity that they may have more to overcome "because their biology has given their condition a firmer reality . . . you have to work harder . . . you have to understand that a lot of what you have is biologically driven." When you grasp the reality that your stress system may be more reactive because of your past, this information in and of itself can help you remain calm in response to a stressful situation. Yehuda has seen individuals use this "aha!" awareness to remind themselves, *I have poor shock absorbers, and I should just let it pass, because my biology is going to have extreme responses before it calms down.*

Being the parent you want to be begins with recognizing your own story, acknowledging the force of what happened to you and the impact it may still have on you and in how you parent. This includes understanding how your reactivity might be rooted in your childhood and observing the impact that it has on your child. Both can feel terrifying. Often, we repress or minimize our own traumatic experiences. And it can be hard, without the help of a third party—a therapist or counselor or wise friend—to have the deep level of insight to recognize when our own trauma is being triggered.

Psychologist Amy Karlen, Ph.D., who specializes in adolescent females, offers up this litmus test: "Being overreactive, even if it's just being internally overreactive and flooded by hard-to-untangle thoughts and emotions, can be a sign that something is being triggered for you from your past. When our children encounter the kinds of experiences that were hardest for us as we grew up, or [when] they enter phases of their lives that we found challenging at their age, understanding this connection to our emotional reactivity can be enormously helpful."

Let's consider a few hypotheticals. Your thirteen-year-old daughter comes into the kitchen after school and slams her backpack on the table. Books spill everywhere. She tells you her two oldest, best childhood friends are having a sleepover without her. Or you hear your fifteen-year-old sophomore daughter quietly sobbing in her room. You go in to see what's wrong, and she gulps out the story: An older boy at school asked her for a photo of her cleavage. She didn't stop to think and texted a photo to him; he shared it with friends, and when she got on the bus to come home, they laughed and joked about her "mosquito bite breasts."

Now imagine, in the first scenario, that you were bullied in middle school, taunted by other girls, or made fun of by your own siblings, who often excluded you while you were growing up. Or imagine, in the second scenario, that your own mother or father shamed you about your body as you went through puberty; or, as is true for nearly one in three young women, you were coerced into having sex when you didn't want to; or you were raped or date-raped.

Whatever the case, your own trauma will be the lens through which you view your daughter's experience, who she is, and how to help her in the moment. Your ability to be present and to listen with compassion—or what's often referred to as your window of tolerance—shrinks when emotions arise inside you that echo your trauma as a child. Your nervous system is more easily overactivated. You might overreact or lash out angrily ("Why are you slamming your backpack around!" or "What in the world were you thinking!") before you listen to what your child is trying to tell you. Or you might say nothing, but she sees your grimace.

However, when your own trauma narrative is explored and addressed, that cloudy lens through which you see your child's struggles begins to clear. Even though what's happening in front of you may be highly stressful, you become better able to note your own galloping thoughts and your physiological sensations of fight, flight, or freeze and to bypass your knee-jerk reaction, so that you can offer up more present-moment awareness, hear what your daughter is saying, seek to understand her feelings, and find out what she thinks about what happened to her. Whether we realize it or not, we are always modeling for our kids how we handle mistakes, manage frustration, solve problems, listen, apologize, ask for help when we need it, speak up for ourselves, and navigate conflict.

The payoff for doing this kind of inner-trauma work is relationship gold: You become safe for your daughter to turn toward when she feels vulnerable, no matter how difficult the topic or situation. (If this resonates, and you're interested in how to assess, address, and begin to resolve your own trauma, see appendix B in this book for a list of powerful resources and for further reading. Or see my earlier book *Childhood Disrupted: How Your Biography Becomes Your Biology* and my online programs to help you on your trauma-healing journey.)

Kids have an inner antenna for knowing when a parent is caught up in their own head, ruminating, tuning out, or sending signals, through facial expressions or gestures, that they might emotionally lash out—versus when they are ready and able to have a clear view of their child, believe the best of them, and engage in active listening. All six senses tell the child when it's possible, versus impossible, to have their emotional needs met. This brings to mind the famous quote often attributed to Maya Angelou, "People will forget what you said, they will forget what you did, but they will never forget how you made them feel."

Your brain is always storing and transmitting information from your nervous system throughout your body. Any pent-up emotional or physical stress from the trauma we experience gets trapped within the nervous system, creating what's known as somatic energy. But somatic energy can also be healthy—meaning your nervous system is grounded in a kind of deep, abiding cellular presence: You are right here, right now. When you offer up your own state of calm for your child, from every cell of you to every cell of her, it helps take the charge out of both your emotional responses.

When a girl is agitated and yet experiences her distress in the presence of a nurturing, loving adult, her nervous system is far less likely to get stuck in fight, flight, or freeze. The amygdala is more likely to calm down, so that her body and brain can return to a state of clarity and purpose. This is the state of calm in which your child knows she can turn safely toward you. Again, this is a high bar and far from always realistic for us human mortals. But merely holding this in your heart as something to work toward as a parent means you are already offering a greater degree of healthy attunement to your daughter when she needs it from you the most.

> *When you offer up your own state of calm for your child,*
> *from every cell of you to every cell of her, it helps take the*
> *charge out of both your emotional responses.*

Of course, simply recognizing how our behavior affects our children is not enough to resolve our own trauma. But it's a good first step toward creating a toolbox of strategies to heal deeper wounds and be in a healthier state of mind to manage day-to-day stressors (and help our children develop and build those skills as well). Where do you, as a parent, begin? Research shows that the safest and most effective trauma-healing approaches are already well known to us: therapeutic modalities.* Whether it's talk therapy, cognitive behavioral therapy (CBT), dialectical behavior therapy (DBT), acceptance and commitment therapy (ACT), psychotherapy, writing-to-heal (e.g., narrative writing about difficult experiences), mindfulness meditation, or neurofeedback—it's important to try enough practices so that you learn which strategies resonate the most for you so that you'll keep practicing them.

Dial Up on Noticing Positive Behaviors and Qualities

There is an old saying that it's better to catch children being good than it is to catch them being bad. This is all the more relevant as we live through

---

*   Many of these modalities require having the financial resources to pay for practitioners, and too many Americans lack these resources. We are not a society that prioritizes access to mental health care. If we want to improve family connection for children and childhood well-being, these approaches must be made available and affordable for everyone. (For more on free resources, see appendix B.)

challenging times, and especially given that adolescents' mental health has been worsened by the COVID-19 pandemic. Yale researchers who study teen resilience have looked at many of the risk factors for higher rates of anxiety, depression, and drug and alcohol abuse. In perusing three decades of data, they found that adolescents attending high-achieving schools (whether public or private) suffered from symptoms of clinical depression and anxiety at significantly higher rates than other teens—three to seven times higher. This was driven by "unrelenting achievement pressures" to excel at school, sports, and extracurricular activities, often with the goal of getting into a good college. And at the heart of this intersection between a high-achievement culture and an increased risk of depression and anxiety stood one central determining factor: Teens were more likely to suffer from mental health concerns if they felt their parents had extremely high standards for grades, activities, accomplishments, and getting into a good college, or if they felt their parents were critical of them when they fell short.

In the spring of 2020, early in the pandemic, when school pressures eased up—exams were canceled, classes became pass/fail, activities stopped, and teens had more flexibility and freedom while learning from home—students' well-being improved. But that was short-lived. Stanford researchers surveyed ten thousand kids and found that although the pandemic might have initially given teens more flexibility and freedom while learning from home, about half of students now say the pressure to do well academically and overall school-related stress levels have increased since 2019. More than a third of students say that since the pandemic, their parents' expectations—perhaps due to the economic uncertainty brought on by the pandemic—have only *increased*.

This research invites parents to step back from evaluating kids for performance-based achievements and to reassure teens that it is their qualities, values, relationships, and their mental and physical health that matter most. One way to achieve this is to underscore, praise, and speak

aloud the positive character traits and virtues you see in your child versus using evaluative terms such as *fabulous* or *excellent* or *tremendous*.
For instance, "One of the things I love about you is that you are so
thoughtful to your friends." Or, "You're so creative, look at how you
thought to do X and Y in this project." Or, "You sure are responsible and
determined." Or, "I notice the way you always follow through on things.
That takes a lot of effort, and it's a wonderful quality." Or, "You get to be
who you are. You don't need to be anything to please other people." Or,
simply, "Your job isn't to be the best; your job is to grow up to be a good
person."

Karlen believes that school systems play into this "be the best" messaging, too. "We have to rethink school systems that relentlessly elevate
and overemphasize attainment through achievement awards and cere-
monies. The push toward ever-elevated levels of attainment promotes
anxiety in young people and infiltrates the climate of a school." Parents,
like schools, often send mixed messages. "Parents may say they value
character traits over attainment while being totally preoccupied with
tangible signs of achievement. The important thing for parents to understand is that ultimate success, both interpersonally and in a career
path, hinges on those character traits parents can note and reinforce—
not which college [their children] attend."

Anna Moralis explains how friends and family helped shift the way
in which she speaks to herself in her head. "So often, female friends rush
to compliment each other on how they look. My parents and my friends
made such an effort when I was really suffering to validate me for qualities they saw in me rather than my physical attributes. It meant a lot to
hear 'You're really brave' or 'You're really hardworking' when I was
struggling, instead of hearing 'But you look good!' or 'I love your dress.'
The family and friends who could see me in that way the most are the
ones I'm really close to now, and I try to reflect the qualities I see in them
back to them, too."

During the half year that Anna spent at home with her parents during the pandemic, she had the sense that her parents were making deeper shifts in the way they related to her. "For a long time, I'd felt people were proud of me for what I was accomplishing or what I did in the external world—my grades, my college acceptances, the awards I'd gotten, the work I was doing by rolling my sleeves up to help underserved communities. But being at home with my family for so long, and not being able to engage in the world in ways that had led to those external forms of validation, I started to have the sense, for the first time in my life, that people who loved me really were proud of me just for me, my parents valued me as me, and nothing more was required of me than that."

Antidote 3

When Your Daughter Turns to You, Make It a Good Experience for Her

The adolescent brain is wired to be hypervigilant around assessment and evaluation. And that means we need to be extra careful about finger wagging or making comments that judge their actions when girls come to us to share what's in their hearts and on their minds. This may be especially true for girls, given the way the world around them assesses every nuance of their appearance and actions. (To wit: Julia pointed out to me that one upside to wearing a mask during the pandemic was that she didn't hear endless male voices calling out to her to "smile more," as if "I owe it to men to do something that makes them feel good by virtue of simply being female.")

The goal here is simple: If and when your daughter turns to you with difficult feelings or dilemmas, do all you can to ensure that the conversation is a positive experience for her. The ability to share overwhelming fears and feelings without overreacting or lashing out at oneself or others with thoughts, words, or actions is the cornerstone of close, healthy relationships, and it is a skill children learn in their interactions with parents and other adults. Stated another way, psychological safety is the interior belief that you can speak your ideas and take risks without fear of ridicule, humiliation, or retaliation. The message you want your daughter to receive is this: You can be insecure, imperfect, angry, confused, needy, anxious, or unhappy (or all the above) and still be loved. For girls, this sense of psychological safety is too often put at risk by the world at large. The last thing girls need is to experience that same lack of safety at home. If your daughter breaks a favorite glass while pouring orange juice or falls off her scooter and skins her elbow, the best way to help her learn how to succeed at either is to make sure she knows she's wholly loved no matter what.

Studies back up the concept that having a parent you can safely turn to is a boon for life. Parents who respond to parent-child conflict with mindfulness, by exhibiting low negative emotions and staying present, also report more positive emotional interactions with their teens, and their teens are less likely to engage in high-risk behaviors like drinking alcohol or having sex. Similarly, teens whose parents practice mindful parenting have a lower risk of depression or behavioral disorders—and this holds true across early childhood, middle childhood, and adolescence.

Perhaps Fred Rogers said it best: "Parents are like shuttles on a loom. They join the threads of the past with the threads of the future and leave their own bright patterns as they go." That is the hope: to weave bright patterns as you go. Offering a state of empathy and engaging in attuned listening, so that your daughter feels heard and understood, will calm her nervous system and help regulate her emotions, which regulates her neural state.

But again, we can't draw forth this deep listening skill from our parenting toolbox if "we haven't first resolved our own story of trauma or, in some meaningful way, come to understand the role of our past in our parental stance and behaviors," says Karlen. And yet, she's found that given the demands and stressors of modern life, even parents who've addressed their own trauma, or who never met up with adversity, find it hard to engage in deeper listening. We are not a culture that promotes empathic listening in general; rather, we tend to be quick to offer advice and judgment. "Listening requires checking one's emotions and remembering to ask questions with curiosity in order to understand what your child is going through. It means that if something your daughter says disappoints you or evokes your fear or anxiety, you step back before you dive in. If we can remember that how we make girls *feel* is key, then we can remember that advice is not necessarily what they are looking for. Being heard is the process by which we help young people to feel safe. There is great receptivity to problem solving and advice once [it is] truly heard."

Imagine how different Deleicea Greene's college experience might have been if, at age eleven, she'd been able to sit at a kitchen table and tell a parent that she felt unmotivated or not smart enough in her classes? Or how Julia Abernathy's teen years might have been if, at the age of twelve, she'd felt she had someone to whom to open her heart when a slew of older boys began sexually propositioning her.

The good news for parents is that no matter the child's age, even when the roots of troubles are deep, relationships can heal. It's never too late to start learning and practicing small-scale approaches to reengineer the climate of family life.

Offering a state of empathy and engaging in attuned listening, so that your daughter feels heard and understood, will calm her nervous system and help regulate her emotions, which regulates her neural state.

Family Connection: "We Can Talk About Anything"

Let's do a short thought experiment. Take a moment to close your eyes and think back to the most difficult moments you've faced in your life as a parent. Maybe you and your spouse weren't getting along; or your family was stressed to the max in a time of crisis, when something bad had happened; or life was just too busy and chaotic; or someone flipped their lid, yelled, or overreacted, and the whole house was miserable. Now ask yourself: *What was the emotional climate like in the house? Was it a climate of parent-child attunement?* Again, it's a tall order, and it's okay if your answers are messy.

Let's add a second, brief reflection. Go back further in time, to your own childhood living room. Ask yourself the same questions. Reflect on the emotional tenor of your childhood home when your family faced difficult times, or when a family member had big, negative emotions. Think, too, of times when you were emotionally hurting as a child or teenager. Could you safely turn to, be honest and vulnerable with, and be validated and soothed by your mother? Your father?

Recently, I sat in on a discussion at the Johns Hopkins Bloomberg School of Public Health with Christina Bethell, Ph.D., and a dozen or so of her graduate students. Bethell is a professor, the director of child and adolescent health at Bloomberg, and a leading architect of much of what we understand about the way parent-child attunement and family resilience safeguard a child's mental and physical well-being. She has spent the last twenty-five years delving into the granular details of what healthy family connection looks like and why it is so neurobiologically protective. Bethell comes to this area as a scientist, but her work is also imbued with her deep, personal understanding of the role trauma plays in well-being. She tells me—with a sense of openness that is rare in academia—that she grew up facing an extremely high level of childhood adversity, and her family had a very low level of connection. Bethell's mother suffered from alcoholism, and her father abandoned the family very early in her life; the remaining family subsisted on welfare. Her mother remarried a man who repeatedly sexually abused his stepdaughters, landing Bethell in the emergency room at the age of nine. As an adult, Bethell also manages a range of inflammatory disorders, including the autoimmune disease lupus. Her life experiences, scientific findings, and curricula interweave in what one senses, as she speaks, is an embodied moral imperative to help every teen thrive. And she is particularly interested in growing strong girls.

Bethell is teaching her students about her most recent work. Using data from the 2016 and 2017 National Survey of Children's Health, she and her colleagues examined predictors for flourishing among children ages six to seventeen. To determine child well-being, parents filling out the survey were asked how well the following phrases described their child: "My child (1.) Shows interest and curiosity in learning new things; (2.) Works to finish tasks he or she starts; and (3.) Stays calm and in control when faced with a challenge." Parents were asked to respond with "definitely true" or "sometimes true or not true."

They were then asked to indicate how well the following six questions described their family, the answers to which form what's known as the Family Resilience and Connection Index (FRCI) score:

1. "When your family faces problems, how often are you likely to talk together about what to do?"
2. "How often are you likely to work together to solve [your] problems?"
3. "How often are you likely to know you have strengths to draw on?"
4. "How often are you likely to stay hopeful even in difficult times?"
5. "How well can you and [your] child share ideas or talk about things that really matter?"

6. "How well do you think you are handling the day-to-day demands of raising children?"

The odds of a child flourishing throughout adolescence were, Bethell tells her students, twelve times higher for children and teens whose parents answered positively ("very well") to a single question: "How well can you and [your] child share ideas or talk about things that really matter?" For children whose parents answered "somewhat well," their odds of flourishing were nearly four times greater than for those whose parents answered "not very well" or "not at all."

"Girls who could talk to a parent about any topic when they felt angry, worried, or troubled, without worrying about their parents' emotional reaction, were significantly less likely to develop symptoms of anxiety, depression, or behavioral health issues." The eyes of the young women in Bethell's class lock on her as she explains that girls who grew up in families that were able to talk and strategize together to solve their problems, recognize one another's strengths, and stay hopeful even in difficult times were far more likely to report strong connections to their mother and father and less likely to develop anxiety or depression. "Overall, the likelihood of flourishing was three to four times greater for children whose parents answered 'very well' to between four and six of the Family Resilience and Connection Index questions, compared to having a score of zero to one. This remained true for those children who faced adverse childhood experiences, grew up in poverty, or who struggled with complex chronic health disorders."

I think, as she lectures, of all the recent research in immunology that speaks to the biological underpinnings of the correlation Bethell has found. Higher levels of parental support and connection are strongly associated with children having lower levels of inflammatory biomarkers, including cortisol and C-reactive protein. Lower levels of these factors are, in turn, linked to a decreased likelihood of children developing mental health disorders. Other studies from the field of neuroscience show that teens with more positive relationships with their parents are less likely to show an overactivation of neural activity in areas of the brain associated with high-risk behaviors.

Unfortunately, only about 48 percent of families today actually exhibit four or more of the strengths assessed on the Family Resilience and Connection Index. Rather than blame individual families, though, Bethell believes that society is a big part of the problem. "We lack the skills and ability, as a society, to support strong family connection, which means too many children are not flourishing. A family's level of connection can exacerbate or heal a problem. Relationships *are* the intervention and the cornerstone of healthy childhood development. This is a biological imperative for well-being." Bethell refers to this state of parent-child attunement with a term I really like: *biosynchrony.*

Think of Deleicea Greene, who grew up in near poverty. The economic hardship her single mother faced limited Deleicea's opportunities as well as her own. But what Deleicea remembers as being most painful about her childhood was the feeling of not having an adult to lean on or turn to with her own suffering. That is what felt relentlessly excruciating and led to her wanting to kill herself when she was only eleven.

Researcher and psychologist Hillary Lianne McBride, author of *The Wisdom of Your Body,* has uncovered similar relationships between family connection and healthy body image in girls. She and her colleagues surveyed ninety-one women between the ages of nineteen and thirty regarding their relationship to their bodies. She then conducted in-depth interviews with five young women who scored very high on positive body image and also interviewed their mothers. Her goal was to better understand how young women's relationships with their mothers contributed to their positive relationship with their own bodies. McBride found that young women who spoke about their bodies in kind and affirming ways and viewed them positively, regardless of their body type, were more likely to say they "always felt able to go to their mother for anything they needed, physical or emotional" and felt "accepted fully by their mother, regardless of their appearance or if they disagreed" with each other. These young women were also more likely to resist bogus societal messages that their bodies defined their worth as women.

And yet, too many girls say they didn't grow up with high levels of family resilience and connection. Julia Abernathy and Deleicea Greene both found it hard to turn to their parents when they were in distress, and Deleicea's family did not come together to solve hard problems. But Julia and Deleicea are not alone. According to a study led by Bethell, females are less likely to report that they "feel their family often stood by them" or that they "always receive the emotional support they need" compared with males. This may be due to a confluence of familiar factors: Girls still often have less power and voice in family life, are often encouraged to care for others before they care for their own emotional needs, and carry the additional psychological stressor of coming of age marinating in our culture's toxic, sexist messaging about how to be acceptable as a female.

Indeed, it became abundantly clear to me as I wrote this book that if there was one thing Anna, Deleicea, and Julia could have benefited from having more of in family life, it was being able to talk to a parent about their problems and knowing they could tell them anything, anywhere, anytime.

So, NOW THAT we understand the role our own story, and our reactivity as parents, plays in parent-child interactions, how do we enhance healthy parent-child attunement given the stressful demands of modern life?

CHAPTER TEN

Make Her Home Her Safe Space

T HE MORE AT home and the safer we feel in our own bodies, the more we get to know ourselves behind our ruminating minds—and the more we get to be in love with this life. But our nervous system doesn't make this feeling of safety very easy to achieve. When your nervous system detects and interprets sensory information in a way that implies an incoming emotional or physical stressor, your body reacts using its ancient mechanisms, reflexively revving up hormones like cortisol, raising the heart rate, quickening the breath, narrowing the pupils, whipping up a sweat, causing the hair on your arms and legs to stand up, and shutting down your digestion. If left unchecked, these fearful responses leave lasting marks on your brain and psyche.

Many of these threat signals are mediated by the body's vagus nerve. The largest nerve in your body, the vagus nerve wanders from your brain stem down throughout your torso, delivering to and receiving info from your heart, lungs, liver, digestive system, and your body's biggest immune organ, your spleen. Among its many jobs, the vagus nerve acts as a bidirectional superhighway, connecting two major regions of the country that is your body: your brain and all your organs, ferrying communiqués about whether you are safe or not safe. This is the case whether a bus is coming too fast as you're crossing the street or if you're simply caught up in the monkey chatter of thoughts dominating your mind, such as ruminating over what a friend or family member might have said about you behind your back.

This means that every event and emotion effects a complex interaction between your immune system and nervous system. Once the vagus nerve is activated in this way, it triggers the nervous system to enter into a fight-flight-or-freeze response. A fight response might be, *They can't do that to me/my child! I'm going to tell them what I think about this! They will regret it!* A flight response might be *I can't believe so-and-so said/did this! I have to get out of here right now!* Fight-flight-or-freeze responses are often accompanied by rage, panic, fear, anger, frustration, and rumination. A freeze response, however, might be *I'm going to curl up in a ball in bed and binge-watch* The Great British Bake Off; *I can't deal with any of this anymore! Everyone leave me the hell alone!* The freeze response is often accompanied by depressive thoughts, helplessness, shame, and feeling trapped. For all three responses, the immune system ramps up to deal with threats real or imagined. Over time, these reactions affect your mood, thinking, cognition, and behavior.

Fortunately, however, human beings (and other mammals) have a way of tamping down these responses: with positive, caring social support. When we turn to others for safe connection, our brain flips a switch and begins releasing signals throughout the body that are physically and neurobiologically protective.

Stephen Porges, Ph.D., professor of psychiatry at the University of North Carolina at Chapel Hill, is the scientific father of our understanding of the vagus nerve and architect of polyvagal theory. Polyvagal theory holds that when we draw upon the power of social engagement, seeking and identifying safe connection, listening, being listened to, smiling, looking into a child's eyes to convey a deep sense of connectedness, reflecting back what we hear and offering compassion, we stimulate what Porges calls the social engagement system. This activates the vagus nerve in positive ways, sending deep safety cues throughout the body, helping you move from feeling fearful or immobilized to experiencing a sense of safety and trust. In essence, what we want to do, as parents, is to minimize the amount of time, and the degree to which, our daughter's stress system stays activated. We also want to bring the parasympathetic nervous system (which helps to restore a sense of calm and well-being) online as often as possible by activating this sense of safety.

The first safe space in life is the family, and it is the most important one of all, the gateway to forming a healthy stress response from childhood to old age. We might think of a child's family as a kind of convoy, a small, nurturing group in which a child learns skills that are helpful for navigating life's inevitable travails and in which she develops a wise inner knowing about whom it is safe to create a convoy with and when. When your daughter has her family convoy to carry her forward, she learns the skills for how to create her own safe convoy later, in her adult life. The next six antidotes will guide you toward creating that sense of a safe convoy.

Antidote 4

When Hard Things Happen (and They Will), Be Prepared to Respond in Healthy, Supportive Ways, Even When Your Daughter Shares Hard-to-Hear Information

As a culture, we have a very low bar for tolerating emotional suffering and negative feelings. We often try to distract or numb ourselves from our own painful emotions and try to fix, diminish, or avoid other people's big emotions when they're struggling with feeling overwhelmed. Hearing another's pain (or feeling our own) is not high up in our cultural skill set or wish list. As parents, too, we often try to spare our children from feeling sadness, disappointment, anger, or frustration. Christina Bethell believes parents often try to erase the hard moments by distracting their children—watching movies, taking them out for ice cream or to the playground, or even going shopping. But meeting the hard with superficial distractions can be—to use the popular vernacular—a kind of toxic positivity. Bethell believes it is better to find ways to help teenagers give voice to their negative feelings: "Deep family connection often emerges through facing what's hard." The best way to make sure hard experiences don't leave a toll on your daughter's development is by inviting her to share negative emotions when they arise, especially in life's difficult moments, so that she knows that her feelings matter to you. This, in turn, tells her that she matters. This takes noticing what hurts.

Indeed, Bethell argues, "it is through the portal of meeting what's difficult with safety that we show children how to have resilience even in the face of life's suffering. It's when you don't allow for your child's negative emotions that you risk diminishing their mental health." This means we have to teach girls how to know when they are in need and how to reach out for help from the safe adults around them. And when they do, we have to be well regulated enough ourselves so that we can sit beside them as they share deep emotions that might be hard for us to hear.

Anna Moralis talks about how her mother, who was often gone during her adolescence, has now become that safe, nurturing adult Anna can talk to about almost anything. "My mom and I are really close now. We've both changed. I've figured out what I needed from her and how to voice to her what I need. I've learned to be super clear with her in communicating my needs and [my] really hard emotions and even [to] say, 'When you said or did this, it hurt me, and I needed you to do X or Y instead.' At the same time, I've had to work within myself to rely less on my parents to solve whatever problems I'm having, or expecting them to be able to make things better, while still being able to go to them as a source of support."

Today, Anna tells me, "my mom is this positive force in my life." When I ask Anna to name the one way in which her mom has changed that has helped her the most, she says, "Listening. My mom has become so much less judgmental. She has become a really phenomenal listener, and that makes me feel I can turn to her with anything."

All too often, when children and teens try to tell us about their fears and worries, adults find it hard to tune in without judgment. This is why children so often stay silent about their deepest worries, which can make it appear that they're happy and coping well even when they are really struggling inside. This kind of deep, safe, attuned conversation can also serve to mitigate the poisonous tone that dominates social media and in which girls' psyches are so often embedded (often to the point that they internalize those critical lashing voices and turn them on themselves).

Moreover, if the adversity a family or teen faces isn't openly discussed, or is treated as a secret, and adults never acknowledge it, children sense something must really be wrong. And when children sense that something is amiss, but it remains unspoken, they assume that something is wrong with *them,* that *they* must somehow be at fault, or bad, or stupid, or unlovable. (*What is wrong with me that this is happening?*) When you meet your daughter where she is and let her know that what she's experiencing and feeling is a normal response to a really painful situation, you help her take an essential leap; instead of thinking, *What's wrong with me?* she gains the wider perspective that the problem lies not inside her, but with the situation at hand (or with society at large). Failure to discuss the truth of what they are feeling, and why, hurts girls. Allowing room for the truth is empowering.

Think of Deleicea Greene, who was well into her teens (when she found the world of slam poetry) before she was able to dig deep, identify, and speak up openly about her feelings. "I can see that because I didn't have anyone to tell my suffering to when I was growing up, I had a lot that had gone unsaid inside of me, and a lot of that unveiling of hard things began to erupt for me on the page. I had never really reflected on or discussed how the neglect or violence I lived with or how taking care of my mom made me feel, because I'd never had the trust required to do so with any adult. All of that ended up imploding inside me in this dark, dark hole." Deleicea's words bring to mind those of author and lecturer Brené Brown: "If we share our story with someone who responds with empathy and understanding, shame can't survive."

Bruce Perry, M.D., Ph.D., professor of psychiatry and behavioral sciences at the Feinberg School of Medicine at Northwestern University, has shown that one of the most important tools we can use to respond to children affected by trauma is the three Rs, "regulate, relate, reason." It's only once a child feels physically and emotionally safe (regulate) and connected in talking to you (relate) that they can tap into the cognitive and neural brain processes that will enable them to freshly consider their perception and interpretation of the situation at hand and start problem-solving (reason). This is yet another reason to brush up on Antidotes 1 and 2—you need to understand your own "baggage" in order to really show up for someone else as they are acquiring their own.

Okay, so how do you prepare yourself for these situations? Getting good at parent listening (versus fixing) takes practice. Trust me, I know. Fixing things was, for many years, my default mode as a parent. And yet, I've learned that doing so only makes it harder for my children to feel safe in telling me how they feel. The bottom line is that you'll want to practice these skills whenever you can, so that they are sharp and ready to go when you need them the most. Otherwise, it's like neglecting a car's maintenance: If you let the engine rust, it might stall when you try to start it up in an emergency.

Let's revisit one of our earlier hypothetical scenarios. Your daughter is clearly upset; she is slamming things around as she tells you her two best friends are having a sleepover without her. When your daughter is feeling emotionally overwhelmed like this, here are a few guidelines:

First, remember what her brain is up to in the moment: Her amygdala has detected a threat, and the stress-threat response (racing heart rate, butterflies in her stomach, muscle tension, sweaty palms) dampens her ability to think through her situation, much less problem-solve. Second, remind yourself of your goals: to understand what's going on below the surface, help her hit the brakes on her body and her brain's stress machinery, and establish safe connection. This means taking your daughter's concerns seriously, even if they seem overblown to you, setting aside your parental desire to interrogate or insert your opinion, and focusing on her distress, not your own.

Start with empathic validation, reflecting back what you hear from her and offering reassurance and comfort. An empathic statement might be "I hear you" or "That sounds so frustrating" or "That sounds incredibly hard" or "Your feelings are real and understandable and important." Or even "Anyone would feel that way. If I were in your shoes, I'd feel that way, too." Validating your daughter's emotions before the conversation moves on to the details of what happened—if it does move on; it might not—will help her express and process her feelings with you rather than try to deal with them on her own. It's important to remember that it's not just your words that matter here, but also the cues you send through your body language (facial expression, tone of voice, gestures). Offer up soft, reassuring eye contact. When a child sees their parent looking at them lovingly, it soothes their nervous system. The point here is to stay connected as the positive neurobiological power of attunement does its big magic and as your daughter's nervous system (and your own) begins to produce calming hormones such as the feel-good oxytocin.

You can then move forward in a high-stakes conversation by reflecting back whatever you heard your child saying: "Let me see if I've got this right so far . . ." or "So, you feel X about Y?" Then you can begin to ask open-ended questions: "What does it feel like when your friends don't include you?" or "Can you say some more about that?" Again, frame these questions nonjudgmentally, bearing in mind that your daughter's perception of how open she can be with you is being formed in response to your words and body language—all of which she's studied hundreds of thousands of times since the moment of her birth (or from the very first moment you met, if she was adopted).

If you are dealing with a highly complicated and higher-stakes situation—let's use our earlier hypothetical, in which your daughter confesses to having sent a picture of her cleavage to an older boy who shared it with classmates—you might walk up to the fact that this is going to be hard to discuss. Set the stage for your conversation with something like "This topic is hard to talk about—even for me, as an adult. Let's just talk. I promise I won't react. And I want you to feel free to say or ask whatever you want."

When we are filled with difficult emotions, we want to unpack that burden with someone we trust. It feels good to be listened to; you know this yourself, no doubt. Think back to a time when you were trying to convey difficult feelings during a conversation, and you'll recognize the following as true: When researchers compare listening approaches, they find that when people are talking to inattentive listeners, they volunteer less information. Conversely, when we talk to attentive listeners, we tell them more information, offer up specific details, and elaborate more, *even when the listener doesn't ask a single question.* Having someone listen with presence and kindness calms the nervous system, which in turn regulates the brain. By being an attentive listener, you also open the door to your daughter to decompress. When teens don't feel heard, seen, or validated, they often get louder or terribly irritable; or they act out or, conversely, quiet down or withdraw—all of which obscures their underlying feelings from your view.

You might ask your daughter if she can name her feelings with emotional detail: "Are you feeling angry about this, or sad, or afraid?" Research shows that the more specific we are in naming difficult emotions, the more we activate areas of the brain that help the amygdala quiet down, which serves as an antidote to a heightened stress response.

If your daughter wants to know what you think, or solicits your advice for brass-tacks next steps, and you're still processing the information you've just heard or you feel you still need to know more, you can offer up a simple response that further underscores her autonomy while also buying yourself time for your own regulation. A good response I've used is "I promise I will tell you what I think, but first, I really want to know what you think, because what you think right now is more important than what I think." Or simply "I'd like to hear more about your thoughts." If she doesn't ask for advice but you would like to offer your thoughts, ask your daughter's permission to tell her what you notice or think before sharing your observations: "Would it be okay if I offered a suggestion?" Or try: "I just want to run something by you."

You can further ensure that your daughter feels respected, suggests Ron Dahl, M.D., professor and director of the Center for the Developing Adolescent at UC Berkeley's School of Public Health, by asking her how she thinks she can better approach her situation—versus evaluating her actions and strategies and/or telling her what you think she should do. Let her know, too, that you appreciate her coming to talk to you: "I'm so glad that you are willing to talk with me about it." Finally, wrap up the conversation by amplifying the good that you see emanating from your child: "Wow, you really dealt with this very complex and confusing situation well."

"Teens will only voice themselves when they feel heard," says Karlen. "But parents often fall into one of several traps which keep them from listening. Parents often become a detective or judge or the inevitable problem solver, jumping in with 'Let's figure out how you got into this,' or 'Who started it?' or 'Here's what you need to do.' Or, in our fear, we jump in with quick, judgmental responses like 'Give me your phone!' or 'Where exactly did you meet this guy?' or 'Oh my God! What were you thinking? I told you every text is public forever!'" When you step back from your role as problem solver, your daughter can start to figure out her own strategies and solutions, a skill that will serve her long into the future.

Even when kids are quite young—long before teenagerhood—we need to switch these reflexive reactions into listening responses, Karlen urges. "Instead of telling our child on the playground, 'Go apologize!' we need to sit with them and say, 'It sounds like you got really angry and frustrated and didn't know what to do,' and listen. Later, you can get to the apology."

Even if your daughter says very little, keep showing up. Sit down beside her on the couch; or if that's closer than she wants you to be, sit quietly nearby. Offer a snack or a glass of water or a cup of tea. Offer your empathic presence until she trusts she can share her feelings. If there are actions that need to be taken, behaviors that need to be addressed, and problems that need to be solved, you can get to those later, after your daughter has soaked in the sense of safety of being vulnerable with you.

Remember to Apologize and Make a Repair

If you mess up in high-stakes parenting interactions, that's really okay. It happens to every parent, especially when we're in the process of identifying and resolving our own trauma. It has certainly happened to me. Loving your children doesn't mean that parenting isn't challenging. The most important thing to do if you make a mistake is to make a repair and come back to a state of reconnection with your child. Don't judge yourself by your immediate reply. It's normal and often warranted to react if your daughter acts or behaves in a way that's worrying, especially if she's in your face, criticizing you or your actions. The point isn't to have no reaction, but to become more mindful so that you have choices for how you respond in the moment, so that you can stay rooted, available, and open even when things get intense: the giant redwood tree in the storm.

Remember, your first, reflexive response doesn't define who you are as a parent or a person. Often, during my own parenting journey, it's been in that moment, just after I've reacted, that I've recognized that my initial response was rooted in old emotions or experiences from my own life. Understanding why I said the wrong thing, and the link between my past experiences and the present moment, helps me to see more clearly. Over the years, I've learned to note this link, pause, take a moment to regulate my own nervous system, and remind myself that my ability to make a repair is rooted in who I am now, in the present, and that I have at my disposal all the skills I've worked hard to develop over years for just these moments.

I learned and developed these skills (and teach them in my courses) because I've needed them myself. If I notice I'm not self-regulated during a discussion with my child, I might call to mind the face and presence of someone I love who has loved me unconditionally and who's been a mentor—like my father, who died when I was a teen. I bring in the sense of calm I felt whenever I was with him. I might even imagine what he might say to me in this moment if he could. Or I might quickly look at one object in the room that is meaningful to me (a vase made by a dear friend, a favorite tree outside the window, the curve of my daughter's cheek) and silently note a few details about it in my mind (the color and shape, the beautiful way the light falls upon it). This helps me truly ground myself in the present. I always note my breathing. If it is shallow, I use one of many different exercises to shift my breathing pattern and soothe my nervous system. Or I might do a vagus nerve relaxation technique—but subtly, so no one can tell. I might even use my own name to calm myself: *Donna, you are safe. You've got this.* (Using your own name to calm yourself mentally helps the brain switch gears.) If I'm still feeling muscle tightness, or if my brain is caught up in monkey chatter, I'll see if I can make a small, gentle, calming movement, such as stroking my fingers down my arm or along my opposite palm. This opens me up to be able to move forward more gently and be more in the moment with the child I so love, who is standing in front of me. As my breathing, tension, and demeanor relax, my child is also more likely to relax. For this, we can thank the mirror neurons in our brain. Ideally, our child starts to mirror not just what we're doing (breathing more deeply and relaxing), but also our sense of calm.

In this moment—for, that is all it takes to choose to do two of these things—I have not said or done more wrong things. This is a win! (True confession: For many years, my go-to when I felt overwhelmed in a parent-child conversation with my daughter was to secretly pinch my thigh so I wouldn't blurt out the wrong thing. Regulating myself feels a whole lot better.) Once I'm regulated, I'm also ready to make a repair. One of my go-to lines for this has been "Hey, when I said XYZ, that came out wrong. I'm sorry. Can we hit the reset button and try this again?" As my children have gotten older, they've said these same words back to me, to make a repair when they've said something in the heat of the moment they later regretted uttering.

Once you've begun a repair, you can be more specific. Acknowledge that something said or done in haste didn't come across the way you intended. "I made a mistake. I raised my voice and that might have scared you; I wish I hadn't done that." Or, "My behavior wasn't okay. I lost it, and I wish I hadn't said that; I'm sorry." Or, "You're right. I wasn't listening to you. But I am listening now." The sooner you make a repair, the less likely it is that an unhappy memory will stick in your child's mind. Moreover, when parents make a repair after having overreacted or yelled, a child's amygdala stops lighting up; they calm down. The nervous system relaxes again. You can make a repair while still imposing limits—after apologizing, and regulating your nervous system, return to the topic at hand: for example, "Our family rule is no cellphone in your room at bedtime."

If you aren't sure why what you said came off as hurtful, you can try to find out, so that you can be more validating in the future. For instance, let's say your daughter tells you, "I bombed my chemistry exam!" and is clearly distraught. You might blurt out something blaming, like, "Did you study as much as you should have?" Or, "I told you you should have been studying harder last night!" She storms out of the room, yelling, "You never take my side!" Or, "You think I'm stupid!" When something like this happens, you might try: "I want to be helpful, and clearly, that wasn't helpful. I can see I hurt you. I love you and know how smart you are and what a good person you are, and I never intended to do that. Can you help me understand what would help you the most right now?" It can also help to admit your own imperfections: "I clearly don't know everything; I don't have all the answers." Sometimes, a more blanket, or retrospective, apology is in order for past events in general. As therapist Nedra Tawwab writes, "There is still time to tell your children: 'I did not have the proper tools, and I apologize that you didn't get what you needed.'"

Psychologist Amy Karlen often works with parents on how to make repairs. "Parents often fear that if they apologize, it will make them look weak or flawed. But if we think about it as if the tables were turned, we can more readily recognize the importance of owning mistakes made, and it's critical that we model that for them." Apologizing is also good for parents' mental well-being, she points out. "Ruminating on what you did or said or how you screwed up with your child is not helpful. Moms especially often beat themselves up and ruminate over their interactions with their kids, or what they did wrong to set their kid off. The only way to settle your own brain back down is to model how to own it, repair it, and let it go. Apologizing is a positive first step."

*"The only way to settle your own brain
back down is to model how to own it, repair it,
and let it go. Apologizing is a positive first step."*

Antidote 5

Power Up on Joy (Especially) in Difficult Times

Negative and positive experiences coexist every day in the lives of our children. As we've seen, trying to push away our daughter's anxiety or angry mood just makes that mood grow bigger. But that doesn't mean that, once we've acknowledged our daughter's emotions around big problems, we move on. After we notice and validate what's hard, we can also help our child to notice small but powerful positive aspects of their lives and to interweave enjoyable experiences. This might mean focusing on the taste of the apple pie you've just made together or noticing how cute and funny the new puppy is. Interweaving the habit of noticing what is good, after we've accepted that things are really, really hard, helps children and teens understand that even when things feel miserable and life seems overwhelming, they can still connect with the positive; they still get to be happy.

Christina Bethell believes that this two-step process of recognizing and helping children to feel their negative emotions with care and compassion, and then having the positive experience of feeling seen, safe, and supported, "mitigates the negative impacts of adverse childhood experiences to the extent that it can interrupt damage to neural pathways associated with mental health concerns." You can even explicitly agree as a family "that you still get to be happy even when really hard things are happening."

At the same time, we don't have to wait for crises to strike to take in the good. We can seek out the more joyful moments throughout our day and savor the good feelings that arise. This can be as simple as making the most out of small, serendipitous moments (powdered sugar on everyone's faces while baking, enjoying the way your usually stern grandmother lets out a big belly laugh that starts everyone else laughing, getting caught in a sudden downpour walking home from the bus and racing to the front door). Or *create* moments: When you spot a bluebird on a branch outside the window, you might turn to your child and say, "He has a worm in his beak! Let's watch and see if he takes it to his nest." During that last hour of the day, when the sun is going down, soak it in: "Let's sit on the front steps and enjoy this sunset together." Or when another driver lets you merge ahead of them on the highway: "That's really kind of that driver, to let me go ahead; people can be generous."

Searching for joy and finding pleasure is the antithesis to nonstop doing and productivity. When you model amplifying pleasurable experiences and sitting with them, it helps regulate not only your child's nervous system, but your own. You teach your nervous system and your child's that it's safe to inhabit a soothing mental space throughout the day. Taking a few moments to create a deliciousness around an experience also helps to create a happy, and sticky, memory, one replete with tiny, pleasurable visual images that the mind can return to and draw solace from at any time in the future.

Learning this has been key to Anna's healing. She puts it this way: "I learned, in the face of my struggle with disordered eating and anxiety, that I had to actively seek out what gave me joy and stack up those positive experiences every day for myself." This lesson served Anna well during the COVID-19 pandemic. "I had to go back home from college and stay with my family for six months, and I was just basically in my room the first two months, writing papers. I couldn't be out in the community doing the work I love to do. So I had to make something good come out of it and find my self-worth and excitement in other places." Somewhere in the middle of being in a funk about having to be home all the time, Anna had this "realization that when I was in high school, we couldn't all be together because my mom was overseas, but now we could. And this was a chance for me to refocus on rebuilding family relationships." She started creating menus and cooking three-course dinners for her family once a week. She says, "We binge-watched silly TV shows. When the weather was nice, I planned hikes for us as a family, and we took our three dogs. And this time of reconnection has turned out to be really meaningful to me, a gift in the time of crisis."

Antidote 6

Don't Solve All Her Problems for Her—Leave Room for "a Little Wobble"

I want to be really clear here: Establishing psychological safety and family connection shouldn't be confused with overprotecting children and teens. Tracy Bale, Ph.D., neuroscientist at the University of Maryland, puts it this way: "Wobble is good, but falling down is not." Understanding this difference between wobbling and falling down is crucial to building resilience in girls. "There are developmental windows during which children have to learn certain lessons about how to get through bumps in their friendships, or in meeting small challenges in their life, and see that they can manage a little kid-size failure, not fall apart, grow from it, and move on," Bale says. In response to child-size adversities, the brain develops certain structures "or matrixes, that are a really important part of the architecture of the brain," she explains. "This wiring is really complex and intricate. It results from not only the good stuff you learn from healthy connection; it's also formed from all of the bad stuff you learn from your screw-ups." Bale draws upon her earlier analogy for adolescent brain remodeling, likening it to a house under renovation. The creation of these healthy and necessary brain matrixes is like "putting very strong, resilient plumbing in your house during a renovation, before you put up the walls. If you don't allow this to happen as children are growing up, it's going to be a lot, lot harder to go back later at age twenty or twenty-five and try to help the brain build this neural structure."

At the Yale University's Child Study Center, known as SPACE (for Supportive Parenting for Anxious Childhood Emotions), researchers are examining the way American adults approach parenting to glean insight into what goes wrong when this wiring up of healthy, protective matrixes fails to occur. One of SPACE's streams of research centers on reexamining what researchers call "accommodating behaviors," in which a parent tries to reduce a child's anxiety by accommodating them in small but constant ways. Studies show that nearly 95 percent of parents of anxious children engage in such accommodating behaviors, and higher degrees of accommodation are linked to more severe anxiety symptoms. For example, repeatedly retying your child's shoes for her because she complains they are too tight or uncomfortable; coaching your daughter through the rest of her history assignment after she dissolves into anxious tears; driving her to school because the bus is too noisy for her; double-checking her homework every morning as you pack her backpack for her; and so on. As a mother who raised an anxious daughter, I know of what I speak: When she was a toddler, I would find myself searching the house in a panic looking for her "bunny," a five-inch-high stuffed rabbit I'd given to her one Easter and without which she would not leave the house.

This kind of overaccommodating behavior is more likely to happen when parents are busy and tired and overwhelmed. It's easier to retie a four-year-old's shoes three times than it is to deal with tears or tantrums during the walk to the post office. It's quicker during the morning to race back into the house and quickly reassemble her lunch in her favorite lunchbox than it is to negotiate through her tearful insistence that she can't go to school without it. But there is another reason that parents remove even small hurdles from their children's lives, according to William Stixrud, Ph.D., a clinical neuropsychologist, and Ned Johnson, coauthors of *The Self-Driven Child*: not so much to protect our kids from feeling distress, but to shield ourselves from the discomfort our child's distress causes us.

And here, once again—and not surprisingly—your own story of trauma plays a role: When a parent's stress response, brain, body, and nervous system are set on high alert because of the way in which their own early adversity shaped them, the entire family is likely to have a higher baseline level of stress. This, in turn, makes it more likely that a child's stress response never has a chance to shut off. When children are marinating in their parents' anxiousness, they might resist taking on the kinds of normal, everyday risks and challenges that help most children grow.

In the SPACE therapy program at Yale, parents learn how to begin to reduce their accommodation—but to do so while also showing empathy for their child's distress, discomfort, and suffering and while expressing confidence in their child's strengths and capabilities. In other words, the stepping away from accommodating behavior happens within the container of safety and family connection.

Life will always present us with another problem or disappointment. Without the ability to wobble and regain our inner footing, it will be very difficult to get through the small, frustrating moments life inevitably serves up. "If we are always stepping in and taking over when our kids make mistakes, they will never learn 'Hey, I can't treat a friend this way. I need to do better,'" says Bale. "Or it could be that the lesson is the opposite: 'Some girls can be bullies, and they are not my friend, and I'll remember this and notice the signals that someone is a bully earlier the next time.'" All these lessons and experiences in social groups and in relationships—where kids make mistakes, get feedback, and grow from the experience—create wiring between existing synapses and new ones; in other words: this wiring is achieved only by life experience. These lessons can "be awful and hard, and yet that's how the brain learns. We tend to want to protect our kids from everything, but if we do, we will then be pushing them forward into the world when they haven't yet learned the lessons they need to succeed and choose healthy relationships on their own," or make healthy decisions. And by then, says Bale, "the architecture in crucial areas of the brain, like the prefrontal cortex, which helps us to manage our emotions and behavior and make good decisions, will have already been formed."

This is not to say that it's ever too late to change the way you respond when your child meets up with age-appropriate adversities. Nothing is set in stone. Life is an endless process of learning and unlearning. The brain is highly neuroplastic and is always changing to reflect that growth. As your child has more chances to safely develop her resilience, her brain will change and grow, too.

It's important that girls grow up knowing that not all adversity is harmful or threatening and that difficulty and adversity exist along a continuum. Many things happen to us every day that are difficult or unfortunate (the car breaks down; we lose our phone), but they are not threatening unless we register them as such in our nervous system. This means that, as parents, we have to differentiate between healthy stress and toxic stress or safe struggles and unsafe struggles. (Again, we first have to resolve our own trauma so that we can be adept at this differentiation and model it with ease for our daughters.) When we see that a stressor is a safe, bite-size adversity that doesn't require an overt adult intervention, we can offer support, love, stability, and connection to help our daughter find her own way. This might sound like "I can see you have a problem. But you've got this. I know you can handle it. What do you think are your best options?" Or, "What strategies are you going to use?" Or, "What has worked for you in the past?" What won't achieve this is calling another child's parent to complain about their child or showing up at school with a homework assignment your child forgot on the kitchen table.

> *"If we solve our kids' problems . . . their anxiety*
> *will be temporarily reduced, but it will return at*
> *the next hurdle. Parents who hover and helicopter*
> *and are quick to jump in haven't taught their kids*
> *how to manage stress or given them a chance to*
> *develop a picture of themselves as competent."*

When we intervene in child-size adversities, we send the message to our child that the fear of imminent harm is an appropriate response to life's small challenges. We also signal that we lack confidence in their ability to solve the problem. If you've been convinced you cannot handle problems on your own, the implicit message becomes that you're in some way fragile or a victim of the vagaries of an unpredictable world, and that message gets wired into the brain.

"Many parents believe the main goal in family life is having happy children and that we can in part achieve this by keeping stress out of their lives," says Karlen. "But the goal of ongoing happiness is impossible. The main job and goal of parenting is building resiliency. If we solve our kids' problems, if we repetitively intervene on their behalf, their anxiety will be temporarily reduced, but it will return at the next hurdle. Parents who hover and helicopter and are quick to jump in haven't taught their kids how to manage stress or given them the chance to develop a picture of themselves as competent."

Antidote 7

Wonder Aloud Together to Help Build Resilience to Stress

A child's mind is a wondering mind: It flits and floats and makes connections and associations about things in the world that we as adults no longer see; and by so doing, it calms and helps itself. Alison Gopnik, Ph.D., professor of psychology and philosophy at the University of California, Berkeley, and author of *The Philosophical Baby,* uses an old philosophy metaphor to help explain the way children's minds are built to wonder and why it does them so much good. Consider two types of human consciousness as being like two types of light, Gopnik suggests. One is a spotlight: "It comes in," she says. "It illuminates the thing you want to find out about. And you don't see the things that are on the other side." This is the way we as adults live our lives, focusing on the specific things we have to get done, whether it's answering emails or cooking dinner. Your mind might wander a bit as you perform the task at hand, but your focus always returns to it, which requires shutting down your awareness of all the other things you're not paying attention to.

But children live in a state of consciousness that is, says Gopnik, "much more like a lantern." They're "taking in information from everything that's going on" around them, rather than focusing on just one thing at a time. This state of lantern-like consciousness is a kind of open awareness. We experience this as adults, too, of course, when we have moments of awe: We notice the way the light illuminates a field of tall grass that's waving in the wind; or we hear a piece of classical music and we feel a sudden sense that everything in the world is significant and important and that we are just one small part of this interconnected world, Gopnik explains. In these moments, "everything around you becomes illuminated. And you yourself sort of disappear. And I think that's kind of the best analogy I can think of for the state that children are in." Children are not always in this state, of course, but it's "more like their natural state" than it is for adults.

When kids are in this broad-based state of consciousness, they feel "a certain kind of happiness and joy that goes with being in that state." It's the same state children enter into when they're immersed in play. And it turns out, says Gopnik, that offering children the opportunity to experience lantern-like consciousness—in the presence of a caring adult and in situations in which there is no pressure for the child to produce a particular outcome—is really important to development and resiliency.

Entering a state of wondering, in turn, helps children develop a skill that is crucial to resilience and the ability to adapt well to stress—what Rebecca Nye, author of *Children's Spirituality,* calls a sense of relational consciousness, or relational awareness. Relational awareness involves self-awareness (the ability to go within and notice your own responses and patterns and respond with self-compassion), awareness and acceptance of others (including the ability to have empathy or compassion for them), your relationship with nature, and your relationship to something bigger than you.

Our hope, of course, is that our girls will have all these skills as they come of age. This means your daughter will able to ask herself: *How do I feel when I'm in this setting? How is my behavior affecting others? How do I feel when I am with this person/group of people? How do I feel when I'm walking in nature?*

When we instill this sense of curiosity and wonder in girls, we invite them to look inside, rather than to the outside world, for answers. This can help them when they need to discern whom it is safe to turn to and when, or whether to emulate the behavior of others. A girl's sense of right and wrong becomes the voice that matters most, versus the din of voices on social media or in the school cafeteria.

One of the most powerful ways to provide opportunities for children to develop relational awareness is to take the time to "wonder together." In my own years of raising children, these moments have been as simple as saying, "I wonder what a bird feels like in the rain?" Or after reading a story, "What did that story make you think about?" Over time, children internalize this deep sense of awareness and, as they approach adolescence, turn it into larger relational questions such as "Why is that clique suddenly forming among middle school friends?" Or, "Why is my friend Tanya drinking?" Or, "Why did Emily send a selfie of her cleavage to Henry?" Or, "What will life be like after the pandemic?" Or, "What can we do to reverse climate change?"

As the years went by in my own family's life, wondering together as a family led to powerful conversations among us, often at the dinner table: "Why do you think X story in the news got so much attention? Why did this stir up so much controversy?" Or, "If we could choose just one societal problem to change, what it would be, and how would we do it?" (This has led to some very impassioned conversations!) These discussions are robust and good-natured, even when we disagree. Increasingly, my children are my teachers, and I am their grateful student.

We can do this nonverbally, too. My children grew up on Chesapeake Bay and, early on, learned to sail small dinghies, to paddleboard, and to kayak. I would often stand on shore, or on a nearby dock, letting them figure out how to catch the wind in their sails, how to stand and balance on a paddleboard without tumbling off, or how to steer a kayak against the current—before offering suggestions and guidance. As their boat luffed in the wind, or they fell off the paddleboard, or got turned around by the current, they faced their frustration, failed a little, wondered what they could do differently, and succeeded by challenging themselves. These hobbies became some of their most joyful pastimes because by doing them, they so often learned to be their own guides.

Girls who come of age amid our society's gendered, sexist messaging often feel a tremendous loss of power and control as they grow up, as they realize the depth to which sexism permeates so many aspects of our larger culture. This revelation is often particularly hard felt for girls who become immersed in the social media terrain only to quickly realize that many of the loudest, most powerful voices in our society don't have all that much regard for young women's safety, needs, or feelings. In the face of all this, wondering together also sets the stage for a "power-with" dynamic rather than a "power-over" dynamic.

Researcher Bob Whitaker—author of the epidemiological study that showed that girls who face adversity are more likely to later develop mental health disorders compared with boys who face the same level of adversity—offers up an analogy that illustrates the difference between guiding versus acting as the "leader" in family life. If you are headed up Mount Everest, "you need a guide. But that guide is not going to go up Mount Everest *for* you, just as parents cannot go through adolescence for their girls. The best guides don't simply lead while you trail behind; the best guides model how to tackle Mount Everest while standing beside you. A Sherpa might say, 'Hook yourself into the harness this way' or 'Watch how I cross this stream; then you try it.'"

Modeling a power-with relationship can help reinforce in girls the knowledge that their thoughts, needs, and feelings are valued and respected. Guiding rather than leading gives your daughter more voice, autonomy, and the interior skills to choose for herself the best direction to turn toward once she's navigating on her own.

Antidote 8

Go Slow on Development—Keep the Biological Brakes Engaged

The onset of puberty doesn't just occur like clockwork, at a predetermined, time-stamped moment based on genetics; it happens in response to signals from the environment. One potent environmental signal is early sexualization imposed from the outside (as opposed to normal, burgeoning sexuality from within). According to neurobiologists, our constant pop culture depiction of young girls as sexualized objects (from Instagram to advertising) doesn't just act as a "social pathogen." As I touched on in chapter 7, this chronic visual titillation and toxic oversexualization may play a role in signaling the biological pathways that switch on puberty, gearing up the body and revving it into action, thus lifting the biological brakes off puberty before the brain is equipped to navigate this complex emotional time of adolescence.

If neuroscientists are correct in their supposition that social media and traditional media exposure can hasten a potential cascade of estrogen-boosted stress-immune chemicals during a neurodevelopmentally vulnerable window, this suggests that we, as parents, must do everything we can to hold back what we know to be toxic influences. Children and teens lack life experience. The hope is to allow for enough time during girls' development to teach them strong decision-making and coping skills before they encounter toxic sexist influences. That way, when they do, they'll have a solid enough sense of self and will know how to interpret such information, ask questions, engage in critical thinking, and balance the negative barrage of messages they're receiving with core interior values and real-life experience. We want them to have the necessary tools to make choices that are good for them rather than harmful. This is, after all, what adolescence is for—and we have to let our girls have that "lost" period of childhood.

All this underscores the need to ensure that by the time your daughter interacts with social media and the larger world (with its gendered messaging, hate speech, misogynist views, and distressing news of climate change, inequality, and mass or school shootings), you will have constructed a deep sense of safe family connection. With that connection in place, she can be confident about coming to you to talk openly about her feelings without fear, shame, or embarrassment.

Shielding children from "forces that are accelerating in society around them" may be "one of the most loving things you can do for your child and for her neurobiological health," says Whitaker. As in all child development, "it's about the right thing at the right time in the right way." In our modern world, "on average, we have one or more of those rights wrong."

I WANT TO reiterate this one more time here: This science shouldn't be misread as some twisted rationale for shuttering girls away from the world or not letting them wear a bikini. Far from it. It's simply a scientific framework to help shore up your resolve when setting limits for social media use (more on that later) or saying no to a movie rated NC-17. Looked at in another light, it is also to help you keep your child inside the "safe space of childhood" for as long as it is healthy and appropriate for her neurodevelopment. Again, the emphasis here is on the word *appropriate*. We do not want to shelter girls from real-life problems, but in a society where major corporations like Meta continue with business as usual even knowing the harm they may be doing to today's generation of girls, and where media is increasingly marketing adult content to eight- and nine-year-old girls, we do want to exercise "right timing" for what our daughters are exposed to.

In essence, says Karlen, "as parents, we need to ask ourselves questions about the level of exposure our daughter is getting and what message that exposure is sending her. There is never one prescribed, uniform answer that fits for all families, but if parents keep this question in mind, and are aware of the impact of these influences on their child, then some of the ability to know when and where to set safe limits will naturally emerge."

How do we hold the line when our child is pressing us for something we want to keep from her for a little while longer? One of the best examples for how to do this right emerges from a therapeutic technique referred to by the acronym DEAR MAN. Let's say your thirteen-year-old daughter wants to set up an Instagram account on your family computer, and you and your partner agree the answer is no. You can use DEAR MAN to respond to her request:

Describe the situation objectively and simply. State only the facts. Don't bring in your feelings yet: "I know you've asked several times if you can create an Instagram account. I've thought a lot about it, and your dad (or mom) and I would like to talk with you."

Express how you feel ("I feel X because of Y"): "We feel that given what we know about the harmful way Instagram affects girls' sense of self, and because you are still young, being on Instagram could be harmful to you. We love that you are confident and mature in so many aspects of your life, and we want you to have more time to gain skills in decoding and coping with negative and sexist messages before you have an account on social media."

Assert your decision firmly and clearly. Say what you need to say. Don't be namby-pamby: "We've decided it is too early for you to have an Instagram account."

Reinforce for your daughter why this outcome is positive for her. Reward her with a smile and be positive: "You've really shown that you know how to use your downtime in meaningful and creative ways. You've been doing beautiful work with your filmmaking, and we're really proud of your ingenuity. We can certainly revisit this discussion when you turn fourteen."

Be **mindful.** Don't fold laundry or look at your phone. Don't get sidetracked by the expression on your daughter's face. Let her know that you care very much about the conversation by keeping your mind on it.

Appear confident in posture, tone, eye contact, and body language. Sit up or stand straight, look your daughter in the eye, and speak clearly and directly.

Negotiate. Be open. You aren't issuing an order or a demand. You're hoping to ultimately deepen your shared trust and connection. Listen to what your daughter has to say so that she feels heard, even if she's frustrated, prickly, or annoyed. Then make a counteroffer: Perhaps she recently expressed that she wants to download a photography app; or she wants to read a book about sexism to learn more: "I'd be glad to buy that app and download it; that's a wonderful way to use technology! Let's do that today." Or, you might soften the blow of your saying no to her request by offering instead an opportunity for connection: "I've heard that book is really excellent! Why don't we get two copies, and we can read it together and talk about it?"

Antidote 9

Create Routine, Ritual, and Structure—Including a Family Media Plan

Offering children our engaged presence doesn't mean we don't also set limits. Connection and guidance are not mutually exclusive, but they function like two wings of parenting, and together they help kids take flight. Creating structure and routines in family life can help set limits in a way that's protective without being overprotective.

When Deleicea Greene looks back, she sees one routine in her life that helped give her a "sense of consistency, even though we had no other sense of routine in our life." Every Sunday, "my mom took me to church, and that helped me have a sense that there was this bigger community outside my home and classes at school." Later, that felt desire to tap into a broader community led her to join her poetry group, where she found "the home I was looking for."

Anna Moralis's family was very different. "We always had dinner together every night. I didn't realize until I was older how rare and meaningful a lot of our family rituals were, or how much they helped me in ways I didn't understand at the time," she says. "We cooked together, we had a proper bedtime, we were not allowed to watch TV until we were much, much older. Instead, we read together; when other families were watching TV, we were having 'family reading hour.'" Her parents were, she says, "very creative, and they filled the house with books and supplies for drawing or photography or making art." A lot of nights, she recalls, "my dad would read really substantial books to me. We continued this tradition even after I was too old to be read to, and then we would talk about the book. That ritual before bed was idyllic. I'm so grateful for it still. Looking back, I think it made me more interested in talking about and sharing ideas." Other traditions helped create a sense of deep family connection for her, helped her feel close to her family even in adolescence, when she was pushing them away. "During holiday dinners, each time you took a sip of water or wine, you had to say something you were grateful for in the past week. We also did a lot of things with my extended family; we were super close to my grandmother and my aunts and uncles and cousins. I knew if I wasn't feeling great in terms of my friendships at school, I could always, always hang out with my cousins and be with my grandmother."

We might wonder, after reading this, why this wasn't more protective for Anna. The answer is complex. It's true that Anna's family created connection through these positive experiences, but this in and of itself was not enough to fully protect her from all the toxic influences the world has in store for girls. But that doesn't mean these moments weren't protective. They created a sense of family connection that served Anna well when she was ready to accept help from her family for her depression and anxiety. Indeed, as I listened to her, Julia, and Deleicea, it became clear to me that, to help reduce the ill effects of the mounting stressors girls face, the many antidotes in these pages must, to the best of each parent's ability, be applied in tandem. Each antidote in and of itself is protective, but cumulatively they become more powerful and preventative.

When Julia Abernathy looks back on the positives in her family life, she, too, can find many. "My parents and siblings and I were all very close growing up; when I was young, I thought of my parents as my best friends," she says. "And my mom and dad had lots of family traditions and routines that I think helped to make us all feel very connected." Julia's family sat down to a homemade meal "every single night," she says, "to the point that when friends came over, they would say, 'Oh, this is very weird.'" Her mom often took Julia on mother-daughter trips; they learned to scuba dive together. Her father taught her how to play tennis, and they played every weekend. But, she says, "when I hit my teen years, and they started to put a lot more rules in place, I really rebelled. They put controls on my computer, and even though I was fifteen, I went in and hacked and rewrote the code, and they didn't know it. I could not see at the time that they had my best interests at heart." Looking back, Julia realizes, "if I had actually talked to them, I think it would have really helped me. Whenever my mom tried to talk to me, it went right past me because I was pretty stubborn. Now I appreciate their efforts, and I feel really bad for them, that they didn't get to have a normal experience with raising me as their daughter. I regret putting them through so much."

Julia's story tells us that, again, although parents may do their very best to protect their daughters—Julia's parents certainly did—teens often find a way to circumvent the structures we set in place to help keep them safe. This is hardly unusual in adolescence. We try to protect our children, but we can't foresee every path they might choose to walk down. This is not to fault us as parents when things go wrong (which they will). We do the very best we can, often in difficult or even traumatic circumstances. We may not have learned these skills growing up, and we do not gain them magically the moment we bring a child into the world. The new science of why our daughters are struggling gives us renewed impetus to learn and practice these strategies. And it is never too late: We can begin right where we are, right now.

Creating a sense of structure and routine while also allowing your daughter her freedom is a bit of a "Goldilocks and the Three Bears" proposition: It's hard to get it just right. Often, in an effort to be emotionally responsive to kids who are under too much societal stress, we parents fail to take a clear position, especially when it comes to rules about social media and engaging with pop culture. But there is a way to create a warm sense of camaraderie around structure and routines so that, over time, they become part of a positive family identity—"the way our family does things"—and are seen as accepted family rituals rather than demands or chores.

In my life as a parent, these have included (as for many families) evenings devoted to reading books together, versus using electronics, and Friday Family Movie Night. It meant Haiku Night—writing and sharing our haiku poetry over the kitchen table. It meant anyone being able to call out, "Family hug!" and we'd all drop everything and be in a huddle in less than sixty seconds. And it included putting smartphones, laptops, and all other electronic devices outside bedrooms before bed. (Truth talk: As my daughter got older, we let this slip, and I regret it very much now.) When a ritual is seen as part and parcel of who you are as a family—*this is our thing*—it's no longer viewed by kids as a parental demand, but is instead attached to a deeper layer of meaning and identity as a family. The predictability inherent in rituals and routines also helps reduce the chaos kids so often feel in our highly stressful and chaotic times. This, in turn, helps to create a buffer zone against anxiety. In today's world, structure and routine also mean limiting time on social media and monitoring how social media platforms are used.

It's all a matter of choosing a parenting style that locates that ever-elusive "sweet spot" nestled between emotional warmth and responsiveness (spending time together, having good communication, and offering praise and positivity) and establishing agreed-upon family rules and daily rituals (setting and keeping rules, reasonably monitoring activities, and giving your child shared, age-appropriate responsibilities). Once you've found the sweet spot, it's easier to create a plan for how everyone will use and engage with media.* And why not? You've already established an emotional climate for your children in which your efforts have the best chance of succeeding.

No one is saying this is easy to do, especially when it comes to denying kids their devices. And to be clear, this isn't just about limiting smartphone use. (Although that's almost always a good idea: During the pandemic, screen time of any kind—television, movies, video clips,

---

* For helpful insight on how to cultivate healthy media use for children and teens, see commonsensemedia.org or the American Academy of Pediatrics Family Media Plan at healthychildren.org.

using apps or games on any type of device—skyrocketed for youth, rising to six or seven hours a day even for children of kindergarten age.) It's also about having an age-appropriate amount of oversight into how, when, and for what reason a teen's device is used, so that when a girl holds hers in her hand, it's not amplifying her nervous system's stress-threat detection system.

Social media, as we've seen, has made it easier to magnify fear and anxiety in teens. Decades ago, in the food industry, food giants figured out a perfect recipe to hook you and make you come back time and time again for more cookies, chips, and cakes or for that plate of cheeseburger and fries: a perfect blend of fat, salt, and sugar. Similarly, when we're on social media, the onslaught of headlines and data often delivers a blend of fear and anxiety, to imply hidden threats, and to stir conspiracy and restlessness in an alarmist, fear-igniting way. Together, it can act like a Twinkie for the brain's taste buds (if the brain had taste buds). When social media posts make us angry, when we feel superior or more virtuous than other people, or left out, or afraid of being dissed, dismissed, or ostracized, it activates our visceral neurobiological responses. Once our brain gets a taste of this Twinkie, even though we know it's bad for us, it's hard not to come back for more, because our brain has been tricked into thinking that staying glued to these platforms might somehow keep us better prepared for any incoming threats, or that we will find safe respite inside an online community. If this feeling is true for us as adults—and I think it is for many of us—it's only amplified for our daughters' developing brains. To wit: We know from Facebook's own internal research that children and teens say they want to spend less time on Instagram but feel they lack the self-control to do so.

Young people aren't the only ones who can't put their phones down. We can all recognize ourselves in this truth. If you're out shopping for clothes with your daughter and spend half your time typing into your phone while she tries things on, she won't feel seen. If she's feeling unsure about her body or how a dress looks, how can she share her worries or insecurities with you if she first has to attract your attention? Letting devices intrude on family and parent-child moments also means unwittingly modeling for your child the message that being addicted to devices at the expense of relationships is normal and okay.

When teens are allowed to use their smartphones in bed—alone, in the dark—the Twinkie effect is magnified; there's no one around to help them interpret or respond to what they're hearing or seeing, which is all the more problematic if what they're seeing is stressful. What's seen visually on a smartphone is felt emotionally and in the body; what is felt is interpreted, and often inaccurately: *I should be afraid,* or *I don't measure up,* or *No one likes me.* A phone that dings at 2 A.M. with texts or tweets is an alert system, one that goes off during the very time when a child's body and mind are trying to dial down. Let bedtime be about sleep, rest, and restoration.

This is true for older teens and college-age students, too. In 2020, Boston University School of Public Health researchers surveyed 33,000 college-age students. They found that worsening trends in young people's emotional suffering are due in large part to three core factors: the aftereffects of pandemic stress, the impact of social media, and the shift toward societal values that are "extrinsically motivated" (getting more followings and likes, scoring top grades, positioning oneself for a successful, high-paying career) as opposed to "intrinsically motivated" (being a good member of your community, connecting in meaningful relationships, and so on). Knowing that our teens are marinating in this messaging makes it all the more crucial that we, as parents, underscore that it's more important to us that they grow up to be good people who enjoy good relationships than that they achieve big things.

A phone that dings at 2 A.M. with texts or tweets is an alert system, one that goes off during the very time when a child's body and mind are trying to dial down. Let bedtime be about sleep, rest, and restoration.

Growing up immersed in the online portal is also making our children feel lonelier. Twenge and her colleagues found that rates of loneliness in schoolchildren doubled after 2012, long before the pandemic. In looking at possible causes, they found that "smartphone access and internet use increased in lock step with teenage loneliness." Other factors—including income inequality, increases in unemployment, general declines in family size—appeared unrelated. Growing up relying on texting, Instagram, or TikTok to be your community is not a substitute for real human connection. Most of us can look back on times in our own lives when we felt terribly anxious, worried, or sad. We didn't turn to social media for consolation; we turned to a flesh-and-blood friend or family member. If we recognize this deep human need as being true for adults, it makes sense that it's even more crucial for girls as they navigate adolescence.

If you need backup for setting family limits with social media, consider consulting with your family pediatrician. Faith Hackett, M.D., a Hopkins-trained pediatrician who's been in practice in Annapolis, Maryland, for forty years (and who, in full disclosure, was my own children's doctor), minces no words with families and children on this topic. "Every day I listen to what's going wrong in kids' lives. By the age of eleven or twelve, so much of it comes down to social media, especially for girls. And yet, it's extremely rare to see families establish limits. So, when I talk to families, I don't sugarcoat it." Hackett sits parents and children down together and tells them: "Your child should not be on social media at eleven or twelve, period. Your job as a parent is to teach your children things about the world. Right now, every minute they are on social media, you're not teaching them, the rest of the world is teaching them, and what they are learning is hurting them physically and emotionally." She asks families to, at a minimum, commit to removing devices from breakfast, dinner, and bedtime hours. "These are the moments when kids are most likely to talk about their day—what their coach said to them during basketball practice, their worries over the family dog who's sick. When kids are eating or falling asleep, that's when they spill their feelings. It's only when you shut out the rest of the world that you get to hear what's going on and model for them how to handle things. None of that happens when the family is on their cell phones."

All the tech bashing in these pages aside, not all tech is bad, of course. Nor is all social media bad. In the right circumstances, it can be a tool to help teens better connect and offer each other mutual support. Also, numerous apps and online programs are now available that train the developing brain in positive ways with tools that promote breathing, meditation, brain fitness, executive function, and attention. It's simply a matter of finding a middle ground.

Julia Abernathy talks about how giving up social media changed her life. "I found I was happier when I didn't have social media to blare these high expectations for myself," she says. But, she adds, "there was still a place for tech in my life—I began to put my love of technology into computer engineering and coding and seeing how tech could be used for positive things—and honestly, that became much more rewarding than staring at photos of girls talking about makeup and clothes and what they did over the weekend."

APPLYING THESE ANTIDOTES, together, in family life can help dial down the stress response. And yet, even though healthy family connection and a home that promotes flourishing are protective factors for any teenager, they are not enough in and of themselves to combat the mounting societal and environmental toxic challenges coming from so many different directions and across all media platforms during this sensitive developmental window. Moreover, as any teacher, coach, or therapist knows, too many kids do not get that essential healthy adult connection at home. This means we need to ensure that girls also feel safe and valued in the wider spheres of influence in their lives.

CHAPTER ELEVEN

Bring in What the
Wider Community Can Provide

THE WORLD IN which our children are coming of age is nearly alien to us adults. School and mass shootings have escalated, the global reality of climate change is creeping toward everyone's backyard, lives and livelihoods have been lost in the COVID-19 pandemic—and on top of all this, every second of their lives, our children can be liked, disliked, included, or excluded via the phone in their hand. On some level, all these reflect some degree of moral failure on the part of adults and leaders.

You may tell yourself these environmental factors don't affect your child; perhaps they haven't touched them personally. But children who report third-party exposure to serious or traumatic events in the lives of others also suffer from trauma exposure. And this can, in turn, influence their well-being. A child's growing anxiety might be considered an understandable response to the anxiety-inducing chaos of our modern lives.

Even as a relationship with one loving parent or caregiver is the single most protective factor for any child, it is clearly not enough to protect girls against the mounting challenges they face from so many directions. Indeed, you may know this yourself. You may already have established a strong sense of family connection at home with your daughter—and she might *still* be falling prey to difficult times. The messages from the world at large may be slipping into and distorting her interior sense of who she is and could be. This can be confusing and frustrating for a parent trying hard to do everything right. But if girls' exposure to pressures and stressors, including those that are social-media generated, is increasing at a faster rate than we are offering up protective factors, then our girls are going to continue to flail.

This means that in addition to having all that she needs at home, a girl also needs to have a convoy of nurturing, invested adults outside the home, which includes meaningful relationships with mentors, teachers, coaches, schools, and even, if needed, a healing professional. It can be a relief to hear this truth. We often assume as we raise our girls—especially when we are the mother—that the onus is on us to provide all that our daughter needs to grow and thrive. But that is not the case. Sometimes, through no fault of our own (trauma, illness, separation, distance, divorce), a deep and constant sense of safety is not as fully in place at home as we would like it to be. (I know, in my own daughter's life, for example, that my battle with a serious neurological autoimmune disease, a heart condition, and a hematological disorder, which often put me in the hospital for a month or longer, interfered with her sense of safety throughout her childhood.) Or, sometimes, as our daughters grow, they simply want and need space from Mom.

If, for reasons outside your control (and despite your best efforts), your daughter doesn't seem to feel she can come to you with her problems as you wish she would, you can help to ensure another adult is there to be her person and catch and hold her unspoken fears. If she enjoys an utter sense of safety at home all the time, even better. But she will also need to know the wider world is safe, too. Simply put: If we are to raise girls to become healthy adults with a secure and self-realized sense of who they are in the world, certain conditions outside the home must also be realized. No family can go it alone.

To return to psychologist Mary Pipher's very early metaphor—that of reviving Ophelia—reimagine, for a moment, how very different the outcome might have been if the community had flocked to Ophelia, activating in her a positive, affiliative, relational stress response. Unfortunately, her centuries-old literary tragedy, but with a modern twist, is playing out for girls across our country every day. But with our newer neurobiological understanding of why girls today are flailing, and why so many of our efforts to revive this generation of girls have failed, we have a new opportunity to create environments and communities that rewrite this narrative.

George Slavich at UCLA, the scientific father of Social Safety Theory, argues that developing and maintaining friendly social bonds is "a fundamental organizing principle of human behavior." Human contact and kinship help turn off the stress response. This makes sense, given that across human history, we were safer (and therefore, less anxious) when we traveled in numbers.

A sense of safe connection can be harder to create not just in our postpandemic world, but also because extended family often lives all over the country. And then, of course, there are our electronic devices, which create physical and emotional distance between us even as we try to connect through them. So how do we begin to help our girls create safe connections and develop relationships with safe others so they know whom they can turn to, and when, in response to whatever challenge has arisen in their day and so they come of age within a beloved community, one that stands behind them and will serve as a buffer against the inevitable adversities that affect every life?

Antidote 10

Engage the Power of Benefactors, Mentors, and Avatars to Help a Girl Feel She Matters

Again, we can't always erase the negatives or the adversity girls face. So we have to help create additional positive relational experiences in their lives. And it turns out that when we succeed in doing this, we help protect against the negative epigenetic shifts that lead to anxiety and depression. Christina Bethell calls the factors that contribute to a child's or teen's resilience positive childhood experiences, or PCEs. Instead of looking at children's well-being solely in terms of the adverse childhood experiences they've suffered, we would do better, she suggests, to consider child health through a lens that looks at both ACEs and PCEs combined. This more comprehensive view of a child's good and bad experiences is what public health experts now refer to as positive and adverse childhood experiences, or PACEs.

We know a lot more about the association between adverse childhood experiences and the risks for poor adult mental health than we do about how positive childhood experiences may protect against the effects of ACEs. Bethell is trying to remedy this. She examined seven different types of PCEs, as reported by adults who looked back on their lives, and considered how these individuals might have benefited from positive relationships with family and friends and in school and their greater community. The PCEs identified were: (1) feeling able to talk to family about feelings; (2) knowing family stood by them at difficult times; (3) feeling safe and protected by an adult in the home; (4) having a sense of belonging in high school; (5) feeling supported by friends; (6) enjoying participating in community traditions; (7) and having at least two nonparent adults take a genuine interest in them.

Bethell then looked at the study participants' mental health histories, including whether they had been diagnosed with depression and whether they had reported experiencing poor mental health fourteen or more days during the previous month. She found that adults who reported higher PCE scores had significantly lower rates of depression and enjoyed stronger social and emotional support in adulthood. For instance, the odds of having depression or fourteen or more poor mental health days in the previous months were 72 percent lower for those reporting six to seven positive childhood experiences, compared to those reporting zero to two PCEs. "Even for those reporting three to five PCEs, the odds of depression or poor mental health were 50 percent lower than for those reporting zero to two PCEs." All these associations held true even when respondents reported multiple ACEs.

"Adults with fewer PCEs were nearly four times more likely to experience depression and poor mental health compared to adults who had more PCEs." Bethell tells me something else that surprises me: "People assume eliminating adversity automatically results in good health outcomes, but many people reporting lower adversity in childhood still experience poorer mental and relational health in adulthood if they don't report having had these positive childhood experiences." Even kids who don't face adverse experiences need protective and positive childhood experiences if they are to thrive.

I think of Anna, Julia, and Deleicea and of how some of the most formative positive childhood experiences they reported having occurred with meaningful adults other than their parents, or what we might call benefactors (adults who show a teen they care). Most of us adults know who our own benefactors were while we were growing up. Think back to those individuals who loved and supported you, knew how to comfort you, really believed in you, offered words of encouragement (perhaps with words you still recall today), and in whose presence you felt special, safe, protected, seen, known, and valued. This can be true even if a benefactor, such as a teacher, coach, grandparent, aunt, or therapist, was in your life for only a brief period. Experiencing positive childhood experiences with mentors, says Bethell, "helps girls to internalize a sense that they are safe in the larger community, on a biophysical level, which helps to create and rebuild needed neural networks even for children who are facing challenges and adversity."

Having these positive relational experiences also shores up young people's sense of mattering. Mattering, says Bethell, is defined as being seen and valued "just because you exist." This includes, she explains: being the positive object of another's attention (*he/she notices me, is aware of my presence, focuses attention on me, does not ignore me*); feeling important or being the object of another's concern (*he/she invests resources in me, promotes my welfare, is attentive to my needs, provides emotional support for me, inconveniences themselves for me, listens to me*); feeling others choose to turn to them or rely on them (*others seek my advice, depend on me, seek support from me, miss me, trust me to be there, value my contribution*); and having voice and opportunity in the community.

University of Toronto researchers recently examined whether ACEs contributed to a young person's sense of mattering. They found that those who experienced early adversity felt less of a sense of mattering and experienced more loneliness, social anxiety, and feelings of being stigmatized. And yet experiencing positive childhood experiences and relationships within the greater community conferred a sense of mattering that was highly protective against the negative effects of the adversity and trauma they faced.

"Emotional abuse and emotional neglect in particular deeply shape our sense of whether we matter," says Bethell. We can see this play out in girls' lives in a society in which male voices are given more value than girls' and in social and work environments where strong female emotions are seen as a weakness. And we see it play out every day when children grow up facing discrimination due to racism. "However you get to a lack of feeling [that] you matter—via family, the sexism that pervades our society, or through systemic racism—it can lead to self-stigmatization and a toxic inner identity." Conversely, "when we can instill in kids a sense of mattering, it not only reduces loneliness, [but] also creates a sense of self-worth and competence, which over time, leads to more positive relationships."

Adolescent therapist Bronagh Starrs, who directs a center for adolescent psychotherapy at the University of Northampton in the United Kingdom, underscores that the most important form of mattering comes from what she calls receptive parenting, in which a girl has "the experience of being received," so that she comes into adulthood with the "expectation of being received and supported by her environment." And yet too many young people, Starrs believes, emerge from adolescence feeling "the shame of being overlooked."

If we see that a child feels the shame of being overlooked, or lacks the positive aspects of relational health, then we need to intervene. "Noticing which children will benefit from our attention and interventions without their having to reach out requires our being present and aware so that we can pick up on cues, especially ones that are subtle," says psychologist Amy Karlen.

Everyone in the community can play a role in introducing positive relational experiences into children's lives. Even small moments of checking in, offering support and caring connection, can have a lasting impact on children and teens by helping them internalize a felt sense that there are many people in the world who care about them. "We have good evidence that just offering up forty seconds of compassion to a child makes a difference, regardless of whether that sense of caring comes from a teacher, a coach, an aunt, or a secretary in the principal's office," says Bethell. "We *are* the medicine; it's within and between us."

Evoke the Power of Female Avatars—or "Shared Parenting"

In ninth grade, Julia Abernathy was assigned an advisor. "I was able to tell her a lot that I could not have told my parents," she tells me. "She thought that I was really, really funny. She saw that in me. And she helped me see that things I saw in myself as weaknesses were often strengths when I flipped them around." Julia's face breaks into a wide smile in a way it has rarely done since we first met. "My advisor had been through a lot of things in her own life and struggled with depression herself. Her mother had committed suicide. She was openly gay. So, when I was going through the hell years of not wanting to be alive, she was totally open about her own mental illness and her own journey and how she figured out how to embrace herself wholeheartedly, warts and all." Julia's advisor became a female avatar.

I am using the word *avatar* here in a way it hasn't been used in a long time. Long before it was commandeered by popular movies, social media, and videogames, this ancient Sanskrit word referred to the mythological Hindu concept of someone who promotes the spiritual growth, inner development, and personal transformation of one in need. In today's context, avatars are trusted, exemplary adult women (other than a parent) with whom a girl feels known, seen, understood, and valued for exactly who she is and to whom she can turn when in need.

Julia's advisor "modeled for me how not to hate myself just because there were these aspects of myself I didn't yet understand or even like. I thought that was really, really cool. Seeing how she wrangled with her own pretty big mental health issues and made it work, how she could love those parts of herself that she struggled with—that made me think that maybe I could come to love certain aspects of myself as I got older. Maybe I could be at peace, too. When I first met her, I'd never seen a woman in midlife handling mood issues and just living a normal, happy life. She also modeled for me what a kick-butt woman could be: She always stood up for herself; she didn't take any crap from any men. I remember, one time, there was a much older teacher making really homophobic remarks, and she just handled him. Bam!" Julia gleaned something else, she says: "Even women with difficult childhoods or who've suffered through really bad things can emerge as very powerful women."

"Have you had any female avatars in your life since high school?" I ask her.

"In computer engineering, most of the role models are men," she says. "I knew that aspect of it wasn't going to work for me." She flashes that grin again. So Julia sought out and landed a part-time job at a company in her college town that "is led by this very impressive woman who is a rare female leader in our field. She's created an all-female team. She gives me random girl advice about surviving in this business. She's tough on me, in that she's demanding that I give everything my complete best, but so respectful, and I know she's rooting for me. The team will be working on a problem, and she'll kick it over to me for a minute and say, 'Julia, what would you do if you had to figure this out?' She's given me confidence that I'm a very good computer engineer. I think a lot about the aspects of her that I admire as I make my way through a field that can be pretty hostile to women's ideas."

Anna Moralis has similar memories of avatars, the first of which was in her family: her mother's mother. "My grandmother was always a big part of our lives. She was a real symbol of strength. Her husband died when she was still a young mother. She'd worked and raised her kids as a single mom by teaching piano." Whenever her grandmother was around, Anna says, "she would tell me that we were very similar, that I was very strong. I felt really understood by her, that we were in a lot of ways sympatico. That was a powerful thing to have in my life as a young girl." Anna and her grandmother loved Broadway musicals, and they'd sing off-the-cuff duets. Once, Anna started singing a song from *The Sound of Music*—"I am sixteen going on seventeen . . ."—about a teenage girl pining for the young man she's met. "My grandmother said, 'Anna, you're a young girl. You don't need to be singing a song about needing a man; you don't need a man to be happy.'" Her grandmother often took Anna on short trips: to go see plays and out for dinner, just the two of them. "She made it clear she was interested in everything about me," Anna says. "What I saw in her eyes when she looked at me made me feel really seen."

Later, in high school, she says, "I had this amazing, brilliant English teacher who let me do an independent study on inner-city crime in my area, and she encouraged me to engage as an activist. This teacher was the bright spot in my high school experience, especially since my high school said it prized the ethos of learning as more important than grades or getting coveted awards—which was so false."

In college, this trend continued. "I had a brilliant professor my senior year of college who took my thinking so seriously. She was an editor at a law journal. In seminars and writing workshops, she led with kindness. She put forth the idea that social justice is also about creativity and love for all of humanity. She never judged me, even when I was writing about very weighty things. I ended up doing my senior thesis with her, and she treated our time together in her office as if it was the most important thing happening for her at that moment in time. She had this kind of excitement, not just about my writing, but about who I was becoming. It made me want to be that kind of kind and caring person myself, but more than anything, it made me see those things in myself."

As Anna got involved in social justice and voting rights, she saw "kick-ass women living these really complex, fearless existences, doing what they wanted to do and not fitting into any mold as females. I got the sense I could achieve that, too. There was a path for *me*. It made me less judgmental of myself."

When I think of the relationship between Julia and Anna and their respective avatars, my mind momentarily flicks to an image of the fictional island of Themyscira, the cinematic home to the female Amazon tribe in the film *Wonder Woman*, where women train girls to be strong and resilient enough to take on any challenge, while also encouraging a deeper relational awareness to lend a hand in bettering humankind. This is, of course, a completely unrealistic standard for mortal girls, but the loose concept is not terribly far afield: Many girls report that the most potent and protective childhood experiences that mitigated the stressors they faced took place with older female adults who were not their mothers.

Time spent with avatar women who exhibit characteristics of females thriving even in the face of stressors (teachers, mentors, aunts, or good family friends) is, in a word, neuroprotective. As was the case for Anna and Julia, it creates a deep vagal and neural sense of safety in the brain and nervous system, a biophysical, felt sense that there is a larger community to which it's safe to flock. This, on some level, reassures girls that the world is full of what we might call shareable parents, adults who have the girls' best interests at heart (versus other parents who want only their own child to succeed, aka the starling effect).

How do we help girls to benefit from avatars in their lives? While these mentoring relationships might occur at school or through sports, that's not always the case. Sometimes parents have to help create the conditions for avatars to emerge, especially for younger girls. When parents find other trusted, valued adults for this kind of shared parenting, it helps their daughters feel safe. Anna knew that if something happened to her mother and father, or if she couldn't reach them, she could go to her grandmother. "I knew she would be there for me, no matter what, even if we didn't talk about big or difficult things." This was one of Anna's positive childhood experiences in the face of adversity. It did not prevent her from developing anxiety and depression, but it may be part of what gave her the sense of self to pursue getting help and to find her way back to well-being.

Time spent with avatar women who exhibit characteristics of females thriving even in the face of stressors (teachers, mentors, aunts, or good family friends) is, in a word, neuroprotective.

If a girl doesn't have this person in her life—or if (as was the case for Anna) that support is not wide or deep enough—we as parents can arrange for there to be someone, or several someones, our daughter can turn to and confide in when life gets confusing and hard. You can begin this process by asking your daughter to "identify the helpers"—that is, to name adult women she'd feel safe approaching in a crisis or when you weren't available. These should be women who model values shared by your family, self-regulatory skills, and openness. Look for or create opportunities for your daughter to spend time with these avatars, whether by inviting them to the family dinner table, arranging walks with them and your daughter, or asking them to play a mentoring role in an area that interests your daughter. Having this strong female avatar network in place helps girls feel physically, psychologically, and socially safer as they move closer to adulthood themselves. In the process, you'll also help your daughter activate an inner sense of safety. Female avatars help to counter the negative messaging girls receive about strong, powerful women under the male gaze by allowing them to witness the unique strengths and other aspects of being female close up, thus recoding as wholly worthwhile and empowering what it means to be female.

Think again of my analogy of the Russian nesting dolls. We can each locate ourselves in the neuroprotective spheres those dolls represent. How can we work within our sphere of influence to affect others and help girls? Ask yourself: Are you an avatar for the young people in your life, beyond your own children? Make an effort to become the reason a girl in your community or sphere of influence feels welcomed, heard, valued, known, and supported. You don't need to wait to be asked; you can begin by showing a genuine interest in how the girls in your life are doing and noticing when they are struggling. Noticing and caring are not the same as stepping in with all the answers for their problems. If you are concerned about a teen girl, you might offer up: "I feel like you're struggling a bit here, and maybe you've been struggling for a while now.

I want you to know it doesn't have to be this way. You deserve to feel better. If it's helpful, I'm here to listen." (This, in turn, might lead to an agreement to have her share with her parents, or a school counselor, how she's really feeling.) Or in less serious situations: "You okay?" Focus the conversation on a topic that's not obviously laden with psychological meaning. For instance, saying "Tell me what's going on at home" might feel intrusive. Instead, begin with a statement that lets a girl know you see her and you care. "I notice you really seem to like the photographs we have hanging in our dining room," you might begin. "Would you like to hear more about the artist? I have a book of her photography I'd love to loan to you."

Rachel Yehuda, at Mount Sinai School of Medicine in New York City, suggests that simply acknowledging the possibility that something bad has "happened to someone and inquiring about them is really at the heart" of how we can check up on each other. Rather than assume that everything is okay, create the space for the possibility that it might not be. "Just really taking a second to inquire, in a real way, about how someone is doing . . . will probably have a beneficial effect." Yehuda, who has worked with and studied the lives of many Holocaust survivors, is struck that many survivors "got through because there was one person" who made a difference for them. "So how we behave towards one another, individually and in society, I think, can really make a very big difference in the effects of environmental events on our molecular biology."

Michelle Obama has championed this idea through her Girls Opportunity Alliance, opening doors for adolescent girls around the world and eradicating barriers that prevent them from reaching their potential. This includes supporting grassroots leaders who provide education for girls in rural areas, providing them with bikes so they can get to school, and funding scholarships.

Avatars may not always be female adults, of course. Deleicea Greene, who so often found herself taking care of her mom and making sure *her* needs were met, tells me, "I had no one I could look up to, really, just examples of women I didn't want to end up like."

So whom did she turn to for a sense of comfort or when she needed advice? I ask.

"The females who helped me become who I am when I was younger were more my contemporaries, my best friend and one of my cousins."

"How about male mentors?" I ask.

She pauses to think and then gives a soft smile. "When I was younger, my father, who I didn't see as often, encouraged my writing. That really meant a lot to me. Later, my male poetry coaches saw something in me, and that really made me feel safe to express what I was feeling. That set me on this path of finding myself literally through voicing my words."

Today, in her work as a poet and youth coach, Deleicea tells me, "I see girls struggling, and I realize that the true help I can give them lies in offering them caring and helping them feel seen and confident in their voices. And in that process, I can see how feeling valued and loved is, for them, kind of like a rebirthing. I think the fact that I had no female mentoring growing up made me want to *be* that person to younger girls who are in similar positions to mine. In some ways, being the healer helps me to heal from not having had one—and rebirth myself."

Seek Out Multigenerational Female Groups

By the time Julia Abernathy entered her sophomore year of high school, she'd become so good at coding that her teachers asked her to help the girls in a nearby elementary school learn to code. In so doing, she became a kind of avatar to other girls. "At that time, everyone teaching coding to girls in my community was a much older male and really not very innovative in their teaching," she says. "I felt I needed to be there. I wanted to be the cool older girl who is going to major in computer engineering. I felt like they needed to see that there were people like me out there, and I tried to make our projects really fun and exciting. I hoped it would help those girls feel they had more options." Julia created teaching presentations and tried "to shake things up in a good way. It was so nice to share my love of computer engineering with them, especially when I would see this light come over a girl's face. The lightbulb would just go off. I felt I was giving something back. A lot of high school was about churning out the grades or hooking up with some guy who was just objectifying me because he was into my ginormous boobs." But with the girls she mentored, "I felt really responsible and valued. It was different than the way I was seen in most other moments of my life."

Neuroscientist Ron Dahl, at the University of California, Berkeley, has looked at how social support in teen life provides the neural scaffolding for resiliency, especially in nine- to fourteen-year-olds—a period when kids become more interested in being respected by others and belonging. Reputation becomes much more important during the transition from childhood to adolescence. Yes, kids in this period of life still care about what their parents think, but they start to care more about what other adults think, too, as well as how peers perceive them. The fear one feels that someone's going to evaluate you, or what researchers like Dahl call "social-evaluative threat," starts to become more worrisome to kids than the fear of physical threats. This is because, as Social Safety Theory argues, for much of human history, being accepted within the tribe was essential to our survival. Over time, says Dahl, "neural systems evolved to be extra vigilant in adolescence with respect to: *Am I valued here? Do I fit in here? Do I belong?*" For adolescents, the emotional intensity and physiological response that accompany being negatively evaluated can be so intense that they may find themselves ruminating over scenarios in which they felt slighted. And if your child mentally replays scenarios in which she worries that others think poorly of her, those neural systems fire and wire together even more.

Deborah Tannen, Ph.D., professor of linguistics at Georgetown University and author of *You're the Only One I Can Tell: Inside the Language of Female Friendships,* writes that girls often fear being left out of something, especially during adolescence, when such a great amount of energy goes into forming female friendships and girls try to find their friend group. This period of life can be rife with difficulty: Some types of friends may be what Tannen likens to wolves saying wolflike things while wearing sheep's clothing, while others are snuggle friends, like friendly puppies. It can be hard to tell the difference. Indeed, recent studies show that adolescents are more likely to be bullied by close, social-climbing "frenemies" who use cruelty to gain attention and status than by classmates they don't know as well. In one study, researchers at Harvard and Johns Hopkins evaluated middle-schoolers' friendships and had these same students undergo brain scans and report symptoms of depression and anxiety. They found that middle-schoolers subjected to hurtful words from verbally abusive peers showed changes in their brain scans and reported feelings of depression and anxiety that were similar to those of children with a parent who was verbally abusive.

One way you can help temper the effects of negative social experiences is to search for ways in which girls with shared interests can spend time together during what adolescent female psychologist Amy Karlen, Ph.D., calls the crucial "in-between years" of ages ten to fourteen. "We need to restore those lost formative years of late childhood to girls, so that they are free to engage in self-directed pursuits and enjoy positive bonding relationships that are not marked by competition, criticism, or social and societal judgments." It's during these years that girls can learn what a safe community is and what being one's genuine self in the world feels like on a visceral, perhaps intuitive level. They can then carry that sense forward as a benchmark for friendships throughout their lives.

For many girls, this respite is found in female-centric groups that pair young girls with older women in dedicated fields of interest—like Julia's coding group for girls. These are often mini safe zones for girls, away from school-friend dynamics and academics—spaces of safety in which girls can learn how to find and broadcast their ideas and cultivate their own voice among other girls in their own age group, while being led by older women who may serve as avatars. Such groups serve as a kind of petri dish in which girls grow their sense of autonomy.

These groups might revolve around a girl's growing interest in just about anything: filmmaking, pottery, poetry, car mechanics, or rescuing animals. For instance, the group Row New York brings together girls to teach them rowing and offer them intensive academic tutoring. Female leaders at the Pentagon recently launched a program called Girl Security, in which they invited girls to play war games, strategize, and voice their ideas for how to meet real-world crises. Girls on the Run brings together female coaches and girls as young as eight, not just for running, but also for exercises and discussions about emotional and physical health and to practice skill building. And Girls Who Code, a national nonprofit, pairs girls with adult women in technology, who help the girls learn to be "brave, not perfect" as they develop confidence in their own voice.

Antidote 11

Help Her Find "a Sense of Something Bigger"

"I'm not very spiritual," Julia Abernathy confides. "Maybe part of the reason is that the church we went to growing up was very male-dominated. All that preaching about Eve coming from Adam's rib, and Eve being the bad one who ate the apple, that didn't work for me." But, she says, "we also went hiking and camping a lot as a family. And I really loved being in nature; I still do. Hiking is therapeutic; it's always helped me to get in touch with serenity." Julia still hikes with friends in college. "When I'm out hiking, I feel connected to something larger. It's like the façade of the world falls away, and I gain this immediate sense of perspective. I feel like I get a chance to be with the me that lies beneath all my ruminating."

Anna Moralis finds very similar comfort in nature. "We took long summer vacations to the big national parks growing up," she says. "My cousins and aunts and uncles and grandmother would come, and we'd go whitewater rafting and sit around family campfires. My family loves to sing, and when I'm feeling stressed out, there is a place inside me that I can call upon, just remembering those evenings together singing under the stars in front of the fire." To this day, she says, "when I remember to immerse myself in nature, my mind gets tricked into relaxing; the anxiety washes away."

As for Deleicea Greene: "I always carry with me this feeling that the universe has my back. I can relax into the feeling that there is something bigger that connects all of us. And that allows me to do what I know I need to do in my heart and let go of the rest."

One of the most protective factors for flourishing involves helping girls develop this sense of unity with something larger than themselves. The more often a girl enjoys a felt sense of safety across myriad settings, the less risk there is that the biophysical effects of stress will become long-lasting. This sense of unity and safety can come through immersion in the natural world, in spirituality, or in being part of a larger, safe, purposeful community that extends beyond one's home. Connecting in trustworthy, relational spaces (at multifamily naturalist clubs or camping trips, family-centric mindfulness retreats, or the neighborhood soup kitchen) serves as a counterbalance to the increased sense of unsafety so many of today's girls feel as they come into adolescence.

Lisa Miller, Ph.D., professor of clinical psychology at Columbia University and founder of the Spirituality Mind Body Institute, has spent her career delving into the science of spirituality. She's found that children who have a positive relationship with spirituality (as defined by a child's relationship to a higher power: nature, the universe, God, or even a tree) and a sense of spiritual awareness in daily life are 60 percent less likely to be depressed as teenagers and more likely to enjoy a greater sense of purpose and do better academically. (Spirituality is not the same as being religious; Miller argues that religion without spirituality can have the opposite effect.) In one study of 615 adolescents from a wide range of socioeconomic, ethnic, and religious backgrounds, Miller found that this was uniquely true for girls compared with boys: For girls, a lower sense of spirituality was more likely to be associated with depression in adolescence.

Hillary Lianne McBride, who has studied the effects of mother-daughter relationships on a daughter's well-being and sense of self, found that girls with the highest scores for positive body image also said their mothers encouraged them to focus on nonappearance-related aspects of life and to develop an identity rooted in their spiritual life. This was, she says, "hugely influential in supporting their self-worth" and in helping them ignore gendered cultural messages of being sexually objectified or devalued as females. Whether they were involved in gardening or had an everyday spiritual practice, girls benefited from "other ways of finding value and joy" and "learned to connect with themselves and with the earth and experience themselves as a whole self."

Fostering in your daughter a sense of interconnectedness to something larger and an ability to experience transcendent moments and feel safe within them can help keep depression from rearing its head throughout her life.

A great deal of data support the notion that time spent in nature downshifts the stress response. Researchers at the University of Georgia and the University of California, San Francisco, found that just thinking about the natural world "in an interconnected and harmonious way" corresponds to improved psychological health. One study looked at the mental health of six hundred teens between the ages of ten and eighteen during the COVID-19 pandemic and found that outdoor play and nature-based activities (going for walks or runs, skating, camping, hiking, fishing, and paddling) buffered the negative mental health impacts of the pandemic for many and offered them tools to cope with other crises looming over their lives, including natural disasters and climate change. This is likely why so many college orientation programs revolve around nature adventures, which build relational spaces and, by so doing, foster mental resilience. Fostering in your daughter a sense of interconnectedness to something larger and an ability to experience transcendent moments and feel safe within them can help keep depression from rearing its head throughout her life.

Stressful events become toxic, and the biophysical effects of stress long-lasting, when a teen's experienced emotion is that she is being (or will be) harmed or threatened by an event (or possible future events). Feeling part of something bigger can help girls change the emotional context in which they process stressful events, allowing them to put toxic societal or emotional threats in their proper context.

Antidote 12

Take the Pressure Off Your Parent-Child Relationship and Get Some Professional Help

When Anna was in high school, she briefly tried therapy, but she wasn't yet ready to do a deep dive into her feelings. When her parents gently insisted she begin therapy during her sophomore year of college, Anna thought immediately of her former therapist. "I found myself wishing that I'd stayed in therapy with her, but when I was fourteen or fifteen, I wasn't motivated to do the work." Still, she felt an affinity for the therapist and sought her out again. "Specifically working with a female therapist has been empowering for me in ways I didn't anticipate it would be," she tells me, after having been in therapy for over a year now. "As a teenage female, I'd so rarely had a time that was completely devoted to my own emotional well-being. Growing up female, you're so often placed in a position where it's your job to support everyone around you and to somehow know what people around you need before they even ask for it themselves. And if you have big feelings, you know you'll be judged as being too emotional or too sensitive, just by virtue of being female, so you try not to show your feelings, because you don't want to be seen as weak or hysterical. Working with my therapist has been very affirming for me. When I'm in her office, I have this deep sense that I am understood and that what I feel has value. Being seen in this way, while also being pushed to recognize and break my negative thought patterns, has been so beautiful and powerful for me."

In her day-to-day life, outside the hours spent in therapy, Anna finds that "mantras my therapist has taught me are always circulating in my mind. She's taught me small ways to touch base within myself and remember to offer up a kinder voice when I'm talking to myself and to know that it's okay to make mistakes. And she helps me find a way to not be so freaked out by new stressors when they arise." For instance, during the COVID-19 pandemic, like so many young people, Anna experienced a recurrence of some of her depressive symptoms. "School stopped, work stopped. There was no break from being saturated in the online world. Work, news, social media—every aspect of life went online. When I saw other young women on Twitter or Instagram talking about their lives or work and sharing savvy opinions, I felt exactly the same way I did in eighth grade, when I saw other girls all going to a party I wasn't invited to. I felt utterly alone." Anna knew she was falling prey to old anxieties. "I felt very freaked out and like I didn't measure up. So whenever I was having a strongly negative thought about myself, my therapist had me do this very simple thing where at the end of a thought like that, I added the words 'in COVID' to remind myself this was just a period of time in my life that would pass. She's helped me learn how to be inside the space of a negative experience and yet still apply lessons and skills so that I feel safe. The lovely thing is that I'm learning how to do this regardless of what stressful thing shows up in my life." She looks reflective before adding, "I wish I hadn't resisted therapy for so long. It took me years to really commit to it, and now it's my favorite moment of my entire week. I worry that we don't do a good enough job of destigmatizing and normalizing asking for help, regardless of where a young person's symptoms fall on the spectrum of severity. Even if your concerns are seemingly small, that's the best moment to begin."

Julia Abernathy feels similarly about the role of the therapeutic relationship in her own story. "I think most of my success in how far I've come is due to therapy," she says. "For most of my teen years, I thought I could fill my insecurity by finding people who I thought seemed to like me. This was rooted in the fact that I had come to see myself as men saw me: as an object, as an 'other,' not as me, or who I really am. After I was raped and no one really stepped in to help me or comfort me—which I know is not really fair to say, since I didn't even tell my parents it happened—and I felt abandoned by everyone, I began to slowly get it that no one was going to save me from myself and from my pain. No one could do it for me."

At first, seeing a therapist was hard, she admits. "Obviously, I was in dire need of help. But it was hard to open up. When I didn't have anything to say, my therapist was cool, and we'd just toss a ball back and forth. We spent a whole session like that once. I was afraid she would be very judge-y, like my parents, but she never was. Even if I said, 'Oh, I did something really bad,' and told her about it, she didn't judge me for it. I was struggling to shake the feeling of *Oh, I'm so pathetic,* and she made me feel that I was not pathetic. She thought I was very smart, and it was nice to be seen as that for a change."

Julia's therapist also instilled in her the sense "that my identity was not created by grades or who I had sex with—she made me see that I was a lot more than a vagina and a brain." She also helped Julia advocate for herself. "I'd talk about something a supposed friend had said or done and tell her I felt bad because I didn't know what to do about it. And she'd say, 'Why do you feel terrible, Julia? She sounds really awful! She sounds like a terrible friend!' She helped me to understand that being loyal doesn't mean sticking around when someone treats you badly or taking the pain that someone dishes out on you. I started to realize I didn't need to constantly have a friend around or be dating a boy; it was okay to eat alone in the lunchroom, or spend a Saturday night at home listening to music or coding for fun." Julia gives a bright laugh. "Now that I think of it, she was definitely another female avatar in my life." To this day, says Julia, "when I'm flooded with feelings, I can just imagine her face in my mind, and that small moment of association with her in my head is very grounding. I still go in to see her and touch base when I'm home, and she talks to my therapist at college, which is really helpful. She's really, really good at what she does. Therapy with her has been one of the most positive experiences of my life."

When Deleicea Greene came home from college, she says, "I knew I needed more help. Therapy has been like opening a door to understanding all that's happened to me and connecting the dots. It also has really helped me with my writing."

At UCLA, George Slavich recently did a meta-analysis of fifty-six studies and found that psychotherapy is consistently associated with improvements in immune health. Patients randomly assigned to receive psychotherapy showed reductions in levels of inflammation, and these effects lasted for up to six months posttreatment. Other studies show that therapy changes gene expression, resulting in a greater ability to calm one's brain and oneself. Rachel Yehuda has found that "some epigenetic changes occur in response to psychotherapy." This makes sense, she argues: "If we're saying that environmental circumstances create one kind of change, a different environmental circumstance can create another kind of change."

All this argues for ensuring that you send the message to your daughter that in your family, there is no stigma associated with seeking therapy and that, as parents, you see therapy as a helpful, powerful tool for building the capacity for resilience in the face of life's stressors—not just as a last resort or something you do only once you have a difficult psychiatric diagnosis. If you see a therapist, you might let your daughter know how helpful it is in terms of coping when you feel overwhelmed. Or if the topic of a family member or friend going to therapy arises, be sure that rather than stigmatize that person—"I wonder what's wrong with *her*?"—you send the message that you think that's great.

These findings also underscore the need for greater accessibility to therapy as a proactive measure. As a society, our norm is still to wait until young people show serious signs of mental health issues before acting rather than intervening when their issues are still relatively small. Even though the average age for the onset of symptoms of mental health disorders is fourteen and a half—and the most common age for the first signs of anxiety disorders is even earlier, at five and a half years old—we so often wait until children and teens fall, and fall crushingly hard, before we offer them the outside help and support they need. (Imagine if we waited until people had heart attacks to pay attention to their heart health or cholesterol.)

Karlen points out that "once multiple stressors pile up (emotional trauma in the home, at school, on social media) in combination or in an individual who is predisposed to emotional vulnerability, that can make addressing the impact of all of these more challenging to treat in therapy." Moreover, once a teenager presents with obvious signs that she's struggling, all too often there are not enough school counselors, college counselors, or affordable therapists in the community to go around.

To do better requires that our government, medical system, and health insurers prioritize mental health services as necessary and preventative rather than requiring psychiatric diagnoses to receive reimbursement through insurance. Services must be made available and affordable for those who suffer from social-environmental threats due to race, gender, socioeconomic status, or history of trauma. (A topic that could fill another book entirely.)

Most of us think we will recognize the first signs that our daughter is struggling, but studies show that too often we're overconfident in our ability to see our child and her moods clearly. In one study, ninety percent of parents rated themselves as either very confident or somewhat confident they would recognize the signs of depression in their child. And yet two-thirds of these same parents admitted it was difficult to distinguish their child's normal ups and downs from depression or that their child was too good at hiding her feelings or didn't like to talk about her feelings very much, which made accurately assessing her mental health difficult. Other studies have found that half of parents are unaware of it when their child is having suicidal thoughts.

Meanwhile, we have good evidence that when you do intervene, even a short course of cognitive behavioral therapy (CBT), trauma-focused CBT, and/or dialectical behavioral therapy (DBT) can lead to small but helpful improvements in depression and anxiety and can reduce suicidal behavior in teens and young adults. Short-term psychoanalytical therapy (thirty weeks), when combined with sessions in which parents also receive therapy, is as effective as CBT, especially when combined with educational sessions, for both family and teen, about depression and how and why various interventions help alleviate symptoms.

And yet, regardless of what therapy is chosen, therapy is only as successful as the relationship a teen forges with her therapist and how well she feels her therapist understands her feelings and difficulties in life. To listen to Anna and Julia, one gathers that the power of being seen, known, and valued within their therapeutic relationships was as transformational to their healing as the specific coping skills they learned in their therapists' offices. Feeling seen, known, and valued—that you matter—is what we seek in every relationship.

If your daughter resists traditional talk therapy, or if you want to help her add to her toolkit of healthy, healing strategies, explore other approaches, like mind-body techniques we've long known about (meditation, mindfulness, guided imagery, breath work, yoga, exercise, qigong, chanting the *ohm* sound, singing, dancing). These are simple-seeming but powerful tools for soothing the nervous system, the vagus nerve, and promoting emotional resilience. In fight, flight, or freeze, the thinking brain goes offline, and the body and brain stop talking to each other. These mind-body methods help the brain and body connect again in healthy ways and help us enter a calming cycle. Yoga, meditation, and breathing exercises have been shown to help reduce levels of inflammatory cytokines and neuroinflammation and have a positive impact on depression, anxiety, cognition, and pain levels. Breath work can be a crucial part of soothing modalities: One of the ways body and brain communicate is through the breath. We take in twenty-five thousand breaths a day, and when it comes to getting the brain's attention, respiratory messages take top priority. If your breath is coming quickly, your brain gets the message to act and respond as if you were in physical danger. Slow, deep breathing naturally soothes the nervous system.

In a 2021 study, researchers looked at four hundred and nineteen clinical trials involving fifty thousand participants who fell into three groups: those with mental health conditions, those facing physical illness, and those generally in good health. They found that techniques such as mindfulness, meditation, and conscious breathing increased well-being across all groups. Even short periods of meditation have been found to help reverse negative, stress-induced epigenetic effects. Meditators show not only positive epigenetic changes in genes that regulate the stress response, but also increased gray matter in the hippocampus, frontal lobe, and other areas of the brain involved in learning and memory, emotional regulation, perception, interpretation, mood, and perspective.

What we are looking for here are methods and approaches that help create balance in body, brain, and nervous system while creating a sense of self-agency. For Deleicea, meditation serves this role. "Meditation is a must to keep me grounded after I get up in the morning and to deal with my anxiety." Anna, too, works with meditation and mindfulness. "I'm still terrible at any of this," she says, groaning. Yet she's working on it. Mindfulness has helped her create "a place inside where I'm not putting pressure on myself to constantly accomplish the next thing or plan things out. To get comfy with myself being messy and complex and pull back from expectations and allow everything to be and just show up in my life as I am."

Julia chooses a combination of weightlifting, meditation, and self-calming breath work for her reset. "I go to the gym a lot and do mostly weightlifting. It's a really good way to get out of my mind. I find a lot of solace in taking care of myself. I'm not doing it for looks. I do it because it lifts my mood." She also does "a lot of breath work and meditation. Every night, I listen to a meditation tape, which really helps me, because if I'm left to my own devices, I can't help but think of all the cringey things I've done or what happened during the day." If she's feeling really stressed, and if her mind is stuck in rumination and meditation isn't cutting it, she will "count to four on the in breath, hold for four, and breathe out to the count of five. It's like a manual reset, like when you hold the button down on your computer and it reboots everything." Sometimes she practices breath work in the bathtub, with bubbles and candles, for a "combination relaxation effect." At first, Julia says, when her therapist had her try breath work and self-care approaches in general, "I was like, 'Yeah, yeah, sure, okay. Breathing is going to help me with my anxiety. Uh-huh, sure.' Even when I tried it, I wasn't convinced. At a certain point, I thought to myself, *Okay, I'm either going to keep having these panic attacks, and they are going to rule my life, and I'm going to look back in twenty years and regret later that I didn't do this work, so I might as well give it everything I have now.* Either I was going to let the panic get me or I was going to find ways to calm it down. So I made the internal decision that this is going to be work; and it's going to take time, maybe years. It's something you have to keep working and working at. But eventually, you come to see that all the efforts you've made to wake up on your own side have added up, and it's all been worth it."

Catch Kids Before They Fall—with the Help of Schools

Given that many parents may fail to pick up on subtle changes in their child's mood or behavior, some schools are stepping in with screening tools, using surveys and data analytics to identify mental health issues and suicide risk in school-age children and teens. With parental consent, students log in and complete a brief survey, which generates new questions based on the students' answers to previous questions. These screening tools have identified students who were struggling in ways teachers and parents were not aware of—and the students received help earlier. Such real-time analytics of how teens are doing helps schools gather data to present to school boards to push for more school counselors. Many schools already do this to establish baselines for physical health. (Take concussion-prevention programs, for instance.)

In an ideal world, we would have enough school counselors to step in at the first sign that a child is struggling, but we do not. So nurses and teachers are stepping in to fill that gap. In Connecticut and Maryland, school nurses have begun trying brief interventions for reducing anxiety, using a method called CALM, for coordinated anxiety learning and management. The goal isn't to diagnose students, but to notice the red flags: A student displaying anxiety, for example, is introduced to anxiety-reduction techniques. Warning signs often include somatic complaints (headache, stomachache, nausea, lightheadedness), distorted cognition (becoming preoccupied with failure or perfectionism, feeling they always mess up), and changes in behavior (such as avoiding raising their hand or answering questions, not turning in their work, or not showing up for class).

With the CALM model, teachers—rather than telling kids to calm down, which the children might not have the skills to do—are taught to help children do so with the use of relaxation strategies, by encouraging them to face their fears, by showing them how to listen to scary thoughts and turn them into coping thoughts, and by strategizing with them about how to manage future problems. At a three-month follow-up in a pilot program, researchers found that students who had completed the CALM program showed improvements in anxiety levels.

One program, Youth Mental Health First Aid, has teamed up with Lady Gaga's Born This Way Foundation to recognize early signs that a student is struggling, initiate a conversation, and connect the young person to a professional. Other schools are bolstering children's sense of safety and belonging by focusing on relationship building between teachers and students. Students might spend half of each school day with one teacher and peer group—not unlike the "pods" formed among teachers and students during the pandemic. When middle schools in Maryland implemented such a program, called Project Success, they found that kids were "more likely to feel that their teachers valued and cared about them and that their peers wanted to help them."

In a recent story that circulated on Twitter, one teacher took a more proactive role and gave parents a handout on Back-to-School Night that read: "I want to make sure I can best support your child this year. If your family is experiencing any difficulties or challenges at home, you may email me these three words, 'Handle with Care.' Nothing else will be asked or said. This will simply let me know that your child may need some extra space, time, or help during the day."

In Austin, Texas, schools have opened mental health clinics on middle and high school campuses. Trauma-informed therapists' offices are housed right on school grounds, where counselors treat students in situ, a few yards from where they go to class. Therapists work with students to address school-related and interpersonal stress, while advocating for their needs with teachers and parents. When researchers compared high school students in one on-site therapy program to those not in the program, they found that substance use and behavior-related issues dropped, while students' GPAs went up. The program has been so successful in reducing student anxiety and depression that other school districts in several states are pursuing similar on-site therapy clinics.

But programs like these are few and extremely far between, not to mention expensive to implement. This means that rather than wait for school staff to spot signs and reach out to families with concerns, parents need to take a proactive role, too, by making it clear to teachers that they're open to having a transparent conversation with them about not just grades but also any possible changes to their child's mood, friendship dynamics, and so on. Parents must also let schools know if and when their child needs more support because of events at home or because they're struggling with anxiety, depression, or other mental health concerns.

"Parents often hesitate," says Karlen, "because of the stigma. They fear they'll be judged as being inadequate as parents or seen as somehow responsible for all their child's issues." The point is to open the door to a two-way communication with your child's teachers and agree to share insights about their child's mental well-being in the same way you would partner up with a coach to make sure your child's physical health was being considered if they were at higher risk for injury.

CHAPTER TWELVE

Ready Her to Stand on Her Own

THE POWER OF the previous twelve antidotes resides in their ensuring that girls have the support, experiences, skills, and qualities that will help them feel safely seen in the world, that they belong, and that they matter. The hope is that, over time, as she steeps in these feelings, a girl will learn to embody this sense of well-being in an autonomous way, inside herself. The power of these wider community approaches isn't just to help your daughter feel safe and valued through caring relationships with others, but to help her learn to carry that feeling within herself, whether she's seeking the support of others or flying solo. To help her heal from adversity and be resilient in the face of future stressors, we must help her feel safe in her own body and mind.

Think again about my earlier analogy of the wooden nesting dolls. Tucked deep in the heart of the myriad circles of influence that shape each girl's life stands that core solid figure at the center of everything. It is, of course, the self. But *self* can be a tricky word here, especially for girls who've already encountered a lot of toxic stress. As we've seen, girls who've come of age with significant adversity and trauma often show changes in connectivity in areas of the brain that give rise to self-related thoughts: your sense of who you are, your *me-ness,* that interior feeling that you deserve to be here and to be loved. These beliefs are formed deep in the brain's neural structure early in life in response to the messages you receive from your caregivers and your wider environment. The degree to which a girl grows up feeling (or not feeling) that she is of intrinsic worth, that she matters, shapes the narrative she carries with her throughout adolescence and the rest of her life.

When this interior sense of being connected to oneself is lacking, it makes it hard to turn inward and dive into self-awareness and emerge with insights, wholeness, and self-love. The goal here is to help girls feel safe not just in their connection to others, but also in connection to themselves.

Antidote 13

Encourage a Sense of Mastery

A girl's sense of herself doesn't emerge only in response to her relationship with parents, mentors, and caregivers. Feeling good about ourselves is also shaped by our experience of "actually being competent," writes Ron Dahl, at Berkeley. Adolescents (who are by definition engaging in the process of defining themselves) need, he says, "a mastery curve experience"—to work at something, struggle, and get better and better at it over time. A mastery curve experience is one of the most powerful support systems an adolescent can have beneath them.

In the teen years, having access to meaningful work and an opportunity to contribute is often referred to by psychologists as "an identity project" (pursuing projects or activities that help them to figure out what they love, what they're good at, and, by extension, who they are). In studies of adolescents, finding a purpose and passion is associated with increased feelings of hope, optimism, and life satisfaction. Hope and optimism aren't just feel-good emotions; they matter to our physiological well-being. In one study, when researchers looked at optimism levels among women, those with the highest levels of optimism versus the lowest had a 15 percent longer life span. (The findings were similar for men.)

An identity project can't be a pursuit you choose for your daughter. The whole point is that it be *self*-desired, *self*-driven, and *self*-motivated. When parents suggest or orchestrate projects and opportunities for teens, it often has the opposite effect, making the teens feel less capable, diminished. And so they lose interest.

Having the opportunity to see one's talents being realized over time helps girls to internalize a sense of being worthwhile and having equal status in her community. Again and again, the girls I spoke with talked to me about the importance of finding their passion projects—and these tales loomed large in their healing narratives. When Deleicea Greene walked into her high school poetry club for the first time and dug out the poems she'd been keeping in notebooks and hiding in her backpack, for the first time in her life, she was, as she put it, "standing with a group of other people thinking about my poetry, not about who or what was tormenting me." She continues: "Walking into that room, being asked to share my poetry, hearing other people sharing their work . . . I'd never seen anything like that in my life. Poetry club made school so much better. The mentors and friends I met there made life so much better. On the days our club met, I looked forward to school. Poetry became a passion for me, yes, but it turned into something more—doing what I loved, and learning to get better and better at doing it, helped me find myself not just within the art medium of poetry, but also within the community of people it brought into my life. Poetry introduced me to my soul tribe, people I felt safe with, and somehow that made me feel safe within myself." That year, Deleicea's self-harm behaviors stopped.

Now the student has become the teacher: "My favorite days in the past year have been teaching poetry workshops to students in middle school, many of whom don't have much access to the arts. I've never felt more alive and inspired than when I'm coaching students and helping them to go within and create and share their words with me and with each other. Things get deep even though they barely know me. Seeing poetry create the same change in some of my students that it has created in me inspires me in a way nothing else has in my life."

Anna Moralis's passion project has been the pursuit of social justice, community organizing, and voting rights for underserved populations. "My work in community organizing helps me to derive a positive even out of a negative," she says. "When I see that there is a wrong in the world, I ask myself, *What can I concretely do to root it out and help give people in communities a platform to organize, so that we can help see that justice is recognized?* It's so important to me that the disenfranchised feel understood and that we help them to speak truth to power and that those in power are held accountable for their actions."

In the process, Anna has found out a lot about herself. "I'm often completely on my own out in the field or with a few other organizers, creating or managing an event. At times, I've felt thrown in at the deep end. But that allows for this sense of opportunity. I am starting to see—no, *feel*—what might happen if I can weave together my love of social justice with helping the underserved. There is so much that I want to do and so much that I think I can do now to help the world." Anna smiles wryly. "I know I can't save the world, but I do have a sense of how my skills and talents can meet the deep needs of the times we are in."

Anna, recently, has been working on voting access for women who have been victims of domestic violence or gender-based violence. "I want people to wake up to injustice, and at the same time, I've come to recognize that there is so much generosity among so many people in every community in terms of wanting to help those who don't have access to equal rights or justice."

For Julia Abernathy, "teaching myself how to code, and then finding out, *Hey, I'm really pretty good at this,* and teaching younger girls how to code—that has been the thing that, along with therapy, has brought me out of my suffering. In hindsight, I can see I was so, so, so self-involved in my own head. Falling in love with coding and realizing that I'm actually good at logic—that took me out of my own head in a healthy way. I started to see how I could shape the world around me by creating code." Julia smiles and says, "I heard this saying recently, that 'if you want to build self-esteem, you have to do self-esteemable things.' For me, computer science has allowed me to give back to my community and help younger girls find their passion and identity, and, wow, that gives *me* a ton of joy."

For parents, of course, the question becomes: How do I get my daughter some of that? How do you simultaneously start your daughter down this healthy passion project path without choosing the project for her? You might suggest a fairly wide range of options and then stand back and see what ignites her excitement. Let your daughter choose what to pursue, allowing room for trial and error. Options might include rowing for a cause, creating a film, learning pottery, taking a glass-blowing or carpentry class at a community college, developing a coding project, campaigning for climate change, tutoring younger kids, attending drama classes, volunteering, or participating in sports, from kick boxing to track and field. All these can lead to an empowered sense of "who I am." As your daughter finds her passion, encourage her by recognizing and appreciating her hard work, but don't insert yourself or tell her how to do it—unless she solicits your advice. As teens take a constructive step in the right direction, appreciate and admire their hard work, but do not jump in to help or tell them what to do. If we push too hard toward a goal, or place emphasis on performance, we can derail that motivation.

Of course, this poses a significant problem for families from disadvantaged backgrounds who may have few options available to them at school or during after-school hours. This puts the onus on community and school leaders to create opportunities for arts clubs, sports, and other options for every child, regardless of background. Passion is a natural motivator. If we provide exposure and opportunity, we may spark an interest, and self-motivation and mastery can follow.

Developing a deep inner well of self-mastery helps girls move away from extrinsic evaluation (evaluating herself through the eyes of others, as in *I will lose weight; get better makeup, a new haircut; exercise; buy new clothes*) and toward intrinsic values, such as working toward a goal for the sake of learning itself rather than for the outcome, and feeling connected to others by sharing a common passion.

Antidote 14

Help Her Develop a Voice of Resistance

When girls respond to stressors or perceived threats by blaming themselves (e.g., *Those kids posted trash about me on Insta because I'm so* [insert self-deprecating adjective]), over time, neural circuitry forms around those self-beliefs. As we've seen, self-blame and rumination over what we did wrong, or what others did to us, or what others might be thinking or saying about us, is associated with changes in the brain's default mode network (the "self space") and overactivity in the amygdala (the brain's danger alert center). These changes in the brain can show up later as behaviors, including a decreased ability to care for oneself, ask for help, or take proactive steps to try to change one's situation or mindset. And that's a path to more severe depression and anxiety.

One intervention that has been able to reduce the tendency toward self-deprecation in girls and, in turn, lessen the likelihood that a girl will blame herself when she is the brunt of sexist, misogynistic messaging is helping her unlearn traditional feminine gender roles. Sociologist Nicole Bedera at the University of Michigan has written about the importance of unlearning gender roles and moving away from self-blame. This includes, says Bedera, basic stuff like teaching girls that you don't have to continue a conversation with a guy that "you aren't enjoying, just to be polite." Or she suggests occasionally letting your daughter blow off her dad's opinions sometimes and question his authority. Let her "talk back and leave the room in the middle of an argument." Let her see that she "has the right to set her own boundaries" and have them respected. This is often especially important between fathers and daughters. In one recent study, University of Minnesota researchers found that over half of girls (compared to one-third of boys) feel unable to talk to their father about anything important.

But mothers, too, can practice helping their daughters develop a voice of resistance. Letting your daughter walk out of the room in the middle of a discussion, and especially after she's blown off some steam, can help her find the strength of her own voice. Many a mom who has heard her daughter let her feelings and opinions rip in heated discussion has learned not to take such moments personally. But in many homes, girls feel more comfortable doing this with their mothers than their fathers. (This doesn't mean you allow your daughter to be disrespectful or put you down, just that you recognize the difference between her blowing off steam and her attacking you.)

Ultimately, when fathers do this, too, Bedera says, this helps build a stronger relationship between a father and daughter, "one that teaches her that she is equal to men." Working to reduce female self-blame is especially important in the face of the never-ending performative, pretty-filtered posing that girls see in the beauty, fitness, and wellness porn that permeates Instagram and other social media platforms. Reducing self-blame has been found to help girls who later face sexual harassment, or even sexual assault, to process those traumatic events without self-loathing or self-recrimination, says Bedera. "They knew they should have been treated better. They knew they didn't deserve what happened to them."

Julia tells me how moving away from a negative view of herself, and unlearning traditional media-spun female roles of being polite and acceptable in behavior and appearance, has made a tremendous difference. "I've traditionally been pretty hard on myself. I've had to go in and manually unlearn caring about what other people think. It is a *manual* process. I follow a set of steps: Stop. Notice that I'm worrying about what others might be thinking of me. Allow myself to sit with the discomfort of those thoughts and sometimes even deliberately make those thoughts bigger than life, so that I increase my ability to tolerate the fear rather than be afraid of it. And then intervene by saying to myself, *I'm not responsible for what others might think of me, what other people think of me is none of my business, that's not my problem.*" This is, Julia says, "painstaking, painstaking work. But I'm getting better at it now."

Recently, she says, during the pandemic, "I got tired of wearing a bra, and I have these pendulous boobs. My dad was giving me a really hard time about it. At one point, some male relatives were coming over, and he was telling me I had to go put a bra on. I finally told him, 'Hey, Dad, if you are telling me that I should be worried about whether a male relative is going to sexualize me, then maybe we shouldn't have that male relative over!'"

"How did that feel?" I ask.

"It is amazing, learning not to take shit. It's changed how I am in my academic life, too. I've realized that the male egos in my classes are not going to celebrate my achievements. Yes, there was a time when that would have been hard for me, and I would have blamed myself for the fact that they weren't recognizing my contributions. I might have felt less than. But I am not that girl anymore. I don't need external validation from men to tell me I'm a good computer engineer. I know I am. I don't need to do everything perfectly all the time to believe in myself. If I have something to say or want to show how I worked out a problem, I speak up. I won't let being ignored or dismissed for my opinions silence me when I have something to contribute." And this, says Julia, "this feels like the reverse engineering of female shame. I feel proud of making my way in what can be a misogynistic environment without giving up any part of myself."

Julia's desire to have greater belief in her own voice and abilities in academic settings is understandable. Research shows college classrooms are still chilly for women: In a recent Dartmouth study of gender inequities in classrooms, men spoke 1.6 times more often than women, and women were more hesitant to speak and used more apologetic language. Men used more assertive language and were more likely to interrupt and to engage in longer conversations with their professors. When professors allowed for open discussion (students didn't have to raise their hands to participate), men talked even more—three times more often than women.

Julia is far from alone in feeling fed up. In her 2019 book, *The Witches Are Coming,* Lindy West argues that women are, by and large, seething. The way in which we socialize girls to put themselves second, "to be nice, and compliant, and to be caregivers," on top of centuries of gender inequities and injustices, she argues, has created a well of frustration for girls and women, especially since "women's anger is stigmatized; it's caricatured."

Worrying about being seen as angry can make it hard to step out of the voice of female self-blame. For Anna, it has been hard "to recognize and redirect my cycles of female self-blame. I can still find myself wanting to overapologize or seek others' approval. I'm learning to break that by applying self-care in those moments instead, and asking myself, *What do I want right now in this situation?*"

This hard work served her well recently, she says, when an older activist started hitting on her during a series of community organizing events. "I'd heard in advance that he had a reputation for doing this to younger women, that he was kind of radioactive and to stay away. This guy was totally lecherous. But he was in town for an event, and I couldn't always stay out of his line of sight. At first, he kept telling me over and over what a great job I was doing. Then he started to intimate that he had a great job in mind for me. It was so creepy. I knew through other people that the job he was telling me about didn't exist." Anna grimaces, as if both disgusted and exhausted by the memory. Then her voice reignites with energy. "So I just more or less gave him the message to fuck off. I didn't stress too much over it. I just said, 'Look, I'm super busy here, and I'm not interested,' and then I ignored him. He was so shocked and miffed by my response. And in that moment, I got to see how competent I could be completely on my own. I saw I'd developed these incredible muscles for shutting down situations which in the past might have triggered a lot of interior doubt or shame. That was a big moment for me."

Hillary Lianne McBride refers to this "reverse engineering of female shame" (as Julia calls it) as "the voice of resistance. This is the voice women use when standing in opposition to the voice of idealized femininity, when standing up against values and media that oppress women or cause them to believe their bodies are bad or undesirable, when resisting silencing gender roles and the objectification of women's bodies. It is the voice women use when speaking truth about their value." Once a girl embodies her own resistance to the myth of the idealized female and pushes back against the cultural script that she as a woman should be submissive or please others, she becomes freer, too, to speak up for other girls and women and be their advocates when men try to silence them.

You can start by modeling for your daughter how to respond to everyday sexist remarks. Let's consider a few hypotheticals. (One very important caveat: Do not try these comebacks if you or your daughter is at risk for retaliation from the person you're responding to or if your words might put you in danger—e.g., walking down an uncrowded street or responding to someone who is emotionally or physically reactive in your home life.) All these responses, when used safely and with the right timing, help our daughters to internalize the message that casual sexism is a form of intimidation, not an invitation to a conversation, and to learn how and when it's appropriate to speak her mind. Just as important, it's not her job to make men feel better when they're throwing out sexist remarks or belittling women.

Let's say you have an uncle who often dishes up "lighthearted" sexist jokes or spouts sexist comments.

Sexist uncle: I don't want to sound sexist, but . . .
You: Then don't be sexist! [Or,] Then I'd rather you stop right there.

Sexist uncle: [Says something about women drivers.] Ha ha ha.
You: That's neither humorous nor accurate.
Sexist uncle: Hey, I was joking!
You: It has to be funny to be a joke.

Sexist uncle: Wow, don't be so sensitive!
You: That's what people say when they're being insensitive.

Sexist uncle: Don't tell me you're a feminist.
You: You mean someone who believes men and women are equal?

Sexist uncle, *watching women's sports on TV*: That girl has a great body. Wow, she really fills out her uniform! She could be a model instead of playing basketball!
You, *pretending not to hear what he said while remaining calm and serious*: What?
Sexist uncle: [Repeats comment.]
You: What?

The point here is the more someone has to repeat an offensive re-mark, the more likely he is to see his behavior and realize how sexist and ridiculous he sounds.

> **Sexist uncle:** You're getting so emotional/hysterical/worked up!
> **You:** You're sounding like a seventies sitcom; have you been watching Archie Bunker again?

> **Sexist uncle:** You aren't listening to me, I'm telling you, women today . . .
> **You, *referring to yourself and your daughter*:** Jane and I are too busy working to change the world and create equality for all human beings to sit here listening to more misogyny/sexism.

Perhaps one good use of social media is this: various Twitter feeds offer comebacks to sexism. (Again, these are appropriate only if your daughter is in a safe situation.) Someone honks from a car as a girl walks down a busy street. The girl yells, "I'm a woman, not a traffic jam!" A boy at a party tells a girl, "You have *huge* boobs!" The girl looks down and screams at her breasts as if she's never seen them before. A guy at a party says to a girl, "You have great breasts. Don't be shy about it!" The girl responds, "I guess you're not shy about being a creep!"

Ultimately, the point is this: We need to raise girls not to feel ashamed or blamed by our toxic male culture. Helping girls move away from this misplaced blame opens the door to tremendous self-liberation for them.

Antidote 15

Have Her Write It Down to Break the Cycle of Negative Self-Talk

Here's another quick thought experiment: Think back to middle or high school, to a scenario when you felt chagrined, left out, made fun of, or embarrassed. Recall one or two details. What was said to you? Who was there? See what your brain did there? Feelings of being disrespected during adolescence create a powerful and lasting biophysical response— so potent that even decades later, you can still replay the same painful tape and feel the angst of that moment.

My work over the past thirty years has taught me a great deal about the intricate machinery behind the mind-body connection, and one of the overarching realizations I've come to is this: Unchecked rumination (looping thought cycles that focus on what others did or said or what we should or shouldn't have done) eventually harms our long-term mental and physical health. High rumination and negative self-talk, coupled with not taking healthy steps to break that cycle, is a trauma headspace. Your mind wants to create a story line to make sense of what it's experiencing, and more often than not, that story line casts you in the role of having messed up or been unlovable or the problem. That story of who you believe you are can shadow you for a lifetime—not just as emotional or behavioral patterns but in the neural networks of your brain.

And because young people care so much about reputation and being respected, rumination more easily locks down their thinking brain. Replaying altercations, resentments, or losses not only leads to an increased likelihood of anxiety and depression and a sense of helplessness, but it also makes us dwell in harmful, inflammatory stress chemicals and hormones that promote anxiety and depression.

George Slavich at UCLA explains the mind-body connection between rumination and physiological health this way: "The more rumination we engage in, the more we activate key stress pathways, which, over time, leads to more inflammation and depression. When the brain gets the message that there is a threat in the environment, it affects the body in stages." Slavich likens this process to being "like a note that gets passed from hand to hand. Imagine that, along the way, this note has to get delivered through a series of different locked gates. Once the danger message has passed through these gates, it tells the immune cells hanging out everywhere in your body to pump out cytokines, which cause inflammation." Ultimately, when adversity occurs, the factor that determines whether there will be long-term epigenetic changes that influence health comes down to whether this warning note gets passed from the brain to the body's immune system. And yet "all of these related biological stress responses are mediated by how we think and what we think about. As girls grow up and begin to face social challenges, stressful situations can only influence the health of their immune system through their thinking and how they perceive these events." This means that we as adults have a responsibility to help girls manage and modulate the way in which they perceive, interpret, and respond to the stressors in their lives. Because, adds Slavich, "one thing we *know* is modifiable is how people think about the world. And the earlier in life we can modify exaggerated perceptions of threat, the more we'll protect brain and immune health."

When Julia talks about having to "manually unlearn caring about what other people say and think" as "painstaking, painstaking work," she is talking about breaking the cycle of rumination and, by so doing, taking one of the most important steps she can take toward flourishing. "I've had to learn to give myself the benefit of the doubt by changing my thinking," she confides. "Getting caught up in those thought traps, misinterpreting things that happen, dwelling on them, coming to the wrong explanation of why bad things happen, or hating on myself, can poison my life. I realize now it will have an impact on how I feel over the months ahead of me, too. I've learned to give myself a chance. I remind myself I don't need to put on a show for anyone based on what I think they need or want. I do a lot of pulling myself back from the edge." This reframing process relies, Julia says, "on first seeing what words I am spewing at myself in my head and doing small manual things to rewrite that thought process. The past two and a half years have been a hell of a lot of hard work on that. But it is becoming second nature to me."

Another way to break rumination and create a new, healthier narrative is through narrative writing. As a writer, I am admittedly biased toward writing as a healing tool. I believe what Maya Angelou wrote is true: "There is no greater agony than bearing an untold story inside you." Research supports the idea that bringing worry and trauma out of the body by getting it out onto the page causes beneficial physical and emotional shifts. Writing-to-heal for just twenty minutes a day has been shown to lead to positive changes in immune function, improved stress biomarkers, and a reduction in symptoms of depression, anxiety, PTSD, asthma, and chronic pain.

For many years I have taught a narrative writing-to-heal program, Your Healing Narrative: Write-to-Heal with Neural Re-Narrating™. With neural re-narrating, I use a series of curated writing prompts to elicit insights, coupled with science-based mindfulness techniques, to help participants recognize their brain's old thought patterns and internalized stories and create new, more powerful inner healing narratives that calm the body, brain, and nervous system. In the years that I've taught this program to organizations, universities, parents, healing practitioners, and educators—no matter the time, place, or location—it is overwhelmingly women who sign up. Women come to the program, they often tell me, because they realize their history of chronic toxic stress or trauma is casting a shadow over their parenting, their relationships, and their ability to thrive mentally and physically. They want to better understand their story of adversity; identify old, painful thought patterns and negative self-talk; and ultimately, amend those toxic thought patterns into a new inner narrative that is more positive, realistic, hopeful, and empowered. This requires first understanding why they're experiencing such strong reactions in certain situations and what their feelings tell them about their story. They're often surprised by how the process of using writing-to-heal techniques helps them break deeply ingrained patterns of rumination and shift the nervous system's habitual responses. It's not always easy work, but as Brené Brown writes, "Owning our story can be hard but not nearly as difficult as spending our lives running from it."

I believe expressive writing is so powerful because getting difficult feelings down on the page and naming painful emotions with specific words is an "action" that breaks the rumination cycle. This allows the amygdala and nervous system to calm down. By putting pencil to paper, you're also able to operate in the past, present, and future all at once. You're in the present moment even as you choose words that call up feelings from the past, and you create a document you can revisit later and learn from.

Although my program is for parents and other adults ages eighteen and older, the benefits of writing-to-heal can be profound for girls, too. From among the one hundred strategies we use in my class, here's a quick, beginner exercise anyone can try anytime on their own: If your daughter is feeling overwhelmed you might suggest she set a timer and spend ten minutes writing down all her negative thoughts on a piece of paper and then tear the paper up into tiny bits and throw it in the trash. Next, suggest she write for ten minutes about how she thinks she might be able to make meaning out of her experience now and in the future. Just so she knows this isn't for anyone but her, suggest she tear up and toss this page, too.

In writing-to-heal and neural re-narrating classes, we delve into an array of targeted, neuroscience-based exercises that elucidate a participant's unique story, including the parts of her story that are most "sticky" or "heated" and still bring up strong emotion. Often, in these stories, we spare very little compassion for ourselves. Once we see a unique pattern in our story, we engage in steps to create a more positive reframing, one that can help change how we feel, think, and respond to life's stressors. I've seen how, with key prompts and strategies, this process helps participants shift from interior rumination punctuated by harsh self-criticism or self-blame, or anger and judgment toward others, toward a powerful reframe. Participants begin to recognize the deep well of resources they hold within them to cope with life's hardships, acknowledge and revel in all the courageous efforts they've made on their own behalf throughout their life, talk to themselves as a benefactor or avatar might, view themselves with affection and a new sense of loyalty, and create new habits of self-talk that help create interior joy.

Anxiety often emerges from over-focusing on potential danger signals in our environment, and under-focusing on our own interior and exterior resources. But the bigger point is this: By pairing narrative writing with new tools, we can help to reset the brain and bring forth a centered calm that is not easily shaken in the face of future stressors or by the behaviors or actions of others. We come back to the truth of who we are. And we become more of who we want to be. Here are a few simple examples of reframing:

Rumination: "No one ever helps me," or "They don't care about what I need," or "I'm always on my own."
Reframing: "I see times in the past when I felt overwhelmed and I did what I needed to keep myself safe, including reaching out for or accepting help. I will be loyal to myself and keep myself safe now. I'm proud of how far I've come."

Rumination: "I can't believe I did that," or "I'm an idiot," or "I always mess things up."
Reframing: "I've been creative and resilient in the past, even in-

cluding when I was a child and didn't always have the support I
needed. I have even more interior and outside resources now." Or,
"When I felt this way in the past, I realized this was not true, and
these feelings did not last. I know how to bounce back."

Rumination: "I am not lovable," or, "No one understands me."
Reframing: "There have been many times in the past when someone helped me through or showed me they loved me, I can name
many benefactors in my past, and I can bring them to mind now."
Or, "What would my benefactors say to me if they were here?"—
and imagining them saying, "You are caring, lovable, kind, resilient,
and capable."

And in this new meaning making, we begin to recognize and draw
upon core inner resources that have always resided within us and to
marinate in positive self-truths about our worthiness—which, in turn,
helps clear the old cache of habitual, ruminating negative thoughts. We
can think of the process of writing-to-heal as helping create new software programming for the brain to run on, programming that better
enables us to find and dwell in a soothing feeling of interior safety. (If
you, as a parent, want to try a few exercises from my Write-to-Heal with
Neural Re-Narrating™ program, see my website, where I offer up a brief
free sample. There, you'll also learn more about a course designed specifically for parents.)

However you do it, shifting from a negative lens through which to
view yourself and your experiences to a more neutral or positive lens
can have beneficial effects. Rachel Yehuda, at Mount Sinai School of
Medicine in New York City, reinforces this idea: Our experiences are
going to change us. But even as what happens to us matters greatly, so
does the way in which we respond to it in our bodies and minds. By
observing our own story in a way that "promotes more reflection . . . in
a way that shows you where you've come from, in a way that honors

your past," we can develop more self-compassionate options to draw upon when we feel overwhelmed by feelings or events.

> *We can think of the process of writing-to-heal*
> *as helping create new software programming for*
> *the brain to run on, programming that*
> *better enables us to find and dwell in a*
> *soothing feeling of interior safety.*

For Deleicea Greene, writing about her most difficult experiences from when she was young, and sharing them with her mother, has helped heal their relationship. "I've been able to read my mother some of the poems I wrote about her and how hard things were for me growing up. My mom would probably not call what happened to me neglect—she was doing her best in a difficult situation as a single mom. When I first shared my feelings, she was upset. But she has held herself accountable. And she's happy that I don't feel that way anymore. Now my mom and I have a much closer connection. I can talk to my mom about a lot of things and our relationship has become a safe space for me."

Writing slam poetry as a form of social justice has also been a potent pathway to help Deleicea move past shame and suffering. "I let myself go really deep into the darkest emotions and experiences, and in the process of letting all that dark bubble and percolate up, I eventually get a glimmer of what is incredibly resilient in me. There is ultimately this power that is unleashed by naming and expressing what happened to me at different, really horrible times in my life. I start to see that it doesn't define me for the rest of my life. And that removes a lot of the confusion and panic away from it. I find I go from being tormented by certain memories, or feeling *Oh, I never tried hard enough to make it in college, I'm a loser, I don't deserve to be here,* to *Whoa, wow, all these events of my life did not derail me. They did not stop me.*" And that shift leads to "appreciating all that I've survived and what I had to draw on in myself to get where I am. So I can take my story forward to help not just myself but others, whether it's people in the audience who are listening to my poems when I'm performing or the kids I am mentoring and coaching. My hope is that it gives them hope—hope that maybe you can't change what happened to you, but you can create a context of meaning around it and honor the good and the bad. For me, feeling empowered starts by naming what happened to me on paper and re-writing the possibilities for where I'm going next."

CONCLUSION

Aɴɴᴀ Mᴏʀᴀʟɪs, Dᴇʟᴇɪᴄᴇᴀ Gʀᴇᴇɴᴇ, and Julia Abernathy each faced unimaginable stressors in difficult times and found herself, by mid-adolescence, standing on the edge of a precipice, poised either to fall or to find terra firma. And yet each of them, with support from multiple directions and spheres of influence, coupled with her own extraordinary, hard-won efforts to find healing, began to rewire her sense of herself and find solid footing by the time she hit her late teens and early twenties. Slowly, if painstakingly, Anna, Deleicea, and Julia have all moved toward thriving even amid hardship and uncertainty.

This does not mean they were able to put their mental health struggles completely behind them. Rather, they developed deep self-awareness around their journeys, made new meaning out of their experiences, and internalized powerful coping skills. This allowed Anna, Julia, and Deleicea to emerge with a clear sense of self and with strong, confident voices. Each has come through the worst of her suffering and gone on to live a rich, meaningful, and independent life. They have become the women they wanted to be.

Today, at age twenty-one, Anna Moralis works as a community organizer as she preps for the LSAT exam for law school. "I plan to use my law degree to work to ensure voting rights and immigration rights for underserved communities and people of color," she tells me when we meet for one last time, more than a year after we began our series of conversations. "I can't wait to get going." Her tone shifts to one of caution as she adds, "I just want other girls to know this is *not* a 'now I'm all better' scenario. It's sometimes three steps forward, one step back, that's for sure. But over time, between the changes I've made and with the help of a ton of other people, I feel more whole. It's a process—sometimes I still struggle with eating issues and anxiety, but it's rarer now. And I know what to do about it when it happens. Learning to acknowledge my feelings and understand that a healthy sense of validation really comes from inside of me—that's been really powerful and healing."

Deleicea Greene, now twenty-two, former Youth Poet Laureate of Baltimore, works today as a poetry coach for inner-city teen poets, helping them in their writing, and healing, journeys. "I was literally forced by circumstances to dig deep and find the light in the darkness within myself, to identify it, understand it," she says when we meet again. "I avoided doing this inner work for the longest time, but now I realize that nobody gets around having to do that. It's only by doing that that I've found ways to help me manage and get on top of my depression and anxiety, and mobilize myself toward feeling better. It's been like a re-birthing."

"How did you begin the process?" I ask.

Deleicea gives a small, knowing nod of her head. "I had to begin with first learning that even though I *thought* I knew how to cope and push my way through really difficult feelings and experiences, I didn't know much about how to cope at all."

Julia Abernathy, now twenty, is wrapping up her junior year of college, where she majors in computer engineering. A paper she coauthored with a professor on biohacking and ethics is soon to be published in a prestigious academic journal. She's been in a caring, steady relationship for over a year. She tells me when we take a walk in a park near her house that she has a clear sense of her capabilities: "The future feels pretty exciting for me." She peers at me questioningly. "I don't know if you're interested in hearing this for your book, but I've also figured out something else about myself that's been pretty life-changing."

"I am interested," I say.

"I'm not straight. I can see now, looking back, that some of my self-hatred about my body was coming from a place of not yet recognizing that I'm gay. I think all the gendered messages I got about my body and being endlessly leered at by older men and boys when I was really still a kid created so much trauma for me that I couldn't hear the deeper voice in me, which was trying to help me hear the truth about my own sexual identity."

Anna, Deleicea, and Julia have worked hard for their well-being. They define flourishing with adversity.

WHAT ANNA'S, JULIA'S, AND DELEICEA'S stories tell us is that in the face of mounting toxic stressors, American girls have grown increasingly weary, overwhelmed, and fearful by layers. Every day, every year, teenage girls' general levels of anxiety have ratcheted up. Girls and young women are tired of being resilient and bucking up. They want to feel safe in our world.

Now that we understand how and why ubiquitous social and environmental threats can affect the developing female brain in unique ways, and how this plays out in the way girls feel, think, grow, and love across a lifetime, we must begin a new conversation about how we raise girls. This goes beyond preventing trauma for girls; it means rethinking the social context that shapes girls' lives and no longer accepting that things are okay just the way they are.

In so many ways, we've come pretty far as a human race. But we haven't always been honest about the remaining challenges girls still face. We know that toxic stress is a leading cause of mental health concerns and, yet, as a culture, we pay very little attention to how stressors affect young people's well-being. Meanwhile, we've raised this generation of girls to expect equality at home, at school, and in the workforce while ignoring the reality that they're marinating in the wider message that not only are they not equal, but that they are never truly safe. It may be 2022, but young women are clearly still in danger of being victims of the male gaze; of bias, misogyny, and stereotype. And this feeling of unsafety becomes more insidious and intrusive when delivered and amplified through the toxicity that is social media.

To borrow a term of art from an MIT lecturer and the author of *Leading from the Emerging Future,* Otto Scharmer, as adults, we must first begin by leading "from the future." We must create the very environment we want to look back on, so that five or ten or fifteen years from now, we can say, with our whole hearts, yes, this was a good and safe society for girls to grow up in. This means discussing our own adult behaviors, values, priorities, and skill sets as parents, educators, and mentors; admitting where we fall short; and setting out to do better. We, the adults, are responsible for the chaotic world we've created and its effect on girls. Yet too often we urge girls forward without being honest— with them or ourselves—about the level of toxic stress they will meet up with in their lives. We may even place the fault with them when they begin to struggle or when simple coping strategies aren't enough to help them find their way. To change this, we must better support girls with new strategies while simultaneously assisting parents, educators, and practitioners (and all those who strive to help girls thrive) with the necessary resources, services, skills, and strategies to take actionable steps to improve girls' felt sense of safety and belonging. This includes, but is hardly limited to, healthcare, school systems, social services, mental health services, community organizations, Big Tech, media companies, and our justice system. It necessitates reaching every part of our population, including those facing the threats of racism and poverty. The goal here is to help all girls not just be healthy and feel happy and safe as they come of age, but also become the well-regulated, stable, safe, nurturing parents and leaders of tomorrow.

What we do about the fact that our daughters are struggling, and how we treat girls, tells us how far we've evolved in our shared morality as a society. When girls feel safe in our world on a visceral level and when they thrive as their autonomous selves, freed from pervasive fear and anxiety, we'll know that we as a society are doing pretty well.

But because this bright new future has not yet arrived, we also have to help girls learn to flourish despite the background noise of sexism and other adversities they face. This means ensuring they have the tools to adapt and self-manage in healthy ways, even in the face of being bombarded by social and emotional challenges, and to flourish without being impeded by the culture in which they are coming of age. Even as we address the root causes of the trauma girls encounter by working to change systems and society, this dual inside-outside approach is key to furthering each girl's potential and to her future. We must double down on teaching and supporting girls as they acquire the interior tools and skills to feel and be safe. In this, I hope the fifteen antidotes I've offered up in these pages will prove helpful.

This, of course, requires flipping a few entrenched narratives. The first is the idea that girls are inherently fragile—if I haven't successfully done so yet, let me dispel that idea one last time here. A society that objectifies girls is the source of the harm inflicted on them. We don't need to protect girls' development unless they grow up in an objectifying, sexist culture and unless toxic men are ready, willing, and able to inflict harm on them.

We must also flip the narrative regarding what we mean when we say girls are "resilient." Instead of praising girls who have survived adversity or trauma for being resilient or having grit, we must change the communities, systems, and structures generating a culture of sexism and adversity that make them vulnerable in the first place. We must flip our narrative in professional milieus, too. Telling girls and women to lean in, become harder and tougher, is another way of making sexism *their* problem rather than society's. The do-it-yourself approach that requires girls to change their clothes or the tone of their voice when they want to be seen or treated fairly or receive equal pay is what needs rethinking. As well meaning as the idea of leaning in is, it misdirects our attention away from addressing the patriarchal machine that still sends girls the message that if they want to fit in, *they* are what needs fixing rather than the culture at large.

THE LINGERING FEAR I have, as I wrap up these pages, is that having more science on how toxic stress in puberty affects girls might simply give the most sexist members of our society a reason to "explain away" the social injustices and harms of sexism *because* of the biology of sex, in the same way that has been historically done with so many aspects of female anatomy and biology. Or, that in writing this book, I have unwittingly played into the patriarchy of science and the trap of needing to see enough "evidence" to emerge before we start to make real changes and rethink how we raise our girls and put our hearts and minds together to help them.

We might even ask ourselves: Why do we need to have this science to wake us up to the need to do better in how we raise girls and in how we as a society treat them? If we know girls are struggling and suffering—isn't that enough? When it comes to ensuring child well-being, we would do well also to move beyond this basic discussion of gender and biology: If any group of kids faces bias or derision for any reason, we should care about that because we care about youth, period. We shouldn't have to do a deep dive into the neuroscience on how stress is hurting girls' brains and bodies to care enough to ensure that they know they matter, that they belong, to ensure that they are safe on this planet.

At the same time, I believe that once we can make sense of the why behind an entrenched and disturbing problem—why our daughters are struggling more than ever before—it stops being as confusing and exhausting to think about. And once it's less bewildering and fatiguing to ponder, we're better positioned to make big changes. These differences in female and male responses to stress don't make the female or male brain better or worse. But they do give us a clearer idea as to what's behind sex-specific risks for mental health disorders, so that we can work to change the conditions that lead to vulnerabilities. We are more clear-headed and purposeful as we come together to create a planet that is nurturing for all girls.

We can each take what we find most resonant and helpful in this new science and in these fifteen antidotes and go out into the world and do our absolute best. As you do so, remember that you are not solely responsible for each girl's future. You will need to create your own trusted wider community, your own safe convoy to help you as you set out to help your daughter and all the girls and young women whose lives you touch. Remember, too, that there is room for error. We will, of course, make mistakes. We aren't going to get it right every time. No parent, teacher, or counselor is perfect. We know our girls are not okay. We know we must do something, so let's begin where we are. I don't think we can afford to wait for a perfect plan. Bringing in these antidotes now will make a difference no matter where you are in your efforts to help and support the girl you care about. You can add to and perfect them as you go. And we can all share what we learn, and grow together as families and communities, along the way.

After talking to so many leading experts and girls, I know what I hope for. I hope for my daughter and for all girls to come of age with a sense of safety, belonging, and connection and to grow up feeling free to become any version of "female" or "feminine" (or neither of these) that they so choose. I want this to include the time girls spend on social media, even as I urgently want to see them spend far less time in the distorted online world and extract them from the smartphone social media trap. I want to see men—especially those in powerful roles, be it the head of Facebook (now Meta), corporate CEOs, researchers, professors, male supervisors, guys at parties, or simply the guy who is physically bigger than the girl walking past him on the street—wake up to the reality of the fear girls experience growing up female in a world dominated by sexism and male power. In their interactions with girls and young women, I want men to ask themselves, *What words and behavior will reflect my moral character as a human being?* rather than *What's in this for me?* I want us all to sit with this discomfort, then step up to make a change and seek opportunities for a redo; to do better in whatever role we occupy in a girl's life so that we don't have to read a newer version of this same familiar story twenty-five years from now, in our granddaughters' generation, or in *their* daughters' time.

More than anything, I want to see us find enough social will to decide we can change "the way things are" for girls starting today versus staying in a liminal state of denial and avoidance. Because it doesn't have to be this way.

It's a lot to ask for, yes, but it's past time. Time really is up.

APPENDIX A:
GROWING UP FEMALE, BY THE NUMBERS

We've covered a lot of ground in these pages, and I've tossed out a good number of statistics. To be sure that both the problems and the solutions are clear, I always find it helpful to quantify these things at a glance. Therefore, I've compiled the following facts:[*]

Sex and Gender Differences in Adolescent Mental Health

- One out of four adolescent girls reports suffering from symptoms of major depression compared with fewer than one in ten boys.
- The rate of adolescent girls suffering from major depressive symptoms is 2.6 times greater than that of boys.
- Girls and young women today are twice as likely as boys to suffer from anxiety.
- Depression is occurring more often in girls today than in the past and it's presenting earlier, often by ages twelve or thirteen.
- By age seventeen, more than one-third of girls report having experienced

---

[*]   See the notes section of this book for sources.

at least one "major depressive episode" over the prior year of their lives, an episode marked by feelings of "worthlessness and guilt."

- Between 2016 and 2020, girls were, on average, 48 percent more likely to have a depression diagnosis compared with boys of the same age.

- Between 2016 and 2020, girls had a 43 percent higher rate of anxiety compared with boys.

- Nearly 50 percent of young adult females report as many as ten days of "poor mental health" during the "past month," compared with 28 percent of boys.

- Between 2005 and 2017, the rate of major depressive disorder increased 52 percent among adolescents ages twelve to seventeen and 63 percent among young adults eighteen to twenty-five. This increase was far more prevalent in girls and young women compared with boys and young men of the same age. These statistical increases in depression and anxiety among today's girls were, however, *weak or nonexistent* among young women ages twenty-six and over, suggesting a generational shift in mental health disorders.

- In 2019, one in three high school students reported experiencing such persistent feelings of sadness or hopelessness that they were unable to participate in regular activities. Among girls, that number was significantly higher: half of female students reported constant feelings of sadness or hopelessness.

- Every year, the gap between the rates at which girls and boys suffer from depression and anxiety persists—between 2018 and 2019 alone, it widened by 14 percent.

- Sixty-three percent fewer males develop depression compared with females.

- The rate of preteen and teen girls who end their own lives has tripled over the past twenty years, including in girls ages ten to fourteen.

- Over the past ten years, the suicide rate among Black girls increased at twice the rate as that among Black boys.

Sex and Gender Differences in Adolescent Mental Health During the COVID-19 Pandemic

- Nearly half of parents noticed their teenager's mental health worsened during the pandemic, and this downturn in mental well-being was more pronounced among girls.

- Thirty-six percent of girls displayed new or worsening symptoms of anxiety during the pandemic compared with 19 percent of boys, and 31 percent of girls showed new or worsening signs of depression compared with 18 percent of boys.

- Emergency room visits for mental health crises rose 31 percent among twelve- to seventeen-year-olds during 2020 compared with 2019, and these increases were higher among girls.

Sex and Gender Differences in Mental Health and Adverse Childhood Experiences

- Ten percent of men who've experienced two or more types of childhood adversity later develop major depression, but more than twice that number, 25 percent, of women who've experienced two or more categories of ACEs develop major depression.

- Eight percent of men who have a history of three or more types of childhood adversity develop an anxiety disorder in adulthood, whereas nearly three times that number, or 22 percent, of women who've faced three categories of adversity do.

- For each category of childhood stress a girl faces prior to the age of eighteen, the likelihood that she will later develop a serious autoimmune disease (such as lupus, rheumatoid arthritis, or multiple sclerosis) in adulthood increases by 20 percent, compared with males, whose rate of developing autoimmune disease increases by half that, or 10 percent, when they face the same number of ACEs.

Sex and Gender Differences in Education

- In college classrooms, men speak 1.6 times more often than women, use more assertive language, and are more likely to interrupt. When professors allow for open discussion (students don't have to raise their hands to speak), men speak even more—three times more often than women.
- Although women make up more than half of medical school classes, up to half of female medical students reports being sexually harassed during their training.

Sex and Gender Differences in Adolescent Mental Health and Social Media

- The more time a teenager spends on social media platforms, the more likely she is to develop depressive symptoms, poor body image, and lowered self-esteem—and this association between social media use and depression is much stronger for girls compared with boys.
- Facebook's internal documents show that among girls who feel bad about their bodies, 32 percent say that Instagram (which is owned by Meta) makes them feel worse.
- Forty percent of teens say feelings of being "unattractive" began when they started using Instagram.
- Among U.S. teens who report suicidal thoughts, 6 percent trace those feelings to Instagram.
- The majority of girls start using social media apps between age eight and thirteen—even though users are supposed to be thirteen to have an account.

Sex and Gender Differences in Sexual and Other Traumas

- Nearly one in three young women reports having been coerced into having sex when she didn't want to or being raped or date-raped.
- Among college students, 26 percent of females report experiencing rape or sexual assault.
- Women in the United States have a rate of PTSD of 10 to 12 percent, which is roughly twice that of men, who have a rate of PTSD of 5 to 7 percent. Rates of PTSD in women, in general, are closer to that of male

combat veterans. (Marine veterans of the Iraq War have a PTSD rate of 12 percent.)

Sex and Gender Differences in Family Life

- Female teens are less likely to report feeling their family "often stands by them" or that they "always receive the emotional support they need" in family life compared with male teens.
- Over half of girls, compared with one-third of boys, reports feeling unable to talk to their fathers.

APPENDIX B:
RESOURCES AND FURTHER READING

There are many great books out there that explain in more detail or from other perspectives the concepts and strategies I've introduced in this book. Here is a list of some of those I have used as both a writer and a mother.

Gopnik, Alison. *The Philosophical Baby.* New York: Farrar, Straus and Giroux, 2009.

———. *The Gardener and the Carpenter: What the New Science of Child Development Tells Us About the Relations Between Parents and Children.* New York: Farrar, Straus and Giroux, 2016.

Maté, Gabor, M.D. *In the Realm of Hungry Ghosts: Close Encounters with Addiction.* New York: North Atlantic Books, 2010.

McBride, Hillary L., and Janelle L. Kwee. "Intergenerational Journeys." In *Embodiment and Eating Disorders: Theory, Research, Prevention, and Treatment.* Edited by Hillary L. McBride and Janelle L. Kwee. New York: Routledge, 2018.

Miller, Lisa. *The Spiritual Child: The New Science of Parenting for Health and Lifelong Thriving.* New York: Picador, 2016.

Moorman, Chick. *Parent Talk: How to Talk to Your Children in Language that Builds Self-Esteem and Encourages Responsibility.* New York: Simon & Schuster, 1998.

Orenstein, Peggy. *Girls & Sex: Navigating the Complicated New Landscape.* New York: Harper, 2016.

Perry, Bruce D., M.D., Ph.D., and Oprah Winfrey. *What Happened to You? Conversations on Trauma, Resilience, and Healing.* New York: Macmillan, 2021.

Pipher, Mary, Ph.D., and Sara Pipher Gilliam. *Reviving Ophelia: Saving the Selves of Adolescent Girls.* 25th Anniversary Edition. New York: Riverhead, 2019.

Siegel, Daniel J., and Tina Payne Bryson. *The Power of Showing Up: How Parental Presence Shapes Who Our Kids Become and How Their Brains Get Wired.* New York: Ballantine Books, 2020.

Starrs, Bronagh. *Adolescent Psychotherapy: A Radical Relational Approach.* New York: Routledge, 2019.

Stixrud, William, Ph.D., and Ned Johnson. *The Self-Driven Child.* New York: Viking, 2018.

Traister, Rebecca. *Good and Mad: The Revolutionary Power of Women's Anger.* New York: Simon & Schuster, 2018.

Tronick, Ed, and Claudia M. Gold. *The Power of Discord: Why the Ups and Downs of Relationships Are the Secret to Building Intimacy, Resilience, and Trust.* New York: Little, Brown/Spark, 2020.

Twenge, Jean M., Ph.D. *iGen: Why Today's Super-Connected Kids Are Growing Up Less Rebellious, More Tolerant, Less Happy—and Completely Unprepared for Adulthood.* New York: Atria, 2018.

Online Resources

Commonsensemedia.org, on "How to Talk to Kids About Difficult Subjects."

PACEsConnection.com, on resources and networking opportunities to utilize the science on Positive and Adverse Childhood Experiences and improve lives for communities, families, and children.

DBT website—see Therapist AID LLC "Interpersonal Effectiveness Skills."

My Own Work in This Area

The Angel and the Assassin: The Tiny Brain Cell that Changed the Course of Medicine. New York: Ballantine, 2020.

Childhood Disrupted: How Your Biography Becomes Your Biology. New York: Atria, 2015.

www.donnajacksonnakazawa.com (for more on "Your Healing Narrative: Write-to-Heal with Neural Re-Narrating™").

APPENDIX C:
THE ANTIDOTES AT A GLANCE

Cut out this page and keep it handy for reference.

The Antidotes

The Building Blocks of Good Parent-Child Connection and the Importance of Family Resilience

> **Antidote 1:** Get in Sync—Understand the Connections Between Your Stress, Your Trauma, and What You Are Communicating to Your Child at Every Age

> **Antidote 2:** Observe Your Reactions in Parent-Child Interactions and Dial Back on Evaluating Your Daughter

> **Antidote 3:** When Your Daughter Turns to You, Make It a Good Experience for Her

Make Her Home Her Safe Space

> **Antidote 4:** When Hard Things Happen (and They Will), Be Prepared to Respond in Healthy, Supportive Ways, Even When Your Daughter Shares Hard-to-Hear Information

> **Antidote 5:** Power Up on Joy (Especially) in Difficult Times

Antidote 6: Don't Solve All Her Problems for Her—Leave Room for "a Little Wobble"

Antidote 7: Wonder Aloud Together to Help Build Resilience to Stress

Antidote 8: Go Slow on Development—Keep the Biological Brakes Engaged

Antidote 9: Create Routine, Ritual, and Structure—Including a Family Media Plan

Bring in What the Wider Community Can Provide

Antidote 10: Engage the Power of Benefactors, Mentors, and Avatars to Help a Girl Feel She Matters

Antidote 11: Help Her Find "a Sense of Something Bigger"

Antidote 12: Take the Pressure Off Your Parent-Child Relationship and Get Some Professional Help

Ready Her to Stand on Her Own

Antidote 13: Encourage a Sense of Mastery

Antidote 14: Help Her Develop a Voice of Resistance

Antidote 15: Have Her Write It Down to Break the Cycle of Negative Self-Talk

ACKNOWLEDGMENTS

Writing books has meant long swaths of time spent "in my head" think-ing, researching, writing. I give every book my whole heart and mind. After seven books, I've become accustomed to the duality of the writing life: hundreds of interviews with people whose voices you hear in the book, juxtaposed with many days alone writing in my attic, deeply im-mersed in my evolving thoughts. Over time, it's become clear to me that, as I go through this process again, my family and friends are the most generous, patient, and loving people on the planet. They not only put up with me when I'm distracted and overly involved in my work, but they are, even while tackling their own very busy and creative lives, there when I need them most. Thank you to my family and to the crew of ex-traordinary women—Shannon Brownlee, Faith Hackett, M.D., Amy Karlen, Ph.D., Sarah Judd, Kimberly Minear, and Barbee Whita-ker, Ph.D.,—with whom I make my way through this life. Without our friendship, I wouldn't love this life the way I do.

To Shannon Brownlee, an added heartfelt thank-you for your early reading of this book and for cheering me on, but more important, for challenging me to make this a better, wiser read. To Sarah Judd, your thoughts were invaluable.

No book exists without an agent and editor to champion your vision and take the leap with you as you convey your "big idea" onto the written page. In this I am doubly blessed to have worked with two more extraordinary women, whom I think of as teammates: my agent and dear lifelong friend Elizabeth Kaplan; and my beloved editor, Marnie Cochran. (To give you an idea of how great an editor Marnie is, I refer to her editorial changes as "Marnie Magic.") You both make this work a joy even when it is very, very hard. Even when I am alone in my attic, I never feel that I am.

To the researchers and experts who so graciously allowed me to report on their work and who spent valuable time helping me ensure every complex concept, though written through my lens, met the scientific sniff test, this book is your book, too. It wouldn't exist without your research. A bow of gratitude, also, to Tracy Bale, Ph.D.; Christina Bethell, Ph.D.; DeLisa Fairweather, Ph.D.; Amy Karlen, Ph.D.; Peg McCarthy, Ph.D.; and George Slavich, Ph.D. To Peg McCarthy, a special hat tip—you've been the most generous and patient scientific advisor that any English major could hope for. To Christina Bethell, thank you for sharing fine-grained data analyses from your Child and Adolescent Health Measurement Initiative at the Johns Hopkins Bloomberg School of Public Health. These figures on the health and well-being of American girls and boys proved instrumental to this book. And for speedy, stellar fact-checking and wise editorial suggestions and comments, thank you to Ben Kravitz. Thank you, too, to Katherine Leak at Random House for smoothing the editorial process and to Jenna Dolan for your excellent copyediting of this book. And heartfelt gratitude to Sophie Van Tiggelen, who helps me develop and manage my courses, workshops, and so many other work projects; I couldn't do this without you.

Most of all, my gratitude goes to the generous young women who agreed to talk with me in depth about their personal experiences. To disguise their identities, I've changed some girls' names, but trust me when I say, they are all three brave and brilliant. You know who you are. I was the writer, but you were my teachers.

It's no surprise to any reader of mine that I live with a few challenging health conditions. Here, too, I have a treasured posse of helpers and healers. Thank you to Ahmet Hoke, M.D.; Al and Kristin Liao; Lisa Magarill; Joshua Nachman; Megan Rich; Marla Sanzone, Ph.D.; Heather Sateia, M.D.; and William Vickers, M.D., for your kindness in helping me through these pandemic years. I probably wouldn't be well enough to write if it weren't for you.

To those readers who are parents or educators, I want to acknowledge your hard work and heartfelt efforts in helping the girls and young women in your lives to thrive. (Should you feel compelled to help address your own history of adversity and chronic stress by taking my online narrative writing program, Your Healing Narrative: Write-to-Heal With Neural Re-Narrating™, or any of my other available courses, I want to offer you a special gift. Enter code GIRLSONTHEBRINK during the sign-up process.)

Finally, to my family, I love you, and if you don't know this already, you are everything to me. To my husband, Zenji Nakazawa, you know better than anyone that I can't do this without you by my side. That has been doubly, triply true while writing on a short deadline throughout the pandemic. Without your love—not to mention your banana bread and our long walks through the countryside—I'd never have made it across the finish line. To my beloved son and daughter, Christian and Claire, if there is one thing I spend a whole lot more time thinking about than my writing, it's both of you and how very lucky I am to get to be your mom. It has been a joy watching you both emerge into young adulthood as your truest selves, even in the face of adversity.

NOTES

Introduction

page xi **One out of four adolescent girls reports suffering from symptoms of major depression:** This data was provided by Christina Bethell, Ph.D., director, Child and Adolescent Health Measurement Initiative, professor at Johns Hopkins Bloomberg School of Public Health, and was derived from the 2019 Youth Risk Behavior Surveillance System results as reported by the Centers for Disease Control and Prevention.

page xi **Girls and young women are twice as likely as boys and young men to suffer from anxiety:** C. S. Mott Children's Hospital, "How the Pandemic Has Impacted Teen Mental Health," *Mott Poll Report* 38, no. 2 (March 2021); Nicola Davis, "Women Twice as Likely as Men to Experience Anxiety, Research Finds," *The Guardian,* June 5, 2016; O. Remes et al., "A Systematic Review of Reviews on the Prevalence of Anxiety Disorders in Adult Populations," *Brain and Behavior* 6, no. 7 (June 2016): e00497.

page xi **In 2021, the Centers for Disease Control and Prevention reported that suicide attempts had recently increased 51 percent:** Allyson Chiu, "ER Visits for Suspected Suicide Attempts Among Teenage Girls Rose During Pandemic," *The Washington Post,* June 11, 2021; E. Yard et al., "Emergency Department Visits for Suspected Suicide Attempts Among

Persons Aged 12–25 Years Before and During the COVID-19 Pandemic—United States, January 2019–May 2021," *MMWR Morbidity and Mortality Weekly Report Weekly* 70, no. 24 (June 18, 2021): 888–94; D. A. Ruch et al., "Trends in Suicide Among Youth Aged 10 to 19 Years in the United States, 1975 to 2016," *JAMA Network* 2, no. 5 (2019): e193886. As I state later in chapter 1, it is important to also note that, historically, suicide death rates among boys have been higher than among girls. It's often been said that girls attempt suicide at a higher rate, boys die from it far more often. This has long been concerning. But the suicide death rates among girls have increased significantly over the past decades and that gap is closing.

Chapter One: Our Girls Are Not Okay

page 8   **Depression is occurring more often in girls today than in the past:** J. Breslau et al., "Sex Differences in Recent First-Onset Depression in an Epidemiological Sample of Adolescents," *Translational Psychiatry* 7, no. 5 (May 2017): e1139. Figure 1 shows that 16 percent of first-onset depression among adolescent girls now occurs at age twelve or thirteen; 28.3 percent of first-onset depression occurs by age fourteen. Also see: Ariana Eunjung Cha, "More Than a Third of Teenage Girls Experience Depression, New Study Says," *The Washington Post*, May 31, 2017; Phyllis L. Fagell, "Dealing with Disturbing Spike in Youth Suicides," *The Washington Post*, March 18, 2019.

page 8   **Researchers screen teens to find out if they've faced emotional or behavioral concerns:** It is well known that many children experience mental health problems but lack a diagnosis due to poor access to services, fear of stigma, cultural factors, or other reasons. According to Christina Bethell, researchers feel confident that today's rising rates of formally diagnosed mental health disorders in girls are still an underestimate of mental health problems in girls. "We assess mental, emotional, and behavioral conditions in girls both based on reports of diagnoses as well as using our strongly validated consequences-based screening approach. This approach assesses if there are any ongoing mental, emotional, or behavioral problems that have [lasted] or are expected to last 12 months or longer and for which the child/youth experiences consequences either in functional imitations or need/use of routine services or need/use of treatment or counseling. We also look at symptoms of mental health problems and functioning in school and socially to validate identifying chronic mental health problems[,] even if a teen does not have a diagnosis."

page 9   **Recent studies that rely on these metrics show that, by age seventeen:** Breslau et al., "Sex Differences in Recent First-Onset Depression in an Epidemiological Sample of Adolescents," e1139; Ariana Eunjung Cha, "More Than a Third of Teenage Girls Experience Depression, New Study Says," *The Washington Post*, May 31, 2017. A study in the journal *Pediatrics* also found that the rate of girls reporting that they experienced at least one major depressive episode in the past year has increased over a recent nine-year period. Among girls ages twelve to seventeen, the rate of major depressive disorder increased from 13.1 percent to 17.3 percent between 2005 and 2014: Ramin Mojtabai, Mark Olfson, and Beth Han, "National Trends in the Prevalence and Treatment of Depression in Adolescents and Young Adults," *Pediatrics* 138, no. 6 (December 2016): e20161878.

page 9   **Every year, the gap between the rates at which girls and boys:** This data was prepared by Christina Bethell, Ph.D., using results from the 2016–20 National Survey of Children's Health. The NSCH is the source of depression diagnosis data for the Centers for Disease Control and Prevention.

page 9   **Between 2016 and 2020, girls were, on average:** Bethell, using data from the 2016–20 National Survey of Children's Health.

page 9   **The sense of day-to-day well-being that girls experience:** This data was prepared by Christina Bethell, Ph.D., and was derived from the 2015 Wisconsin Behavioral Risk Factor Survey.

page 10   **The gap between suicide rates in girls and boys is narrowing:** Phyllis L. Fagell, "Dealing with Disturbing Spike in Youth Suicides," *The Washington Post,* March 18, 2019; Ruch et al., "Trends in Suicide Among Youth Aged 10 to 19 Years in the United States, 1975 to 2016," e193886.

page 10   **In 2021, suicide attempts increased 51 percent:** Chiu, "ER Visits for Suspected Suicide Attempts Among Teenage Girls Rose During Pandemic"; E. Yard et al., "Emergency Department Visits for Suspected Suicide Attempts Among Persons Aged 12–25 Years," 888–94.

page 10   **According to a 2019 study in the *Journal of Abnormal Psychology,* although rates:** J. M. Twenge et al., "Age, Period, and Cohort Trends in Mood Disorder Indicators and Suicide-Related Outcomes in a Nationally Representative Dataset, 2005–2017," *Journal of Abnormal Psychology* 128, no. 3 (April 2019): 185–99.

page 11   **Roughly one-third of girls displayed:** C. S. Mott Children's Hospital, "How the Pandemic Has Impacted Teen Mental Health," p. 1.

Thirty-six percent of girls displayed new or worsening symptoms of anxiety during the pandemic compared with 19 percent of boys. Thirty-one percent of girls showed new or worsening signs of depression compared with 18 percent of boys.

page 11   **Emergency room visits for teen mental health crises rose 31 percent:** R. T. Leeb et al., "Mental Health–Related Emergency Department Visits Among Children <18 Years During the COVID-19 Pandemic—United States, January 1–October 17, 2020," *MMWR Morbidity and Mortality Weekly Report* 69, no. 45 (November 2020): 1675–80 (for details on sex differences, see Supplementary Figure 2). For further reading on similar findings, see Benedict Carey, "For Some Teens, It's Been a Year of Anxiety and Trips to the E.R.," *The New York Times,* February 23, 2021; R. M. Hill et al., "Suicide Ideation and Attempts in a Pediatric Emergency Department Before and During COVID-19," *Pediatrics* (December 2020): e2020029280.

page 11   **In additional analyses, researchers even pinpointed the specific year that teen girls' mental health:** Jean M. Twenge, coauthor of "Age, Period, and Cohort Trends in Mood Disorder Indicators and Suicide-Related Outcomes in a Nationally Representative Dataset, 2005–2017," in the *Journal of Abnormal Psychology,* expanded on this research in a recent op-ed: Jonathan Haidt and Jean M. Twenge, "This Is Our Chance to Pull Teenagers Out of the Smartphone Trap," *The New York Times,* July 31, 2021. Twenge and Haidt discovered that 2012 was the beginning of the period when social media use became ubiquitous among adolescents and by which major social media platforms had created mechanisms that were "more polarized and more likely to incite performative shaming." Similarly, this is the year Instagram grew significantly in popularity. Also see Twenge's excellent book *iGen: Why Today's Super-Connected Kids Are Growing Up Less Rebellious, More Tolerant, Less Happy—and Completely Unprepared for Adulthood* (New York: Atria, 2018).

page 11   **And yet it is only since 2016—when the National Institutes of Health asked that sex differences:** This understanding is based on my October 2020 interview with Marianne Seney, Ph.D., assistant professor in the Translational Neuroscience Program and Department of Psychiatry at the University of Pittsburgh, a leading researcher in the study of underlying sex differences in depression.

page 14   **According to a 2021 CDC study in *The Lancet*, by the summer of 2021:** S. D. Hillis et al., "Global Minimum Estimates of Children Affected by COVID-19-Associated Orphanhood and Deaths of Caregivers: A Modelling Study," *The Lancet* 398, no. 10298 (July 2021): 391–402. In the Americas (North, South, Central), more than three quarters of a million children had lost a parent or other caregiver (often a custodial or co-residing grandparent) due to the pandemic.

page 14   A Pew Research study recently found that that nearly 60 percent: Nikki Graf, "A Majority of U.S. Teens Fear a School Shooting Could Happen at Their School, and Most Parents Share Their Concern," Fact Tank, Pew Research Center, April 18, 2018, http://www.pewresearch.org/fact-tank/2018/04/18/a-majority-of-u-s-teens-fear-a-shooting-could-happen-at-their-school-and-most-parents-share-their-concern/.

page 15   Add to this the fact that 17 million children in the United States go to bed hungry: "The Impact of the Coronavirus on Food Insecurity in 2020," Feeding America, October 2020; AIR, *America's Youngest Outcasts: A Report Card on Child Homelessness,* American Institutes for Research, November 30, 2014.

page 15   Neuroscientists at the University of Colorado have demonstrated: M. D. Weber et al., "Stress Induces the Danger-Associated Molecular Pattern HMGB-1 in the Hippocampus of Male Sprague Dawley Rats: A Priming Stimulus of Microglia and the NLRP3 Inflammasome," *Journal of Neuroscience* 35, no. 1 (January 2015): 316–24.

Chapter Two: Is This a Toxic Era for Girls?

page 25   Research backs up Cogan's concerns: In 2017, thirty-two hospitals: G. Plemmons, "Trends in Suicidality and Serious Self-Harm for Children 5–17 Years at 32 U.S. Children's Hospitals, 2008–2015," paper presented at the Pediatric Academic Societies (PAS) Annual Meeting, San Francisco, May 7, 2017.

page 25   Today, given the COVID-19 crisis, teens' rates of anxiety, depression, and eating disorders: Therese Raphael, "Teens Are Suffering in Lockdown Isolation. Can Tech Help?" Bloomberg Opinion, February 6, 2021.

page 25   In one internal report, Facebook's own researchers: Georgia Wells, Jeff Horwitz, and Deepa Seetharaman, "Facebook Knows Instagram Is Toxic for Teen Girls, Company Documents Show," *The Wall Street Journal,* September 14, 2021, A1.

page 26   "We make body issues worse for . . .": Georgia Wells, Jeff Horwitz, and Deepa Seetharaman, "Facebook Knows Instagram Is Toxic for

Teen Girls, Company Documents Show," *The Wall Street Journal,* September 14, 2021, A10. Facebook is also aware that sex traffickers run ads on its apps, which trick girls into "jobs" that lead to their being sexually trafficked, but even when staff members flag criminals, the company often fails to act.

page 26   **Other data shows that the majority of children start:** "New Poll Reveals How Young Children Are Using Social Media and Messaging Apps," National PTA, December 4, 2017.

page 26   **Other controlled studies:** Y. Kelly et al., "Social Media Use and Adolescent Mental Health: Findings from the UK Millennium Cohort Study," *EClinicalMedicine* 6 (January 2019): 59–68.

page 26   **Twenge argues that social media induces "feelings of upward social comparison":** J. M. Twenge and G. N. Martin, "Gender Differences in Associations Between Digital Media Use and Psychological Well-Being: Evidence from Three Large Datasets," *Journal of Adolescence* 79 (February 2020): 91–102; M. N. Steers, R. E. Wickham, and L. K. Acitelli, "Seeing Everyone Else's Highlight Reels: How Facebook Usage Is Linked to Depressive Symptoms," *Journal of Social and Clinical Psychology* 33, no. 8 (October 2014): 701–31.

page 27   **They investigated why this turning point in female mental:** Jean Twenge's colleagues, psychologist Jonathan Haidt and technologist Tobias Rose-Stockwell, were the first to write about major social media platforms having changed in harmful ways between 2009 and 2012. For more on this, read Haidt and Twenge, "This Is Our Chance to Pull Teenagers Out of the Smartphone Trap"; see also Twenge, *iGen.*

page 27   **When teens see popular photos, the reward system in the brain:** L. E. Sherman et al., "The Power of the Like in Adolescence: Effects of Peer Influence on Neural and Behavioral Responses to Social Media," *Psychological Science* 27, no.7 (July 2016): 1027–35.

pages 27–28 **Other research shows the more an individual engages in behaviors that activate the brain's reward system:** Deborah Halber, "Motivation: Why You Do the Things You Do," BrainFacts.org, August 29, 2018.

page 28   **We do know that feeling socially excluded in adolescence, in general:** P. E. Gustafson et al., "Do Peer Relations in Adolescence Influence Health in Adulthood? Peer Problems in the School Setting and the Metabolic Syndrome in Middle Age," *PLOS One* 7, no. 6 (June 2012): e39385.

page 28   **Similarly, being excluded—or observing others being excluded:** G. Novembre et al., "Empathy for Social Exclusion Involves the Sensory-Discriminative Component of Pain: A Within-Subject fMRI Study," *Social Cognitive and Affective Neuroscience* 10, no. 2 (February 2015): 153–64.

page 28   **Or consider the Victoria's Secret Fashion Show craze:** Carey Goldberg, "Victoria Secret Models Got Thinner Over 23 Years of Fashion Show, Study Finds," *WBUR CommonHealth,* January 3, 2020.

page 29   **Every platform is a little different:** Georgia Wells, Jeff Horwitz, and Deepa Seetharaman, "Facebook Knows Instagram Is Toxic for Teen Girls, Company Documents Show," *The Wall Street Journal*, September 14, 2021.

page 30   **This world of façades exacts a cost: Youth who dwell:** A. E. Hamel et al., "Body-Related Social Comparison and Disordered Eating Among Adolescent Females with an Eating Disorder, Depressive Disorder, and Healthy Controls," *Nutrients* 4, no. 9 (September 2012), 1260–72. Also see: H. L. McBride and J. L. Kwee, "Inside and Out: How Western Patriarchal Cultural Contexts Shape Women's Relationships with Their Bodies," in *International Perspectives in Values-Based Mental Health Practice,* ed. D. Stoyanov et al. (New York: Springer, 2021), chap. 12. According to McBride (who specializes in trauma, female body image, sexuality, and eating disorders), for girls, eating disorders exist within a social context that places value on appearance, strict constructions of gender, and the implied threat of sexual violence. "A woman's relationship with her body is shaped by the broader sociocultural influences around her, which are evident in the context of personal relationships, organizations, and media." And all these influences express cultural values about women's bodies. "These broader influences can simultaneously feel both invisible and ubiquitous, and they play a significant role in a woman's experience of her physicality: whether she feels she can move freely through the world, enjoy her sexuality, feed herself, go places and know she is safe, dance and play with abandon, and see herself as a holistic agent being rather than as a sexualized object."

page 30   **As Twenge puts it, "Electronically mediated social interactions are like empty calories:** Haidt and Twenge, "This Is Our Chance to Pull Teenagers Out of the Smartphone Trap."

page 30   **(To rework a quote from philosopher):** Adorno's quote "The culture industry endlessly cheats its consumers of what it endlessly promises" appears in *Dialectic of Enlightenment,* Theodor W. Adorno and Max Horkheimer (Stanford: Stanford University Press, 2002), 111.

page 31   **Think of how the social media machine descended on Greta Thunberg, Hillary Clinton, Taylor Swift:** Laura Snapes, "Taylor Swift Discloses Fight with Eating Disorder in New Documentary," *The Guardian,* January 24, 2020.

page 32   **"What we are seeing—and bringing on ourselves":** Oliver Sacks, "The Machine Stops," *The New Yorker,* February 11, 2019.

page 33   **"gender discrimination is so prevalent in the field":** Arghavan Salles, "Sexual Harassment Is Still the Norm in Health Care," *Scientific American,* October 24, 2019.

page 34   **(Meanwhile, the pay gap between male and female doctors):** C. M. Whaley et al., "Female Physicians Earn an Estimated $2 Million Less Than Male Physicians Over a Simulated 40-Year Career," *Health Affairs* 40, no. 12 (December 2021): 1856–64.

page 34   **As Surgeon General Vivek Murthy, M.D., writes:** *Protecting Youth Mental Health: The U.S. Surgeon General's Advisory,* 2021, 3. https:// www.hhs.gov/sites/default/files/surgeon-general-youth-mental-health -advisory.pdf.

page 35   **But we don't really come together as a society anymore:** I first heard this idea articulated by CNN journalist Jim Acosta.

page 35   **Moreover, "a lot has flattened out across the internet":** Emily Nussbaum, @emilynussbaum, Twitter, February 7, 2021.

Chapter Three: The Missing Years

page 40   **Rates of perfectionism have increased in children:** T. Curran and A. P. Hill, "Perfectionism Is Increasing Over Time: A Meta-analysis of Birth Cohort Differences from 1989 to 2016," *Psychological Bulletin* 145, no. 4 (April 2019): 410–29.

page 40   **Researchers believe the top environmental forces disrupting adolescent wellness:** M. B. Geisz and M. Nakashian, "Adolescent Wellness: Current Perspectives and Future Opportunities in Research, Policy, and Practice," Robert Wood Johnson Foundation, July 1, 2018.

Chapter Four: Two Windows in Time When Early Stress Shapes a Child's Development

page 48   **What Bale has found, she tells me, leaning forward as she speaks:** T. L. Bale and C. N. Epperson, "Sex as a Biological Variable: Who, What, When, Why, and How," *Neuropsychopharmacology* 42, no. 2 (January 2017): 386–96; T. L. Bale and C. N. Epperson, "Sex Differences and Stress Across the Lifespan," *Nature Neuroscience* 18, no. 10 (October 2015): 1413–20.

page 48   **But to better understand why the female teenage body and brain:** We've long known that a mother's health during pregnancy can affect her child's lifelong health. If a mother has the flu during certain windows of pregnancy, that viral impact can make it more likely that her child will develop schizophrenia or autism. Similarly, babies who were conceived during historical periods of famine, and who therefore received poor nutrition in the womb, were more likely to have more health problems, and to be physically smaller, in adulthood. Babies born to mothers who encountered emotional stress during pregnancy are more likely to show a hypervigilant stress response after birth and have higher baseline levels of stress hormones compared with other children. In other words, a mother's health during pregnancy can dramatically affect her child's lifelong health. R. E. Kneeland and S. H. Fatemi, "Viral Infection, Inflammation and Schizophrenia," *Progress in Neuropsychopharmacology and Biological Psychiatry* 42 (April 5, 2013): 35–48; P. Dominguez-Salas et al., "Maternal Nutrition at Conception Modulates DNA Methylation of Human Metastable Epialleles," *Nature Communications* 5 (April 2014): 3746; Assad Meymandi, M.D., Ph.D., "The Science of Epigenetics," *Psychiatry* (Edgmont) 7, no 3 (March 2010): 40–41; A. Zietlow et al., "Emotional Stress During Pregnancy— Associations with Maternal Anxiety Disorders, Infant Cortisol Reactivity, and Mother-Child Interaction at Pre-school Age," *Frontiers in Psychology* 10 (September 2019): 2179; Z. M. Thayer et al., "Impact of Prenatal Stress on Offspring Glucocorticoid Levels: A Phylogenetic Meta-analysis Across 14 Vertebrate Species," *Scientific Reports* 8, no. 1 (March 2018): 4942.

page 50   **Different influences and events in your life can crank:** For a wonderful in-depth description of epigenetics and health, see the article by David Dobbs, "The Social Life of Genes," *Pacific Standard,* June 14, 2017.

page 50   **"Just as males have both an X and Y chromosome":** The placenta is built from baby cells and is genetically like the baby, including having the baby's sex chromosomes, so a placenta has a sex, as strange as that might seem. If you, as a baby, were biologically female, so was your placenta, which tethered you inside the womb.

page 51   **Bale has demonstrated in animal models that when a pregnant mother:** B. N. Nugent et al., "Placenta H3K27me3 Establishes Female Resilience to Prenatal Insults," *Nature Communications* 9, no. 1 (July 2018): 2555.

page 52   **And that is, in large part, because the female immune system:** Hormones are powerful chemicals that act as master regulators in practically every process in the human body and brain. Their role extends far beyond the process of sexual arousal and reproduction. Different parts of the body produce hormones that flow into the bloodstream and are carried throughout the body. The adrenal glands, which sit at the top of each of your kidneys, make adrenaline, which helps us react in split-second time to emergencies and triggers the nervous system to go into fight, flight, or freeze. The pancreas produces insulin. In males, testes make testosterone. And the ovaries, which become active in puberty, make estrogen, which is the name we give to a triplet of hormones: estradiol, estriol, and estrone. The lion's share of estrogen comes from the ovaries, but the adrenals and fat cells also produce small amounts. The ovaries produce progesterone, too, which serves to thicken the uterine lining and prepare it for receiving a fertilized egg each month, after ovulation. Once an embryo begins to grow, the placenta also produces progesterone, to help prevent the uterus walls from breaking down. The ovaries also make a little testosterone, which is responsible for much of the female libido. The process of puberty, however, begins in the brain.

page 56   **Early stress can lead to epigenetic changes in specific genes:** T. Klengel et al., "Allele-Specific FKBP5 DNA Demethylation Mediates Gene-Childhood Trauma Interactions," *Nature Neuroscience* 16, no. 1 (January 2013): 33–41; N. Weder et al., "Child Abuse, Depression and Methylation in Genes Involved with Stress, Neural Plasticity, and Brain Circuitry," *Journal of the American Academy of Child and Adolescent Psychiatry* 53, no. 4 (April 2014): 417–24, e5; G. Morris et al., "Socioeconomic Deprivation, Adverse Childhood Experiences and Medical Disorders in Adulthood: Mechanisms and Associations," *Molecular Neurobiology* 56, no. 8 (August 2019): 5866–90.

page 57   **However, this link among cortisol stress levels, epigenetic shifts:** R. S. Lee et al., "DNA Methylation and Sex-Specific Expression of

FKBP5 as Correlates of One-Month Bedtime Cortisol Levels in Healthy Individuals," *Psychoneuroendocrinology* 97 (November 2018): 164–73.

Chapter Five: The Power of Social Safety

page 62   **Not only do females give birth, but mothers provide breast milk:** My understanding of this is based on my conversations with George M. Slavich, Ph.D., professor in the Department of Psychiatry and Biobehavioral Sciences at the University of California, Los Angeles, and the director of the UCLA Laboratory for Stress Assessment and Research.

page 63   **Given the cascade of ill effects that could follow from even a small:** Patrick Soderberg and Douglas P. Fry, "Anthropological Aspects of Ostracism," in *Ostracism, Exclusion, and Rejection*, eds. Kipling D. Williams and Steve A. Nida (New York: Routledge, Taylor and Francis Group, 2017).

page 64   **Slavich, who is also the director of the UCLA's Laboratory for Stress Assessment and Research:** G. M. Slavich and S. W. Cole, "The Emerging Field of Human Social Genomics," *Clinical Psychological Science* 1, no. 3 (July 2013): 331–48; G. M. Slavich and M. R. Irwin, "From Stress to Inflammation and Major Depressive Disorder: A Social Signal Transduction Theory of Depression," *Psychological Bulletin* 140, no. 3 (May 2014): 774–815; G. M. Slavich, "Social Safety Theory: A Biologically Based Evolutionary Perspective on Life Stress, Health, and Behavior," *Annual Review of Clinical Psychology* 16 (May 2020): 265–95.

page 65   **But having this survival antennae also came with a price tag:** G. M. Slavich and J. Sacher, "Stress, Sex Hormones, Inflammation, and Major Depressive Disorder: Extending Social Signal Transduction Theory of Depression to Account for Sex Difference in Mood Disorders," *Psychopharmacology* 236, no. 10 (October 2019): 3063–79; G. M. Slavich et al., "Interpersonal Life Stress, Inflammation, and Depression in Adolescence: Testing Social Signal Transduction Theory of Depression," *Depression and Anxiety* 37, no. 2 (February 2020): 179–93.

page 66   **Teens who experience just a brief episode of social rejection:** A. S. Masten and J. K. Sapienza, "Understanding and Promoting Resilience in Children and Youth," *Current Opinion in Psychiatry* 24, no. 4 (July 2011): 267–73.

page 66   **She faced adversity in her home, her community:** According to the 2015–16 Civil Rights Data Collection on School Climate and Safety, which looked at data from more than 96,000 schools, 23 percent of bullying incidents involved race. 2015–16 Civil Rights Data Collection School Climate and Safety, U.S. Department of Education Office of Civil Rights, https://www2.ed.gov/about/offices/list/ocr/docs/school-climate-and -safety.pdf.

page 66n **As Wanjiku F. M. Njoroge, M.D., a child and adolescent psychiatrist:** W. F. M. Njoroge, M. Forkpa, E. Bath, "Impact of Racial Discrimination on the Mental Health of Minoritized Youth," *Current Psychiatry Reports* 23, no. 12 (October 2021): 81.

pages 66–67 **Even among children twelve and younger, Black children:** Joshua A. Gordon, M.D., Ph.D., *Addressing the Crisis of Black Youth Suicide,* Director's Messages, National Institute of Mental Health, September 22, 2020.

page 67 **Other research shows that during the past decade:** Christina Caron, "What's Going On with Our Black Girls? Experts Warn of Rising Suicide Rates," *The New York Times,* September 10, 2021.

page 67n **Although Njoroge and her co-authors urge us to "distinguish the various outcomes":** W. F. M. Njoroge, M. Forkpa, E. Bath, "Impact of Racial Discrimination on the Mental Health of Minoritized Youth," *Current Psychiatry Reports* 23, no. 12 (October 2021): 81; D. L. Bernard, et al., "Making the 'C-ACE' for a Culturally-Informed Adverse Experiences Framework to Understand the Pervasive Mental Health Impact of Racism on Black Youth," *Journal of Child & Adolescent Trauma* 14, no. 2 (August 2020): 233–47.

page 70 **Girls are also more likely to pump out increased production:** D. A. Bangasser, S. R. Eck, and E. O. Sanchez, "Sex Differences in Stress Reactivity in Arousal and Attention Systems," *Neuropsychopharmacology* 44, no. 1 (January 2019): 129–39. Additionally, in a 2021 review of the scientific literature, Harvard evolutionary biologists reported that females show a more robust immune response, react to social or physical threats with greater fear and concern than males, and, as a result, develop more "threat-based clinical conditions than males." J. F. Benenson et al., "Self-Protection as an Adaptive Female Strategy," *The Behavioral and Brain Sciences* (November 2021), online ahead of print, 1–86.

page 70 **Other data tell us that individuals with heightened levels of inflammatory:** R. Haapakoski et al., "Cumulative Meta-analysis of Interleukins 6 and IB, Tumour Necrosis Factor A and C-Reactive Protein in Patients with Major Depressive Disorder," *Brain, Behavior, and Immunity* 49 (October 2015): 206–15; M. S. Cepeda, P. Stang, and R. Makadia, "Depression Is Associated with High Levels of C-Reactive Protein and Low Levels of Fractional Exhaled Nitric Oxide: Results from the 2007–2012 National Health and Nutrition Examination Surveys," *Journal of Clinical Psychiatry* 77, no. 12 (December 2016): 1666–71; R. Hou et al., "Peripheral Inflammatory Cytokines and Immune Balance in Generalised Anxiety Disorder: Case-Controlled Study," *Brain, Behavior, and Immunity* 62 (May 2017): 212–18; H. Engler et al., "Selective Increase of Cerebrospinal Fluid IL-6 During Experimental Systemic Inflammation in Humans: Association with Depressive Symptoms," *Molecular Psychiatry* 22 (October 2017): 1448–54; C. L. Raison and A. H. Miller, "The Role of Inflammation in Depression: From Evolutionary Imperative to Modern Treatment Target," *Nature Reviews Immunology* 16 (December 2015): 22–34; M. B. Howren, D. M. Lamkin, and J. Suls, "Associations of Depression with C-Reactive Protein, IL-1, and IL-6: A Meta-analysis," *Psychosomatic Medicine* 71, no. 12 (February 2009): 171–86; Y. Dowlati et al., "A Meta-analysis of Cytokines in Major Depression," *Biological Psychiatry* 67 (March 2010): 446–57; Lisa Bain, Noam I. Keren, and Sheena M. Posey Norris, *Biomarkers of Neuroinflammation: Proceedings of a Workshop* (Washington, D.C.: National Academies Press, 2018), 25.

page 70   **To wit, children who at age ten show elevated levels:** G. M. Khandaker et al., "Association of Serum Interleukin 6 and C-Reactive Protein in Childhood with Depression and Psychosis in Young Adult Life: A Population-Based Longitudinal Study," *JAMA Psychiatry* 71, no. 10 (October 2014): 1121–28.

page 70   **Furthermore, females with higher inflammatory factors are three times:** Lisa Bain, Noam I. Keren, and Sheena M. Posey Norris, *Biomarkers of Neuroinflammation: Proceedings of a Workshop*, 34. Also of note: In patients with bipolar disorder, inflammatory biomarkers go up during periods when symptoms worsen and go down again when symptoms improve. E. Brietzke et al., "Comparison of Cytokine Levels in Depressed, Manic and Euthymic Patients with Bipolar Disorder," *Journal of Affective Disorders* 116, no. 3 (August 2009): 214–17; H. Yamamori et al., "Assessment of a Multi-assay Biological Diagnostic Test for Mood Disorders in a Japanese Population," *Neuroscience Letters* 26, no. 612 (January 2016): 167–71; F. Dickerson et al., "Immune Alterations in Acute Bipolar Depression," *Acta Psychiatrica Scandinavica* 132, no. 3 (September 2015): 204–10. Markers of physical inflammation have also been used to predict suicide attempts in patients suffering from suicidal ideation and depression. See F. Dickerson et al., "Suicide Attempts and Markers of Immune Response in Individuals with Serious Mental Illness," *Journal of Psychiatric Research* 87 (April 2017): 37–43; F. Dickerson et al., "The Association Between Immune Markers and Recent Suicide Attempts in Patients with Serious Mental Illness: A Pilot Study," *Psychiatry Research* 255 (September 2017): 8–12.

page 70 **Moreover, when individuals who faced adversity growing up encountered stressors:** K. J. Bourassa et al., "Linking Stressful Life Events and Chronic Inflammation Using suPAR (Soluble Urokinase Plasminogen Activator Receptor)," *Brain, Behavior, and Immunity* 97 (October 2021): 79–88.

page 71 **In a 2020 meta-analysis of the literature, psychiatrists:** E. T. C. Lippard and C. B. Nemeroff, "The Devastating Clinical Consequences of Child Abuse and Neglect: Increased Disease Vulnerability and Poor Treatment Response in Mood Disorders," *American Journal of Psychiatry* 177, no. 1 (January 2020): 20–36; Stephen M. Strakowski, "The 'Single Biggest Contributor' to Medical and Mental Illness," *Medscape*, January 24, 2020. See accompanying video in which study authors cite childhood adversity and life stress as "the single biggest contributor to risk for psychiatric and medical disorders, more than any other single gene, more than any other single factor." Indeed, "[i]f you look at the prevalence of childhood maltreatment or early life stress on mood disorders, you see rates as high as 50 to 60 percent." https://www.medscape.com/viewarticle/923389.

page 71 **Similarly, whereas 8 percent of men who have a history:** These numbers were prepared by Robert C. Whitaker, M.D., M.P.H., using data from the Longitudinal Survey of Midlife Development in the United States (MIDUS). The MIDUS surveys used the Composite International Diagnostic Interview—Short Form (CIDI–SF) scale to measure major depression, panic disorder, and generalized anxiety disorder in adult men and women.

Chapter Six: When the Pump Gets Primed

page 78 **She has found that for each category of toxic childhood stress:** D. Fairweather et al., "Cumulative Childhood Stress and Autoimmune Diseases in Adults," *Psychosomatic Medicine* 71, no. 2 (February 2009): 243–50.

page 80 **"Toxic social signals play out on the same networks in the brain:** M. D. Weber et al., "Stress Induces the Danger-Associated Molecular Pattern HMGB-1 in the Hippocampus of Male Sprague Dawley Rats," 316–24.

page 81   **When the brain clocks that there is scarcity:** G. Morris et al., "Socioeconomic Deprivation, Adverse Childhood Experiences and Medical Disorders in Adulthood: Mechanisms and Associations," *Molecular Neurobiology* 56, no. 8 (August 2019): 5866–90. This link between stress and physical health is borne out not just at the individual level, but at the level of populations: The chronic stress of poverty and racism has a profound effect on the well-being and health of individuals in entire communities. We might place the sociobiology of gendered social stress and sexism trauma alongside the sociobiology of racism trauma.

page 81   **A recent survey of 35,000 LGBTQ youth found that 75 percent:** The Trevor Project, *National Survey on LGBTQ Youth Mental Health 2021,* TheTrevorProject.org. Also see *The 2019 National School Climate Survey: The Experience of Lesbian, Gay, Bisexual, Transgender, and Queer Youth in Our Nation's Schools,* Executive Summary, A Report from GLSEN, www.glsen.org.

page 82   **This is probably why, during the COVID-19:** N. Dehingia and A. Raj, "Sex Differences in COVID-19 Case Fatality: Do We Know Enough?" *The Lancet Global Health* 9, no.1 (January 2021): E14–E15.

page 82   **(That said, "post-COVID," or "long-hauler," syndrome:** Aria Bendix, "Most Coronavirus Long-Haulers Are Women. That May Be Because They Mount a Stronger Immune Response to the Virus," *Insider,* March 11, 2021.

page 83   **And as we've seen, a growing body of research shows:** There is another pathway for switching on these genes, which DeLisa Fairweather is also investigating in her lab. This research examines how the body responds to environmental stressors found in "extracellular vesicles" from our cells' "energy centers" (aka our mitochondria) that signal we are under danger or threat. Our mitochondria communicate these danger signals through extracellular vesicles that travel to cells in our body, alerting systems and organs that a threat exists. Over time, environmental stressors erode the health of mitochondria, which are the powerhouses of cellular health and longevity. Fairweather hypothesizes that this is one more way in which toxic emotional stress leads to physical changes in health, and she is investigating this pathway as contributing to autoimmune diseases such as myocarditis.

page 84   **In one 2020 study, researchers gave twenty-four young adult women:** X. Zhong et al., "Childhood Maltreatment Experience Influences

Neural Response to Psychosocial Stress in Adults: An fMRI Study," *Frontiers in Psychology* 10 (January 2020): 2961.

page 84n   (**For more on exactly why hormonal changes can affect girls':** Thanks to estrogen, which elevates in puberty, girls have higher baseline levels of glucocorticoids (GCs), which include the stress hormone cortisol. This helps to protect a female by increasing her ability to fight toxins—at least this is true when the fight-flight-or-freeze response is working properly (turning on and off as needed versus being chronically stuck in the on position). A female's higher baseline levels of GCs help ensure a pregnant woman facing infection or injury won't miscarry; it helps keep an embryo safe. Elevated estrogen is also why females, in response to stress, toxins, or infections, generate more antibodies (inflammation) and autoantibodies (which are overly abundant in autoimmune disease). As males come into puberty, they have lower baseline levels of cortisol hormones compared with females. This means that when stressors occur, cortisol levels have to rise faster to help males regulate inflammation. In males, levels of GCs go up and down and up and down, hard and fast, in response to stressors. For females, however, a higher baseline level of GCs means the body is less able to regulate chronic inflammation. Levels go up and stay high if stressors keep coming—which further promotes the production of more antibodies and autoantibodies. Because the brain is an immune organ, this also affects brain health.

Chapter Seven: Too Much Too Soon

page 87   **Adolescence, however, refers to a specific age range:** S. M. Sawyer et al., "The Age of Adolescence," *The Lancet Child and Adolescent Health* 2, no.3 (March 2018): 223–28.

page 87   **And that's a problem, because this means:** In my discussions with neuroscientist Margaret McCarthy, Ph.D., I asked her, "Is there ever an instance when a brain that matures early to match the stressors in the environment might be beneficial or protective?" McCarthy explained that when we see early emotional "maturation" in girls (being highly responsible at an early age, what we might also term precociousness), we tend to equate this emotional maturation with "reproductive maturation," which is what puberty is. While it might be beneficial to have advanced intellectual maturation (good decision making, lack of impulsivity, the ability to plan), it is, she told me, "as near as we can tell, never good to have early reproductive maturation, or early puberty."

Additionally, trauma research shows us that when early emotional maturation occurs because a girl takes on a heightened role of responsibility in family life at a young age (due to parents' high expectations; the loss of a parent through divorce or death; or having a parent who is reactive or has a substance use or mental health disorder), it is a trauma in and of itself. Early emotional maturation often involves the caretaking of others' needs (parents or siblings) and not having a safe, stable, nurturing adult to turn to when a child is in need. This is often referred to by psychologists as "parentification," and it, too, is considered a form of adversity.

page 87   **In our anthropological history, females went through a prolonged:** According to Margaret McCarthy, Ph.D., although we often think that, long ago, girls got married and pregnant at thirteen, this was really not the norm. As best as historians can discern, marriage and childbirth occurred later, closer to age fifteen or sixteen.

page 90   **neuroscientists at the Grady Trauma Project:** E. C. Dunn et al., "Developmental Timing of Trauma Exposure and Emotion Dysregulation in Adulthood: Are There Sensitive Periods When Trauma Is Most Harmful?" *Journal of Affective Disorders* 277 (February 2018): 869–77. Study authors write: "Emotion dysregulation scores varied significantly across all covariates (Table 1), with women, middle aged individuals, and those with lower education, income, and employment status having higher emotion dysregulation scores."

page 90   **To begin with, a growing body of research suggests:** B. J. Ellis and M. Del Giudice, "Developmental Adaptation to Stress: An Evolutionary Perspective," *Annual Review of Psychology* 70 (January 2019): 111–39.

page 90   **In one study, researchers at the University of Pennsylvania showed:** C. L. McDermott et al., "Early Life Stress Is Associated with Earlier Emergence of Permanent Molars," *Proceedings of the National Academy of Sciences* 118, no. 24 (June 2021): eprint.

page 91   **Researchers at the University of Washington believe:** T. Reinehr and C. L. Roth, "Is There a Causal Relationship Between Obesity and Puberty?" *The Lancet Child and Adolescent Health* 3, no. 1 (January 2019): 44–54; S. Shalitin and G. Gat-Yablonski, "Associations of Obesity with Linear Growth and Puberty," *Hormone Research in Paediatrics* (June 2021): 1–17.

Chapter Eight: How the Hazards of Growing Up Female in Our Society Shape Girls' Brains over Time

page 97   **Her comments make me think of the words of Rebecca Traister:** Rebecca Traister, "Serena Williams and the Game That Can't Be Won (Yet)," "The Cut," September 9, 2018. Additionally, in work settings, when women speak up and negotiate for salary increases, they're more likely to be labeled as demanding or aggressive and less likely than men to receive the promotions or raises they seek. Financial podcast host Stefanie O'Connell Rodriguez calls the price exacted for female assertiveness an "ambition penalty." Meanwhile, women today earn eighty-two cents to a man's dollar and own even less wealth (home, car, savings account) compared with men (thirty-two cents to a man's dollar). For women of color, this discrepancy is more pronounced. It's a lose-lose proposition: Women who don't push for pay parity are blamed for lacking the confidence to pursue pay parity or promotions, and women who do are deemed demanding or aggressive. For more on this, see Stefanie O'Connell Rodriguez, "Stop Punishing Women for Being Ambitious," Bloomberg Opinion, May 24, 2021. Sports are also permeated with gender bias. Girls can excel on the field or court just like boys, but when they do, they're often treated as doing something less important than what male athletes do. In 2021, the U.S. men's basketball team was given a state-of-the-art gym for tournaments; the U.S. women's basketball team was given a single rack of dumbbells. David Leonhardt, "Massages for Men, Doubleheaders for Women," *The New York Times,* June 4, 2021.

page 97   **Smith spoke out on behalf of all women, saying:** Christine Hauser, "As Texas Abortion Law Nears, Opponent Amplify a Valedictorian's Speech," *The New York Times,* July 13, 2021.

page 98   **"Though you've never seen my body, you still judge it":** Laura Snapes, "'If I Shed the Layers, I Am a Slut': Billie Eilish Addresses Body Image Criticism," *The Guardian,* March 10, 2020.

page 98   **Orenstein underscores the danger of today's "incessant drumbeat of self-objectification":** Peggy Orenstein, *Girls & Sex: Navigating the Complicated New Landscape* (New York: Harper, 2016), 20–21, 162, 218.

page 99   **and that 22 percent of women who've faced three or more categories:** These numbers were prepared by Robert C. Whitaker, M.D., M.P.H., using data from the Midlife in the United States (MIDUS) Study (www.midus.wisc.edu/). The MIDUS surveys used the Composite International Diagnostic Interview—Short Form (CIDI–SF) scale to measure major depression, panic disorder, and generalized anxiety disorder in adult men and women.

page 100 **The fact that the risk is twice greater than the sum of the parts:** R. C. Whitaker et al., "The Interaction of Adverse Childhood Experiences and Gender-Sex as Risk Factors for Depression and Anxiety Disorders in US Adults: a Cross-Sectional Study," *BMC Public Health* 21, no. 1 (November 2021).

page 101 **Given the historical tendency to ascribe negative attributions to female biology:** This science could all too easily misdirect our attention and lead a male-dominated society to cite biology as a source of so much female suffering—as it has done so many times before and across hundreds of years. This includes the ancient Greek and Roman belief that female depression or anxiety (dubbed *hysteria,* a word originally derived from the Greek word for "uterus," *hystera*) was due to the uterus wandering throughout the body and causing irritation. If a woman didn't want to get married or have children, if she had sex outside marriage, or if she didn't want to sleep with her husband, her uterus was thought to be the problematic root of her bad behavior. Nineteenth-century Victorians used smelling salts, which were thought to help settle the uterus back into place, to cure these and other signs of "female hysteria." As late as the mid-nineteenth century, a husband could commit his spouse to an asylum for being a poor wife and mother, for being too intellectual or disobedient, or for expressing distaste for him. All it took was "the request of the husband." Justification for this was based on the belief that women who didn't adhere to the era's prescribed biological-based gender roles were "medically impaired," suffering from "uterine derangement," and "morally insane." Kate Moore, "Declared Insane for Speaking Up: The Dark American History of Silencing Women Through Psychiatry," *Time,* June 22, 2021.

page 102 **"Numerous studies show that women in the U.S.":** M. B. VanElzakker, "Posttraumatic Stress Disorder," in *Neuroscience in the 21st Century,* eds. D. W. Pfaff and N. D. Volkow (New York: Springer, 2015), 40–58.

page 103 **Girls begin to see from a very early age that the violence:** "Criminal Victimization in the United States, 2008 Statistical Tables," U.S. Department of Justice, March 2010. See Table 38: 77.6 percent of all offenders of crime are male and 19 percent are female. According to these results, men commit violent crimes more than three times as often as women.

When it comes to violence against women, estimates indicate nearly 1 in 3 women worldwide "have been subjected to either physical and/or sexual intimate partner violence or non-partner sexual violence in their lifetime." Twenty-seven percent of women aged fifteen to forty-nine years "who have been in a relationship report that they have been subjected to some form of physical and/or sexual violence by their intimate partner." "Violence Against Women," World Health Organization, March 9, 2021.

page 103 **A male police officer seems to commiserate:** "Gabby Petito & Brian Laundrie Utah Bodycam Footage Transcript Before Disappearance," Rev.com, September 19, 2021. https://www.rev.com/blog/transcripts /gabby-petito-brian-laundrie-utah-bodycam-footage-transcript-before -disappearance.

page 103 **Investigators ultimately concluded:** FBI Denver, "FBI Denver Provides Final Investigative Update on Gabrielle Petito Case," FBI.gov, January 21, 2022.

page 105 **"As researchers have started looking more closely at the female brain":** B. Labonté et al., "Sex-Specific Transcriptional Signatures in Human Depression," *Nature Medicine* 23, no. 9 (September 2017): 1102–11; M. L. Seney et al., "Opposite Molecular Signatures of Depression in Men and Women," *Biological Psychiatry* 84, no. 1 (July 2018): 18–27.

page 107 **On brain scans, both girls and boys who've faced emotional forms:** R. J. Herringa et al., "Childhood Maltreatment Is Associated with Altered Fear Circuitry and Increases Internalizing Symptoms by Late Adolescence," *Proceedings of the National Academy of Sciences of the United States of America* 110, no. 12 (December 2011): 1069–77. This is also based on my interviews with Ryan Herringa about his work, which I reported on in my previous book, *Childhood Disrupted: How Your Biography Becomes Your Biology* (New York: Atria Books, 2015), 104–105.

page 107 **Teens who show this pattern in brain connectivity:** At Yale, researchers used neuroimaging to compare the brains of adolescents with bipolar disorder to control groups of adolescents without bipolar symptoms. They followed participants' brain development over a two-and-a-half-year period. Although healthy adolescents showed significant increases in neural connectivity between the amygdala and the prefrontal cortex over time, no significant changes were observed over time in adolescents who went on to develop bipolar disorder; their brains were wired differently, without the same robust connections in areas crucial to regulating feelings and emotions. In other words, the prefrontal cortex, the part of the brain that helps regulate behavior, was not connecting properly to the fear part of the brain. J. Weathers et al., "Longitudinal Diffusion Tensor Imaging Study of Adolescents and Young Adults with Bipolar Disorder," *Journal of the American Academy of Child and Adolescent Psychiatry* 57, no. 2 (February 2018): 111–17.

page 107 **Adolescents who've experienced chronic early life stress:** M. Zeev-Wolf et al., "Chronic Early Stress Impairs Default Mode Network Connectivity in Preadolescents and Their Mothers," *Biological Psychiatry* 4, no. 1 (January 2019): 72–80.

page 107 **When the core network in the DMN is altered or disrupted:** S. Zhang et al., "Association Between Abnormal Default Mode Network Activity and Suicidality in Depressed Adolescents," *BMC Psychiatry* 16, no. 1 (September 2016): 337. This understanding is also based on recent emails with Ruth Lanius, M.D., Ph.D., professor of psychiatry and director of the PTSD research unit at the University of Western Ontario, Canada.

page 108 **In the aftermath of trauma, such shifts in one's ability to access:** R. A. Lanius et al., "The Sense of Self in the Aftermath of Trauma: Lessons from the Default Mode Network in Posttraumatic Stress Disorder," *European Journal of Psychotraumatology* 11, no. 1 (October 2020): 1807703.

page 108 **In response to stressful interactions that involve possible reward or punishment:** K. M. Dumais et al., "Sex Differences in Default Mode and Dorsal Attention Network Engagement," *PLOS One* 13, no. 6 (June 2018): e0199049.

page 109 **Although brain scans of teenage boys and girls experiencing symptoms of persistent anxiety:** A. N. Kaczkurkin et al., "Elevated Amygdala Perfusion Mediates Developmental Sex Difference in Trait Anxiety," *Biological Psychiatry* 80, no. 10 (November 2016): 775–85.

page 110 **It not only deeply distracts the ruminator from the present moment:** Benedict Carey, "Susan Nolen-Hoeksema, Psychologist Who Studied Depression in Women, Dies at 53," *The New York Times,* January 13, 2013.

Chapter Nine: The Building Blocks of Good Parent–Child Connection and the Importance of Family Resilience

page 118   **And yet these brief moments during which mother and child fell out:** For more on this, see Ed Tronick and Claudia M. Gold, *The Power of Discord: Why the Ups and Downs of Relationships Are the Secret to Building Intimacy, Resilience, and Trust* (New York: Spark/Little, Brown, 2020).

page 118   **In this in-sync state, nonverbal behaviors like eye contact:** A. Garner and M. Yogman, "Preventing Childhood Toxic Stress: Partnering with Families and Communities to Promote Relational Health," *American Academy of Pediatrics* 148, no. 2 (August 2021): e2021052582.

page 119   **For instance, within moments of their being held by their mother:** S. F. Waters, T. V. West, and W. B. Mendes, "Stress Contagion: Physiological Covariation Between Mothers and Infants," *Psychological Science* 25, no. 4 (April 2014): 934–42.

page 120   **We can see the impact of maternal stress on an infant's:** L. J. Pierce et al., "Association of Perceived Maternal Stress During the Perinatal Period with Electroencephalography Patterns in 2-Month-Old Infants," *JAMA Pediatrics* 173, no. 6 (June 2019): 561–70.

page 120   **Even when parents are arguing while their baby is asleep:** A. M. Graham, P. A. Fisher, and J. H. Pfeifer, "What Sleeping Babies Hear: A Functional MRI Study of Interparental Conflict and Infants' Emotion Processing," *Psychological Science* 24, no. 5 (May 2013): 782–99.

page 121   **Two-thirds of adults report having faced at least one category of adverse childhood:** V. J. Felitti and R. F. Anda, "The Relationships of Adverse Childhood Experiences to Adult Medical Disease, Psychiatric Disorders, and Sexual Behavior: Implications for Healthcare," in *The Effects of Early Life Trauma on Health and Disease: The Hidden Epidemic*, eds. R. Lanius, E. Vermetten, and C. Pain (New York: Cambridge University Press, 2010), 77; V. J. Felitti and R. F. Anda, "The Lifelong Effects of Adverse Childhood Experiences," in *Child Maltreatment: Sexual Abuse and Psychological Maltreatment*, vol. 2, eds. D. L. Chadwick et al. (St. Louis, Mo.: STM Learning, 2014), 203–15.

page 122   **Millions of interactive moments in which an adult helps a child stay calm:** For more on this, see Tronick and Gold, *The Power of Discord,* 137–40. These quotes are also based on my email conversations with Ed Tronick.

page 122   **As Gabor Maté, M.D., author of *In the Realm of Hungry Ghosts*, writes:** Maté makes this point in his book *In the Realm of Hungry Ghosts: Close Encounters with Addiction* (New York: North Atlantic Books, 2010), 249.

page 125   ***I have poor shock absorbers, and I should just let it pass*:** Krista Tippett, "Rachel Yehuda: How Trauma and Resilience Cross Generations," *On Being with Krista Tippett,* November 9, 2017.

page 126   **Or imagine, in the second scenario, that your own mother or father:** National Sexual Violence Resource Center, "Sexual Violence by Any Perpetrator," nsvrc.org. Nearly one in five women (18.3 percent) reported being raped, and 13 percent of women report having experience sexual coercion (unwanted sexual penetration after being pressured). Taken together, nearly one in three women have experienced rape or unwanted sexual intercourse.

page 129   **In perusing three decades of data, they found that adolescents:** S. S. Luthar, N. Kumar, and N. Zillmer, "High Achieving Schools Connote Risks for Adolescents: Problems Documented, Processes Implicated, and Directions for Interventions," *American Psychologist* 75, no. 7 (October 2020): 983–95; Emily Esfahani Smith, "Teenagers Are Struggling, and It's Not Just Lockdown," *The New York Times*, May 4, 2021.

page 129   **In the spring of 2020, early in the pandemic:** Ibid.

page 129   **Stanford researchers surveyed ten thousand kids:** These findings come from a survey conducted by NBC News and Challenge Success, a nonprofit affiliated with the Stanford Graduate School of Education. The 2020 report, *Kids Under Pressure,* is available at ChallengeSuccess.org. Emily Esfahani Smith, ibid.

page 130   **"That takes a lot of effort, and it's a wonderful quality":** For more on ideas on how to talk to children in nonevaluative language, see Chick Moorman's classic book *Parent Talk: How to Talk to Your Children in Language that Builds Self-Esteem and Encourages Responsibility* (New York: Simon & Schuster, 1998).

page 131   **The adolescent brain is wired to be hypervigilant:** Melanie A. Gold and Ronald E. Dahl, "Using Motivational Interviewing to Facilitate Healthier Sleep-Related Behaviors in Adolescents," in *Behavioral Treatments for Sleep Disorders,* eds. Michael Perlis, Mark Aolia, and Brett Kuhn (Amsterdam: Academic Press, 2011), chap. 38, pp. 367–80.

page 132   **Stated another way, psychological safety is the interior belief:** The term *psychological safety* was first coined, to the best of my knowledge, by Harvard Business School professor Amy Edmondson.

page 132   **If your daughter breaks a favorite glass while pouring orange juice:** For more on this, see Erik Vance's excellent piece "The Secret to Raising a Resilient Kid," *The New York Times,* September 1, 2021.

page 132   **Parents who respond to parent-child conflict with mindfulness:** C. C. Turpyn and M. M. Chaplin, "Mindful Parenting and Parents' Emotion Expression: Effects on Adolescent Risk Behaviors," *Mindfulness* 7, no. 1 (February 2016): 246–54.

page 132   **Similarly, teens whose parents practice mindful parenting:** J. Parent et al., "The Association of Parent Mindfulness with Parenting and Youth Psychopathology Across Three Developmental Stages," *Journal of Abnormal Child Psychology* 44, no. 1 (January 2016): 191–202.

page 136   **This remained true for those children who faced adverse childhood experiences:** C. D. Bethell, N. Gombojav, and R. C. Whitaker, "Family Resilience and Connection Promote Flourishing Among US Children, Even Amid Adversity," *Health Affairs* 38, no. 5 (May 2019): 729–37. Researcher Robert C. Whitaker has investigated the link between family connection and lifelong thriving by looking at adult populations rather than asking parents about their children's well-being. He surveyed more than four thousand adults between the ages of twenty-five and seventy-four. Asking them about the levels of family connection they recalled experiencing growing up, they found that adults who reported having experienced high levels of childhood family connection growing up also had higher levels of flourishing in adulthood. This remained true even for individuals who faced early adversity growing up and for those who faced socioeconomic hardship. By assessing adults' experiences, researchers were able to show that "positive experiences in childhood don't just lead to the absence of poor outcomes or surviving; family connection in childhood actually promotes thriving in adults decades later." There are exceptions, of course: people who thrive and achieve in adulthood despite a childhood spent feeling very little sense of family connection. But, in general, the links between a sense of connection in childhood and a satisfying and emotionally stable adulthood are powerful. In this study, those who suffered from two to three categories of ACEs and who scored between zero and one on the Family Resilience and Connection Index (meaning they grew up in a family in which they experienced one or zero categories of family connection) had a "flourishing score" of 17 percent. Those who also suffered from two or three categories of ACEs growing up, and yet who scored between four and six on the Family Resilience and Connection Index, had a flourishing score of 41 percent. R. C. Whitaker, T. Dearth-Wesley, and A. Herman, "Childhood Family Connection and Adult Flourishing: Associations Across Levels of Childhood Adversity," *Academic Pediatrics* (March 2021): s1876–2859. In another study, of four hundred young adults, researchers found that this association between family connection and flourishing held true even for children who grew up navigating the significant challenge of managing a chronic health disorder that begins in childhood: in this case, Type 1 diabetes. Chronically ill children whose families provided the sense of being safely seen and valued that comes with connectedness did better than those whose families did not provide this sense. R. C. Whitaker et al., "Association of Childhood Family Connection with Flourishing in Young Adulthood Among Those with Type 1 Diabetes," *JAMA Network Open* 3, no. 3 (March 2020): e200427.

page 136   **Lower levels of these factors are, in turn, linked to a decreased likelihood:** S. Angie Guan et al., "Parental Support Buffers the Association of Depressive Symptoms with Cortisol and C-Reactive Protein During Adolescence," *Brain, Behavior, and Immunity* 57 (October 2016): 134–43; G. M. Khandaker et al., "Association of Serum Interleukin 6 and C-Reactive Protein in Childhood with Depression and Psychosis in Young Life: A Population-Based Longitudinal Study," *JAMA Psychiatry* 71, no. 10 (October 2014): 1121–28.

pages 136–37 **Other studies from the field of neuroscience show that teens:** Y. Qu et al., "Buffering Effect of Positive Parent-Child Relationships on Adolescent Risk Taking: A Longitudinal Neuroimaging Investigation," *Developmental Cognitive Neuroscience* 15 (October 2015): 26–34.

page 138   **These young women were also more likely to resist:** Hillary L. McBride and Janelle L. Kwee, "Intergenerational Journeys," in *Embodiment and Eating Disorders: Theory, Research, Prevention, and Treatment*, eds. Hillary L. McBride and Janelle L. Kwee (New York: Routledge, 2018), 159–69. These quotes are also based on my email conversations with McBride.

page 138   **According to a study led by Bethell, females are less likely:** These figures were prepared by Christina Bethell, Ph.D., director, Child and Adolescent Health Measurement Initiative, and professor at Johns Hopkins Bloomberg School of Public Health, using 2015 data from the Centers for Disease Control's Behavioral Risk Factor Surveillance System.

Chapter Ten: Make Her Home Her Safe Space

page 140 **Polyvagal theory holds that when we draw upon the power:** Stephen W. Porges, *The Pocket Guide to The Polyvagal Theory: The Transformative Power of Feeling Safe* (New York: W. W. Norton, 2017), 5, 6, 9, 48–51; E. S. Susman et al., "High Vagal Tone and Rapid Extinction Learning as Potential Transdiagnostic Protective Factors Following Childhood Violence Exposure," *Developmental Psychobiology* 63, no. 6 (August 2021): e22176.

page 141 **We might think of a child's family as a kind of convoy:** T. C. Antonucci, K. J. Ajrouch, and K. S. Birditt, "The Convoy Model: Explaining Social Relations from a Multidisciplinary Perspective," *Gerontologist* 54, no. 1 (February 2014): 82–92.

page 143 **This is why children so often stay silent about their deepest worries:** J. Berryman, *The Spiritual Guidance of Children: Montessori, Godly Play, and the Future* (Harrisburg, PA: Morehouse Publishing, 2013), 111. Jerome Berryman, director of the Center for the Theology of Childhood, writes that when we don't listen to children's and teens' fears and worries, particularly when it ties into their deeper existential concerns about loneliness or death and the meaning of life, it "traps children in a double bind. They must either please the adults and repress their anxiety or express their anxiety and risk having adults ignore, dismiss, and shame them." Berryman said this in reference to the core existential concerns of loneliness, death, meaning, and freedom that face all humans, and he argued that when we do not allow these worries and concerns to be voiced, they can become more difficult to manage.

page 146 **Set the stage for your conversation with something like:** For more, I recommend the website CommonSenseMedia and its guide "How to Talk to Kids About Difficult Subjects."

page 146 **Conversely, when we talk to attentive listeners:** Kate Murphy, "Talk Less. Listen More. Here's How," *The New York Times,* January 9, 2020.

page 146 **Research shows that the more specific we are in naming difficult emotions:** J. D. Cresswell et al., "Neural Correlates of Dispositional Mindfulness During Affect Labeling," *Psychosomatic Medicine* 69, no. 6 (July–August 2007), 560–65; L. J. Burklund et al., "The Common and Distinct Neural Bases of Affect Labeling and Reappraisal in Healthy Adults," *Frontiers in Psychology* 5 (March 2014): 221.

page 147   **A good response I've used is:** This response is taught by psychiatrist Xavier Amador, M.D., author of *I Am Not Sick, I Don't Need Help! How to Help Someone with Mental Illness Accept Treatment,* 20th Anniversary Edition (Salt Lake City: Vida Press, 2020), 121.

page 147   **If she doesn't ask for advice:** Gold and Dahl, "Using Motivational Interviewing to Facilitate Healthier Sleep-Related Behaviors in Adolescents."

page 147   **You can further ensure that your daughter feels respected:** Ibid.

page 148   **The most important thing to do if you make a mistake:** This concept of "make a mistake, make a repair" comes from the work of Dan Siegel, M.D. To learn more about his science-informed approach to parenting, see Daniel J. Siegel and Tina Payne Bryson, *The Power of Showing Up: How Parental Presence Shapes Who Our Kids Become and How Their Brains Get Wired* (New York: Ballantine Books, 2020).

page 150   **The sooner you make a repair, the less likely:** Daniel J. Siegel, M.D., *Brainstorm* (New York: TarcherPerigee, 2014), 212–15; Donna Jackson Nakazawa, *Childhood Disrupted* (New York: Atria, 2015), 212; D. Schiller et al., "Preventing the Return of Fear in Humans Using Reconsolidation Update Mechanisms," *Nature* 63, no. 7277 (January 7, 2010): 49–53.

page 151   **As therapist Nedra Tawwab writes:** Nedra Tawwab posted this idea on Instagram on February 18, 2022.

page 154   **Studies show that nearly 95 percent of parents of anxious children:** For more on this, see Kate Julian's article "What Happened to American Childhood," *The Atlantic* (May 2020).

page 155   **But there is another reason that parents remove even small hurdles:** For more on this, see Kate Julian, "What Happened to American Childhood," *The Atlantic* (May 2020) and William Stixrud and Ned Johnson, *The Self-Driven Child* (New York: Viking, 2018).

page 158   **Alison Gopnik, Ph.D., professor of psychology and philosophy:** Ezra Klein, "Ezra Klein Interviews Alison Gopnik," *The Ezra Klein Show,* April 16, 2021. This is also based on my email exchanges with Gopnik. For more on this, see Gopnik's book *The Philosophical Baby* (New York: Farrar, Straus and Giroux, 2009).

page 159   **Relational awareness involves self-awareness:** The original use of the term *relational awareness* comes from the work of Rebecca Nye, based on her qualitative research in the mid-nineties with British school-age children. She uses it to describe the four key relationships in children's consciousness: our relationship to self, others, nature, and something larger than ourselves (spirituality or God).

page 160   **Over time, children internalize this deep sense of awareness:** Robert C. Whitaker offered two of these examples to me.

page 163   **All this underscores the need to ensure that by the time your daughter:** I highly recommend the website CommonSenseMedia, which offers ideas on how to have these discussions. See commonsensemedia.org for more advice on "How to Talk to Kids About Difficult Subjects."

page 169   **(Although that's almost always a good idea):** R. A. Dore, K. M. Purtell, and L. M. Justice, "Media Use Among Kindergarteners from Low-Income Households During the COVID-19 Shutdown," *Journal of Developmental Behavior and Pediatrics* (April 2021), online ahead of print.

page 170   **To wit: We know from Facebook's own internal research:** Georgia Wells, Jeff Horwitz, and Deepa Seetharaman, "Facebook Knows Instagram Is Toxic for Teen Girls, Company Documents Show," *The Wall Street Journal*, September 14, 2021.

page 171   **They found that worsening trends in young people's emotional suffering:** To read more about this, see Sarah Ketchen Lipson, "Depression, Anxiety, Loneliness Are Peaking in College Students," The Brink, February 17, 2021. For the full report, see D. Eisenberg, S. K. Lipson, and J. Heinze, *The Healthy Minds Study,* The Healthy Minds Network, Fall 2020.

page 172   **Other factors—including income equality:** Jonathan Haidt and Jean M. Twenge, "This Is Our Chance to Pull Teenagers Out of the Smartphone Trap," *The New York Times*, July 31, 2021.

Chapter Eleven: Bring in What the Wider Community Can Provide

page 174   **And this can, in turn, influence their well-being:** J. Herzog et al., "The Association Between Secondary Trauma and Mental Health Outcomes Among Adolescents: Findings from a Nationally Representative Cross-Sectional Survey," *Traumatology* 22, no. 4 (2016): 307–13.

page 177   **She examined seven different types of PCEs:** C. Bethell et al., "Positive Childhood Experiences and Adult Mental and Relationship Health in a Statewide Sample," *JAMA Pediatrics* 173, no. 11 (September 2019): e193007.

page 178   **"Even for those reporting three to five PCEs, the odds":** This quote is based on my interview with Christina Bethell. She also shared this thought in the article: "For Better Adult Mental and Relational Health, Boost Positive Childhood Experiences," Johns Hopkins Bloomberg School of Public Health, September 9, 2019.

page 178   **Bethell tells me something else that surprises me:** Ibid.

page 179   **University of Toronto researchers recently examined:** G. L. Flett et al., "Antecedents, Correlates, and Consequences of Feeling Like You Don't Matter: Associations with Maltreatment, Loneliness, Social Anxiety, and the Five-Factor Model," *Personality and Individual Differences* 92 (December 2015): 52–56.

page 179   **"However you get to a lack of feeling [that] you matter:** This also plays out in the well-being of pregnant mothers. In one study, researchers looked at the role of benevolent childhood experiences as protective factors for well-being in adulthood, even when there was childhood adversity, in women who were expecting. They asked pregnant mothers ten questions about positive experiences in childhood: "Did you have at least one caregiver with whom you felt safe? Did you have at least one good friend? Did you have beliefs that gave you comfort? Did you like school? Did you have at least one teacher who cared about you? Did you have good neighbors? Was there an adult (not a parent/caregiver or the person from question number one) who could provide you with support or advice? Did you have opportunities to have a good time? Did you like yourself or feel comfortable with yourself? Did you have a predictable home routine, like regular meals and a regular bedtime?" They found that higher levels of benevolent childhood experiences turned out to offset the long-term effects of traumatic stress and adverse childhood experiences among pregnant women as these women prepared to become new parents. And this, in turn, decreased PTSD, symptoms of depression, and feelings of distress when these same women were exposed to stressful life events during pregnancy. A. J. Narayan et al., "Positive Childhood Experiences Predict Less Psychopathology and Stress in Pregnant Women with Childhood Adversity: A Pilot Study of the Benevolent Childhood Experiences (BCEs) Scale," *Childhood Abuse and Neglect* 78 (April 2018): 19–30.

page 180   **And yet, too many young people, Starrs believes:** Bronagh Starrs, *Adolescent Psychotherapy: A Radical Relational Approach* (New York: Routledge, 2019), 15–16, 65.

page 183   **This is, of course, a completely unrealistic standard:** One note here: When we talk about female avatars, we are, in a way, talking about the power of the eternal feminine. By feminine, I do not mean gender. I mean the principles embodied by the feminine: to relate to others with compassion, to care about feeling connected to the people in our lives and the well-being of "the other," and to do so while still having compassion for oneself (versus giving while sacrificing one's own needs). This feminine presence of being is far too often suppressed in all of us, regardless of gender. For more on the power of the feminine, read this excellent piece by senior lecturer and cofounder of the Presencing Institute at MIT, Otto Scharmer, "On the Healing Power of Feminine Creativity: 5 Things My Mother Taught Me Through Her Life," *Medium*, November 22, 2020.

page 186   **"So how we behave towards one another, individually:** Krista Tippett, "Rachel Yehuda: How Trauma and Resilience Cross Generations," *On Being with Krista Tippett*, November 9, 2017.

page 186   **This includes supporting grassroots leaders who provide education:** For more, see https://www.obama.org/girlsopportunityalliance/stories /hays-story/.

page 188   **Reputation becomes much more important:** Jill Suttie, "What Adolescents Really Need from Parents," *Greater Good Magazine,* May 25, 2016.

page 188   **Deborah Tannen, Ph.D., professor of linguistics:** Deborah Tannen, Ph.D., *You're the Only One I Can Tell: Inside the Language of Female Friendships* (New York: Ballantine, 2017), 12, 126.

page 189   **This period of life can be rife with difficulty:** Ibid., 148.

page 189   **Indeed, recent studies show that adolescents are more likely to be bullied:** R. Faris, D. Felmlee, and C. McMillan, "With Friends Like These: Aggression from Amity and Equivalence," *American Journal of Sociology* 126, no. 3 (2020): 673–713.

page 189   **They found that middle-schoolers subjected to hurtful words:** M. H. Teicher et al., "Hurtful Words: Exposure to Peer Verbal Aggression Is Associated with Elevated Psychiatric Symptom Scores and Corpus Callosum Abnormalities," *American Journal of Psychiatry* 167, no. 12 (December 2010): 1464–71.

page 191   **She's found that children who have a positive relationship with spirituality:** Lisa Miller, *The Spiritual Child: The New Science of Parenting* *for Health and Lifelong Thriving* (New York: Picador, 2016), 169. Also see: "What Does It Mean to Raise a Spiritual Child?" WBUR Here & Now, October 1, 2015.

page 192   In one study of 615 adolescents from a wide range of socioeconomic: L. Miller and A. Desrosiers, "Relational Spirituality and Depression in Adolescent Girls," *Journal of Clinical Psychology* 63, no. 10 (September 2001): 1021–37.

page 192   Whether they were involved in gardening or had an everyday spiritual practice: This is based on my email conversations with Hillary McBride as well as on her book, McBride and Kwee, *Embodiment and Eating Disorders*.

page 192   Researchers at the University of Georgia and the University of California, San Francisco: B. W. Haas, F. Hoeft, and K. Omura, "The Role of Culture on the Link Between Worldviews on Nature and Psychological Health During the COVID-19 Pandemic," *Personality and Individual Differences* 170 (February 2021): 110336.

page 192   One study looked at the mental health of six hundred teens between the ages of ten: S. B. Jackson et al., "Outdoor Activity Participation Improves Adolescents' Mental Health and Well-Being During the COVID-19 Pandemic," *International Journal of Environmental Research and Public Health* 18, no. 5 (March 2021): 2506.

page 193   This is likely why so many college orientation programs: One recent study of Head Start teachers working with young children in underserved populations found that teachers who reported higher levels of spirituality had dramatically lower rates of depression. Depression rates among teachers with the highest levels of spirituality were half that of teachers who reported the lowest levels of spirituality. This was true even for those who had faced high levels of adversity as children. R. C. Whitaker, T. Dearth-Wesley, and A. N. Herman, "The Association of Daily Spiritual Experiences with Depression Among Head Start Staff," *Early Childhood Research Quarterly* 56, no. 3 (2021): 65–77.

page 196   "Therapy with her has been one of the most positive experiences": We know that when we do introduce therapeutic interventions, therapy is more likely to succeed when it happens in the context of an ongoing, caring, meaningful relationship with a therapist. In one suicide prevention outpatient program, therapists used talk therapy, as any therapist would, but also wrote periodic "caring letters" to the patient for two years to help build a strong bond. This intervention decreased suicide attempts in youth by two-thirds, compared with control groups. Michelle Andrews, "Why Does the State of New York Have the Nation's Lowest Suicide Rate?" *The Washington Post,* February 4, 2020.

page 196 **At UCLA, George Slavich recently did a meta-analysis:** G. S. Shields, C. M. Spahr, and G. M. Slavich, "Psychosocial Interventions and Immune System Function: A Systematic Review and Meta-analysis of Randomized Clinical Trials," *JAMA Psychiatry* 77, no. 10 (October 2020): 1031–43.

page 196 **Other studies show that therapy changes gene expression:** J. P. Jimenez et al., "Psychotherapy and Genetic Neuroscience: An Emerging Dialog," *Frontiers in Genetics* 9 (July 2018): 257.

page 196 **"If we're saying that environmental circumstances":** Tippett, "Rachel Yehuda: How Trauma and Resilience Cross Generations."

page 197 **Even though the average age for the onset of symptoms of mental health disorders:** M. Solmi et al., "Age at Onset of Mental Disorders Worldwide: Large-Scale Meta-analysis of 192 Epidemiological Studies," *Molecular Psychiatry* (June 2021), online ahead of print.

page 197 **To do better requires that our government, medical system:** A. Garner and M. Yogman, "Preventing Childhood Toxic Stress: Partnering with Families and Communities to Promote Relational Health," *American Academy of Pediatrics* 148, no. 2 (August 2021): e2021052582.

page 198 **And yet two-thirds of these same parents admitted it was difficult:** C. S. Mott Children's Hospital, "Recognizing Youth Depression at Home and School," *Mott Poll Report* 35, no. 2 (November 2019): 1.

page 198 **Other studies have found that half of parents are unaware:** J. D. Jones, R. C. Boyd, M. E. Calkins, et al., "Parent-Adolescent Agreement About Adolescents' Suicidal Thoughts," *Pediatrics* 143, no. 2 (February 2019), e20181771.

page 198 **Meanwhile, we have good evidence that when you do intervene:** For a review of the literature on how targeted interventions that include cognitive behavioral therapy can help improve mental health in youth, see the Colorado Health Foundation's rapid evidence review, "What Interventions Help Teens and Young Adults Prevent and Manage Behavioral Health Challenges?" *Academy Health,* January 2018.

page 198 **Short-term psychoanalytical therapy (thirty weeks):** I. M. Goodyer et al., "Cognitive Behavioural Therapy and Short-Term Psychoanalytical Psychotherapy Versus a Brief Psychosocial Intervention in Adolescents with Unipolar Major Depressive Disorder (IMPACT): A Multicentre, Pragmatic, Observer-Blind, Randomised Controlled Superiority Trial," *Lancet Psychiatry* 4, no. 2 (February 2017): 109–19.

page 199 **Yoga, meditation, and breathing exercises:** D. I. Lurie, "An Integrative Approach to Neuroinflammation in Psychiatric Disorders and Neuropathic Pain," *Journal of Experimental Neuroscience* 12 (August 2018): eCollection.

page 199 **They found that techniques such as mindfulness, meditation, and conscious breathing increased:** J. van Agteren et al., "A Systematic Review and Meta-analysis of Psychological Interventions to Improve Mental Wellbeing," *Nature Human Behavior* 5, no. 5 (May 2021): 631–52.

page 199 **Even short periods of meditation have been found to help reverse negative, stress-induced:** R. Chaix et al., "Differential DNA Methylation in Experienced Meditators After an Intensive Day of Mindfulness-Based Practice: Implications for Immune-Related Pathways," *Brain, Behavior, and Immunity* 84 (February 2020): 36–44.

page 201 **These screening tools have identified students who were struggling:** John Thomas Flynn, "Pennsylvania Adopting Data Analytics Strategy to Prevent Student Suicides," Federal News Network, November 8, 2018.

page 201 **In an ideal world, we would have enough school counselors:** There are simply not enough school counselors in the United States. Only one in five high-schoolers attends a school with the recommended number of staff counselors. And roughly eight million children, or one in five students, do not have access to a counselor in their school at all. This is especially common among students of color in low-income communities. For these and other statistics on the shortage of counselors in American schools, see schoolcounselor.org and its 2019 report, *School Counselors Matter.*

page 202 **At a three-month follow-up in a pilot program, researchers found that students who had completed the CALM program:** G. S. Ginsburg et al., "A Pilot RCT of a School Nurse Delivered Intervention to Reduce Student Anxiety," *Journal of Clinical Child and Adolescent Psychology* 50, no. 2 (March–April 2021): 177–86; also see "CALM—Child Anxiety

Learning Modules: From Research to Practice at Scale in Education," Institute of Education Sciences, November 3, 2020, at ies.ed.gov.

page 202 **When middle schools in Maryland implemented such a program:** For more on this, see Phyllis Fagell, "Teen Suicides Are on the Rise: Here's What Parents Can Do to Slow the Trend," *The Washington Post,* March 18, 2019.

page 202 **"This will simply let me know that your child:** There are different versions of "Handle with Care" notes that teachers send home to parents. This is just one version of many being shared online. A longer version of this handout reads: "If your family is experiencing difficulties at home, I would like to provide additional support at school. I understand that you are not always able to share details and that's okay. If your child is coming to school after a difficult night, morning, or weekend, please text me 'Handle with Care.' Nothing else will be said or asked. This will let me know that your child may need extra time, patience, or help during the day." https://www.smartschoolhouse.com/lifestyle/handle-with-care-note.

page 202 **The program has been so successful in reducing student anxiety and depression:** For more on this, see David Leffler, " 'I Began Feeling Like I Mattered': How On-Campus Mental Health Counseling Can Make a Big Difference," *The Washington Post,* August 19, 2019.

Chapter Twelve: Ready Her to Stand on Her Own

page 205 **A mastery curve experience is one of the most powerful support systems:** Suttie, "What Adolescents Really Need from Parents."

page 205 **In studies of adolescents, finding a purpose and passion:** K. C. Bronk et al., "Purpose, Hope, and Life Satisfaction in Three Age Groups," *The Journal of Positive Psychology* 4, no. 6 (November 2009): 500–510.

page 206 **In one study, when researchers looked at optimism levels:** L. O. Lee et al., "Optimism Is Associated with Exceptional Longevity in 2 Epidemiologic Cohorts of Men and Women," *Proceedings of the National Academy of Sciences* 116, no. 37 (September 2019): 18357–62.

page 206 **The whole point is that it be *self*-desired:** D. S. Yeager, R. E. Dahl, and C. S. Dweck, "Why Interventions to Influence Adolescent Behavior Often Fail but Could Succeed," *Perspectives on Psychological Science* 13, no. 1 (January 2018): 101–22.

page 206   **And so they lose interest:** For more advice on helping children find passion projects, see Jill Suttie's excellent article in which she interviews Ronald Dahl, Ph.D., "What Adolescents Really Need from Parents."

page 206   **Having the opportunity to see one's talents being realized:** Two key components to human flourishing are self-realization (becoming aware of your talents and limitations) and self-actualization (developing those talents and using them so that you reach your potential), according to Robert C. Whitaker.

page 209   **If we provide exposure and opportunity:** Suttie, "What Adolescents Really Need from Parents."

page 210   **This includes, says Bedera, basic stuff like teaching girls:** Nicole Bedera, "What to Say to Your Daughter About Campus Sexual Assault," *Slate,* March 2, 2020.

page 210   **In one recent study, University of Minnesota researchers:** D. M. Ackard et al., "Parent-Child Connectedness and Behavioral Emotional Health Among Adolescents," *American Journal of Preventive Medicine* 30, no. 1 (January 2006): 59–66.

page 210   **Reducing self-blame has been found to help girls:** C. Y. Senn et al., "Efficacy of a Sexual Assault Resistance Program for University Women," *New England Journal of Medicine* 372, no. 24 (June 2015): 2326–35. This understanding is also based on my email exchanges with Nicole Bedera at the University of Michigan.

page 212   **When professors allowed for open discussion:** J. J. Lee and J. M. McCabe, "Who Speaks and Who Listens: Revisiting the Chilly Climate in College Classrooms," *Gender and Society* 35 (February 2021): 32–60.

page 212   **In her 2019 book, *The Witches Are Coming,* Lindy West argues that women:** "'The Witches Are Coming'—and They Are Rightfully Angry," *Morning Edition,* NPR, November 11, 2019.

page 213   **"It is the voice women use when speaking truth about their value":** Hillary L. McBride and Janelle L. Kwee, "Intergenerational Journeys," in *Embodiment and Eating Disorders: Theory, Research, Prevention, and Treatment,* eds. Hillary L, McBride and Janelle L. Kwee (New York: Routledge, 2018). This quote is also based on my email exchanges with Hillary McBride.

page 215   **Perhaps one good use of social media is this:** One such Twitter feed is @EverydaySexism.

page 216 **My work over the past thirty years has taught me a great deal:** Benedict Carey, "Susan Nolen-Hoeksema, Psychologist Who Studied Depression in Women, Dies at 53," *The New York Times,* January 13, 2013.

page 216 **That story of who you believe you are can shadow you:** Suttie, "What Adolescents Really Need from Parents."

page 217 **"Imagine that, along the way, this note has to get delivered":** To put this in more scientific terms, the brain signals the body's hypothalamus, pituitary, and adrenal glands (also known as the HPA axis) and the sympathetic nervous system that a threat is incoming, and if the threat is deemed worrisome, they send that message all the way to the immune system.

page 218 **Writing-to-heal for just twenty minutes a day has been shown:** S. F. Allen, M. A. Wetherell, and M. A. Smith, "Online Writing About Positive Life Experiences Reduces Depression and Perceived Stress Reactivity in Socially Inhibited Individuals," *Psychiatry Research* 284 (February 2020): 112697; J. M. Smyth et al., "Effects of Writing About Stressful Experiences on Symptom Reduction in Patients with Asthma or Rheumatoid Arthritis: A Randomized Trial," *JAMA* 281, no. 14 (April 1999): 1304–9; J. W. Pennebaker, J. K. Kiecolt-Glaser, and R. Glaser, "Disclosure of Traumas and Immune Function: Health Implications for Psychotherapy," *Journal of Consulting and Clinical Psychology* 56, no. 2 (April 1988): 239–45; O. Glass et al., "Expressive Writing to Improve Resilience to Trauma: A Clinical Feasibility Trial," *Complementary Therapies in Clinical Practice* 34 (February 2019): 240–46.

page 221 **By observing our own story in a way that "promotes more reflection":** Tippett, "Rachel Yehuda: How Trauma and Resilience Cross Generations."

Conclusion

page 229 **When it comes to ensuring child well-being:** This idea was also suggested to me by Tey Meadow, Ph.D., associate professor of sociology at Columbia University and author of the excellent book *Trans Kids: Being Gendered in the Twenty-First Century.* We spoke about this idea primarily in the context of youth who identify as LGBTQ. According to Meadow: "It stands to reason that the effects of stress take a physical toll on one's body and brain." This is especially true for LGBTQ youth, for whom discrimination "attacks the core of their sense of self or threatens psychological or actual violence . . . [yet] . . . While recognizing or identifying a connection between the stress of coming of age as an LGBTQ youth and a child's brain health may make the discrimination feel more urgent to us, my wish would be that poor treatment wouldn't need to hurt the body to be real. What if we just cared about not hurting these kids' feelings, not making them feel they are less worthy of love or happiness? Wouldn't that be enough?"

Appendix A: Growing Up Female, by the Numbers

page 233   **One out of four adolescent girls reports suffering from symptoms of major depression:** This data was prepared by Christina Bethell, Ph.D., director, Child and Adolescent Health Measurement Initiative, and professor at the Johns Hopkins Bloomberg School of Public Health, and was derived from the 2019 Youth Risk Behavior Survey as reported by the Centers for Disease Control and Prevention.

page 233   **The rate of adolescent girls suffering from major depressive:** Bethell, using data from the 2019 Youth Risk Behavior Survey.

page 233   **Girls and young women today are twice as likely as boys to suffer from anxiety:** C. S. Mott Children's Hospital, "How the Pandemic Has Impacted Teen Mental Health," 1; Davis, "Women Twice as Likely as Men to Experience Anxiety, Research Finds"; O. Remes et al., "A Systematic Review of Reviews on the Prevalence of Anxiety Disorders in Adult Populations," e00497.

page 233   **Depression is occurring more often in girls today than in the past:** J. Breslau et al., "Sex Differences in Recent First-Onset Depression in an Epidemiological Sample of Adolescents," e1139. Figure 1 shows that 16 percent of first-onset depression among adolescent girls now occurs at age twelve or thirteen; 28.3 percent of first-onset depression occurs by age fourteen.

page 233   **By age seventeen, more than one-third of girls report:** Breslau et al., "Sex Differences in Recent First-Onset Depression in an Epidemiological Sample of Adolescents," e1139. Also see: Ariana Eunjung Cha, "More Than a Third of Teenage Girls Experience Depression, New Study Says," *The Washington Post*, May 31, 2017; Phyllis L. Fagell, "Dealing with Disturbing Spike in Youth Suicides," *The Washington Post*, March 18, 2019.

page 234   **Between 2016 and 2020, girls were, on average, 48 percent:** This data was prepared by Christina Bethell, Ph.D., using data from the 2016–2020 National Survey of Children's Health.

page 234   **Between 2016 and 2020, girls had a 43 percent higher rate:** Bethell, using data from the 2016–2020 National Survey of Children's Health.

page 234   **Nearly 50 percent of young adult females report as many:** This data was prepared by Christina Bethell, Ph.D., and was derived from the 2015 Wisconsin Behavioral Risk Factor Survey.

page 234   **These statistical increases in depression and anxiety among today's girls:** Twenge et al., "Age, Period, and Cohort Trends in Mood Disorder Indicators and Suicide-Related Outcomes in a Nationally Representative Dataset, 2005–2017," 185–99.

page 234   **In 2019, one in three high school:** "Youth Risk Behavior Survey Data Summary & Trends Report: 2009–2019," Executive Summary, Centers for Disease Control and Prevention, 59. https://www.cdc.gov/healthyyouth/data/yrbs/pdf/YRBSDataSummaryTrendsReport2019-508.pdf.

page 234   **Every year, the gap between the rates at which girls and boys:** These figures were prepared by Christina Bethell, Ph.D., using data from the 2016–2020 National Survey of Children's Health.

page 234   **Sixty-three percent fewer males develop depression:** K. H. Abate, "Gender Disparity in Prevalence of Depression Among Patient Population: A Systematic Review," *Ethiopian Journal of Health Science* 23, no. 3 (November 2013): 283–88. This was a systemic review and meta-analysis of research on gender differences in depression across multiple studies.

page 234   **The rate of preteen and teen girls who end their own lives:** Fagell, "Dealing with Disturbing Spike in Youth Suicides"; Ruch et al., "Trends in Suicide Among Youth Aged 10 to 19 Years in the United States, 1975 to 2016," e193886.

page 234   **Over the past ten years, the suicide rate:** Christina Caron, "What's Going on with Our Black Girls? Experts Warn of Rising Suicide Rates," *The New York Times,* September 10, 2021.

page 235   **Nearly half of parents noticed their teenager's mental health:** C. S. Mott Children's Hospital, "How the Pandemic Has Impacted Teen Mental Health," 1.

page 235   **Thirty-six percent of girls displayed new or worsening:** C. S. Mott Children's Hospital, "How the Pandemic Has Impacted Teen Mental Health," 1.

page 235   **Emergency room visits for mental health crises rose 31 percent:** Leeb et al., "Mental Health–Related Emergency Department Visits

Among Children <18 Years During the COVID-19 Pandemic," 1675–80; for details on sex differences, see Supplementary Figure 2; for further reading, see Carey, "For Some Teens, It's Been a Year of Anxiety and Trips to the E.R."; Hill et al., "Suicide Ideation and Attempts in a Pediatric Emergency Department Before and During COVID-19," e2020029280.

page 235   **Ten percent of men who've experienced two or more types of childhood adversity:** These numbers were prepared by Robert C. Whitaker, M.D., M.P.H., using data from the Longitudinal Survey of Midlife Development in the United States (MIDUS). The MIDUS surveys used the Composite International Diagnostic Interview–Short Form (CIDI-SF) scale to measure major depression, panic disorder, and generalized anxiety disorder in adult men and women.

page 235   **Eight percent of men who have a history of three or more types of childhood adversity:** Data prepared by Whitaker, from the Longitudinal Survey of Midlife Development in the United States (MIDUS).

page 235   **For each category of childhood stress a girl faces prior to the age of eighteen:** D. Fairweather et al., "Cumulative Childhood Stress and Autoimmune Diseases in Adults," *Psychosomatic Medicine* 71, no. 2 (February 2009): 243–50.

page 236   **In college classrooms, men speak 1.6 times more often than women:** Lee and McCabe, "Who Speaks and Who Listens," 32–60.

page 236   **Although women make up more than half of medical school classes:** Arghavan Salles, "Sexual Harassment Is Still the Norm in Health Care," *Scientific American,* October 24, 2019.

page 236   **The more time a teenager spends on social media platforms:** Y. Kelly et al., "Social Media Use and Adolescent Mental Health: Findings from the UK Millennium Cohort Study," *EClinicalMedicine* 6 (January 2019): 59–68.

page 236   **Facebook's internal documents show that among girls:** Wells, Horwitz, and Seetharaman, "Facebook Knows Instagram Is Toxic for Teen Girls," A10.

page 236   **Forty percent of teens say feelings of being "unattractive":** Wells, Horwitz, and Seetharaman, "Facebook Knows Instagram Is Toxic for Teen Girls," A10.

page 236   **Among U.S. teens who report suicidal thoughts, 6 percent:** Ibid.

page 236   **The majority of girls start using social media apps between age eight and thirteen:** "New Poll Reveals How Young Children Are Using Social Media and Messaging Apps," National PTA, December 4, 2017.

page 236   **Nearly one in three young women reports having been coerced into having sex:** National Sexual Violence Resource Center, "Sexual Violence by Any Perpetrator," nsvrc.org, n.d.

page 236   **Among college students, 26 percent of females:** This statistic is from RAINN.org: https://www.rainn.org/statistics/campus-sexual-violence. D. Cantor, B. Fisher, S. Chibnall, et al., "Association of American Universities (AAU), Report on the AAU Campus Climate Survey on Sexual Assault and Sexual Misconduct" (January 17, 2020).

page 236   **Rates of PTSD in women, in general:** M. B. VanElzakker, "Post-traumatic Stress Disorder," in *Neuroscience in the 21st Century,* eds. D. W. Pfaff and N. D. Volkow (New York: Springer 2015), 4058.

page 237   **Female teens are less likely to report feeling their family:** This data was prepared by Christina Bethell and was derived from the 2015 Wisconsin Behavioral Risk Factor Survey.

page 237   **Over half of girls, compared with one-third of boys:** D. M. Ackard et al., "Parent-Child Connectedness and Behavioral Emotional Health Among Adolescents," 59–66.

INDEX

A

Abernathy, Julia, 20–24, 33, 39, 43, 52, 56, 67, 91–93, 94–97, 98, 99, 103, 114, 131, 133, 138, 167–68, 173, 178, 180–82, 183, 184, 187–88, 189, 190, 195–96, 198, 200, 208, 211–12, 213, 217–18, 224, 225–26

abortion laws, restrictive, 97

academic stress, 5–6, 129–31

accommodating behaviors, 154–56

achievement pressures, 39–42, 49–50, 129–31

adverse childhood experiences (ACEs), 12, 17n, 177, 272n; impact of, 76–77, 134–37; mitigating negative effects of, 152, 178–79; of parent, recognizing and understanding, 119–23, 124–25; sex differences in, 99–101, 161, 235

adversities: age-appropriate, 153–58; helping child stay calm and self-regulated in face of, 122

adversity, use of term, 121

advice, requests for, 146–47

advisor at school, as avatar, 180–82

amygdala, 106, 109, 127, 144, 150, 219

Angelou, Maya, 127, 218

anger, 6, 23, 110, 115, 120, 140, 170, 220; helping daughter deal with, 136, 142, 146, 148, 151–53; of women, negative views of, 97, 115, 212

anxiety, xi–xii, 114, 120, 136, 170, 174, 189; achievement pressures and, 39–42, 129–31; adverse childhood experiences and, 71, 99–101, 235; CALM program and, 201–2; epigenetic changes and, 42, 56–57, 84, 104–5, 107, 177; helping daughter deal with, 151–58, 169, 177, 184–85, 191; inflammatory stress factors and, 66, 70; personal stories of, 3, 6–7, 59–62, 75–76, 153, 167; rising rate of, in girls, 8–12, 18–19, 24–25, 34, 37–40; sex differences in, 9–11, 99–103, 108, 109, 233, 234, 235 apologizing, 6, 110, 126, 148, 212; for messing up in parenting interaction, 148–51

appearance: sexist culture and, 33, 55–56, 98–99; social media and, 21, 29–30; unwanted comments about, 130, 211. *See also* body image

assertiveness, female, 266n

autoimmune diseases, 66, 77–78, 82–83, 135, 175, 235, 263n, 264n

avatar, use of term, 181

avatars, 180–90, 278n; acting as, for girls outside your family, 185–86, 187–88; advisor at school as, 180–82; asking daughter to "identify the helpers" and, 185; female-centric groups and, 187–90; grandmother as, 182–83, 184; men as, 187; neuroprotective effect of, 184, 185; shared parenting and, 184–87; teacher as, 183; therapist as, 196

B

Bale, Tracy, 47–52, 54–58, 154, 156

Bedera, Nicole, 210–11

being heard, importance of, 132–33, 146

benefactors, 178, 220, 221. *See also* avatars; mentors

Bethell, Christina, 134–37, 138, 142, 152, 177–80, 250n

biosynchrony, 137

Black Americans, 90; children, suicide among, 66–67, 234. *See also* racism and racial injustice

body image, 192, 226, 255n; family connection and, 137–38; social media and, 4–5, 21, 25–26, 28, 30, 33, 55–56, 236

body language, 145–46

brain: of boy, toxic gender messages and, 110–11; chronic stress in childhood and, 15–17, 47–58; default mode network (DMN) of, 107–9; development of, in infancy, 120; dorsal attention network (DAN) of, 108–9; epigenetic changes to, in puberty, 50, 54–58, 87–88; of girl, changed by feeling unsafe, 104–11; learning from wobbles and, 153–58; sex differences in, 11–12, 17–18, 48, 51, 56–57; social media's impact on, 27–31, 35

breath work, 149, 173, 198–99, 200

Brown, Brené, 144, 219

bullying, 13, 60, 61, 66, 70, 74, 108, 110, 126, 156, 189, 260n

C

CALM (coordinated anxiety learning and management), 201–2

calm, calming, 118, 122, 125, 132, 135, 145, 146, 149–50, 158; parent's state of, offered for child, 127–28; therapeutic techniques for, 196, 199, 200, 218, 219, 220

climate change, 14, 55–56, 67, 86, 106, 163, 174, 193, 208

Cogan, Robin, 24–25, 29

college, 193, 225–26; getting into, 5–6, 15, 22, 39–40, 41, 62, 75, 129, 130, 131; male behavior at, 94–95, 96–97, 212, 236; professor at, as avatar, 183; women's difficult experiences at, 6–8, 75–76, 133, 171, 196, 197, 222, 236

community: female-centric groups and, 189–90; hunter-gatherer, legacy of, 17–18, 62–65, 71–72, 86, 109, 188; "my kid first" environment vs., 41–42; positive relational experiences with, 166, 177–80; purposeful, being part of, 191–92; safety conferred by, 40–41, 87–88

community stressors, 13–14

consciousness, of children, 158–59, 275n

cortisol, 56–57, 84, 136, 139, 264n

COVID-19 pandemic, 13, 14, 39, 153, 171, 174, 194, 235; achievement pressures during, 129–31
cytokines, 82, 83, 199, 217

D

Dahl, Ron, 147, 188, 205
DEAR MAN technique, 164–65
depression, 132, 136, 189, 193, 199, 202, 203, 218; achievement pressures and, 39–42, 129–31; chronic stress and, 84, 89, 104–7, 120; comfort in nature or spirituality and, 190–93; epigenetic changes and, 42, 56–57, 84, 104–7, 177, 209; personal stories of, 5–8, 59–62, 75–76, 167, 184, 194, 225; positive childhood experiences as protection against, 177–78; recognizing signs of, 197–98; rising rate of, in girls, 8–12, 18–19, 24–25, 32, 47, 234, 250n, 251n; rumination and, 216–17; sex differences in, xi–xii, 9–11, 56–57, 99–103, 109, 111, 233–34, 235, 236; social media use and, 25–35, 66; social threats, inflammation and, 66, 70–72
difficult emotions, naming, 146
dinner, family rules and, 166, 167, 172–73
distractions from hard moments, 141–42

E

eating disorders, 5, 6–7, 25, 255n
Eilish, Billie, 98
electronic devices: family rules and, 167–73. See also social media
emotional abuse or neglect, 179
empathy: listening and, 145; offering child a state of, 132–33
enjoyable experiences, savoring, 151–53
environmental insults, 48–52, 55, 83
environmental stressors, 13–15

epigenetics. See gene expression
estrogen, 17, 68, 88, 162; inflammation and, 52, 77–84, 264n; puberty and, 52–58, 258n
evolutionary origins of social threat response, 17–18, 62–65, 71–72, 86, 109, 188
extended family, 167, 176, 184

F

Facebook (Meta), 21, 25–26, 163, 170, 231, 236, 253–54n. See also Instagram
Fairweather, DeLisa, 77–80, 83, 85, 263n
family life, 237; media engagement and, 167–73; of parent during own childhood, 134–35; rebuilding relationships and, 153; resilience vs. happiness as goal of, 157–58; sense of connection in, 134–38, 142, 163, 166–67; sense of safety in, 139–41; societal shortcomings and, 137; structure and routine in, 166–69; wondering aloud together and, 158–61. See also parent-child connection
Family Resilience and Connection Index (FRCI), 135–37
female-centric groups, 189–90
fetal development, 48–49, 50–52, 257n
fight, flight, or freeze (stress response), 14, 57, 106–7, 119, 126, 127, 140, 199, 258n, 264n. See also social threat response
fixing vs. listening, 141, 144
freeze response, 140. See also fight, flight, or freeze
friendships, female, 55, 188–89
future, leading from, 227–31

G

gender, use of term, 9n
gendered and sexist messaging, 5, 79, 86, 103, 109, 110–11, 115, 192, 226; in social media, 25, 28, 30, 33, 55–56, 161, 163

gender inequities, 31, 33–34, 212, 227
genderism, as trauma for girls, 101
gender roles, traditional, 110, 210, 211, 212, 213
gene expression (epigenetics), 49–52, 81n, 124; environmental circumstances and, 17, 51, 72–73, 196, 263n; fetal development and, 50–52; mental and physical health disorders and, 17, 42, 56–57, 72–73, 78, 83, 84, 104–7, 114–15, 209; possibilities for positive change and, 85, 177; puberty and, 50, 54–58, 88–89; stress and, 17, 49–52, 56–57, 72–73, 78, 81n, 84, 105–6, 124–25, 199, 217; therapies and, 196, 199
genes, 62, 71, 162, 257n, 262n; predispositions and, 49, 65, 72, 114
glucocorticoids (GCs), 83, 264n
Gopnik, Alison, 158–59
Gordon, Joshua, 66–67
Grady Trauma Project, 90
grandmother, as avatar, 182–83, 184
Greene, Deleicea, 59–62, 66, 68, 71, 74–77, 81, 98, 108, 133, 137, 138, 143–44, 166, 178, 186–87, 191, 196, 199, 206–7, 222–23, 224, 225, 226
guiding vs. acting as leader, 161

H
Hackett, Faith, 172–73
Haidt, Jonathan, 27, 252n, 254n
happiness, 64, 157–58, 159
hard-to-hear information, 141–48; empathic validation of, 145, 146; requests for advice and, 146–47. See also listening
high-risk behaviors, 132, 137
hippocampus, 106–7
holidays, family rituals and, 167
hopefulness, 205–6
hopelessness, 234
household stressors, 12–14

hunter-gatherers, social threat response as legacy of, 17–18, 62–65, 71–72, 86, 109, 188

I
identity, 15, 195; girls' loss of safe transitional period for formation of, 37–40
identity project, 205–6
immune system, 16, 49, 51, 85, 90, 101, 120; microglia and, 104–5; nervous system and, 139–40; puberty and, 52, 55n, 79–80; rumination and, 216–17; social threats and, 64–66, 68, 71–72, 79; stress and, during puberty, 79–84, 100–101, 104–5; stress response and, 14, 56, 64, 79–80, 81–82, 104. See also autoimmune diseases
infants: brain development in, 120; parent's connection to, 117–18, 119–20
inflammation, 261–62n; depression and, 66, 70–72, 217; estrogen and, 52, 77–84, 264n; microglia and, 104–5; parental support and connection and, 136; psychotherapy and, 196; reduced by yoga, meditation, and breathing exercises, 199; rumination and, 216–17; stress response and, 14, 16, 52, 64, 65, 66, 69, 106, 216–17
inflammatory disorders, 78, 135, 136
Instagram, 25–26, 27, 28, 29, 103, 164–65, 170, 172, 194, 210, 236, 252n
interconnectedness, fostering, 190–93

J
Johnson, Ned, 155
joyful moments, savoring, 151–53

K
Karlen, Amy, 36–39, 42, 43, 125, 130, 132–33, 147–48, 151, 157–58, 164, 180, 189, 197, 203

L

Lanius, Ruth, 108
Laundrie, Brian, 103–4
LGBTQ youth, 81, 284n
life-or-death stressors, 15
life satisfaction, feelings of, 205–6
listening, 126; asking open-ended
    questions and, 145–46; attentive,
    127, 132–33, 143–44, 146, 148; to
    child's worries, 274n; fixing vs.,
    141, 144; to hard-to-hear
    information, 141–48; importance
    of being heard and, 132–33, 146;
    judging or problem-solving vs.,
    147–48; social engagement system
    and, 140–41
loneliness, feelings of, 172, 179, 274n
lupus, 78, 135, 235

M

male gaze, 34, 185
mansplaining, 23, 94–95, 96–97
masculinity, toxic, 110
mastery, encouraging a sense of,
    205–9
Maté, Gabor, 122–23
mattering, sense of, 179–80
McBride, Hillary Lianne, 137–38, 192,
    213, 255n
McCarthy, Margaret, 87–89, 90–91,
    111, 264n–65n
meditation, 128, 173, 198–200
mentors, 149, 175, 178–79, 184, 185,
    187–88. See also avatars
microglia, 55n, 104–5
Miller, Lisa, 191–92
mind-body connection, 216–17
mind-body therapies, 198–200
mindfulness, 128, 191, 198–200, 218
mindful parenting, 132, 148
mirroring, 149–50
misogyny, 31–32, 35, 163, 209–10, 212,
    227
modeling skills for your daughter, 161
Moralis, Anna, 3–8, 33, 43, 52, 55–56,
    67, 98, 130–31, 138, 142–43, 153,

166–67, 178, 182–85, 191, 193–95,
    198, 199–200, 207, 212–13,
    224–25, 226
multigenerational female groups,
    187–90
Murthy, Vivek, 34–35

N

narrative. See self-narrative
nature, immersion in, 159, 190–91,
    192–93
nervous system: pent-up stress trapped
    within, 127; regulating, 149, 150,
    152–53; sense of safety and,
    139–41; soothing, 77, 199, 219
Neural Re-Narrating™, 123, 218–22
noticing positive behaviors, 129–31
Nussbaum, Emily, 35
Nye, Rebecca, 159, 275n

O

Obama, Michelle, 186
objectification, 31, 34, 39, 67, 96,
    98–99, 188, 192, 213, 228
open-ended questions, 145–46
optimism, 205–6
Orenstein, Peggy, 98–99
ostracism, 28, 55, 60, 63, 110, 170, 189
overprotecting girls, 115, 153–58

P

painful emotions, responding to,
    141–48
parent-child connection, 117–38;
    apologizing for messing up in,
    148–51; challenges from world at
    large and, 174–75; electronic
    devices intruding on, 170–71;
    ensuring that conversations are
    positive experiences and, 131–33;
    hard-to-hear information and,
    141–48; healing one's own trauma
    story and, 124–28, 133; joyful
    moments and, 151–53; leaving
    room for "wobbles" and, 153–58;
    moments of disconnection and,

parent-child connection *(cont'd)*
118, 122–23; noticing positive
behaviors and, 129–31; recognizing
and understanding one's own
trauma story and, 119–23, 124,
125, 128; Still Face Experiment
and, 117–18, 120. *See also* family
life
passion projects, finding, 205–9
peers, being evaluated by, 188–90
Pentagon, female-centric groups at,
190
perfectionism, 40, 201
Perry, Bruce, 144
Petito, Gabby, 103–4
Pipher, Mary, 18, 176
pituitary gland, 52–53, 284n
pleasure, savoring, 151–53
poetry, writing-to-heal and, 222–23
polyvagal theory, 140–41
Porges, Stephen, 140–41
positive childhood experiences (PCEs),
177–80
posttraumatic stress disorder (PTSD),
11n, 102–3, 108, 218, 236–37,
277n
poverty, 13, 17n, 40, 48, 66, 80–81, 136,
137, 228, 263n
power-with vs. power-over dynamic,
161
prefrontal cortex, 89, 106–7, 156, 268n
pregnancy, 257n, 264n, 265n; positive
experiences in childhood and,
276–77n. *See also* fetal
development
problem-solving, developing
competence in, 153–58
professional help, 193–200. *See also*
therapy
psychotherapy, 128, 180, 196–97
puberty, xii, xiii, xv, 12, 17, 19, 52–58, 62,
77–93, 109, 126, 229, 258n, 264n;
earlier onset of, 87–93, 162, 265n;
epigenetic changes to brain in, 50,
54–58, 87–88; process of, 52–54;
social and cultural forces and, 31,
43, 54–58, 67–68, 70, 79, 102; stress-
immune response and, 79–84,
100–101, 104–5; teaching daughter
coping skills before, 162–65
purpose, finding sense of, 205–9

R

racism and racial injustice, 3, 13, 15,
56, 66, 67, 179, 228, 263n
rape, 95–96, 97, 98, 126, 236
reactivity, rooted in childhood, 125–26
reading together as family, 166, 168–69
receptive mattering, 180
reframing, 217–18, 220–22
relational awareness, 159–60, 275n
religiosity, 192
repairing your mistakes, 148–51
resistance, developing voice of, 209–15
ritual and routine, in family life,
166–69
Rogers, Fred, 132
ruminating, 66, 68–69, 127, 140, 151,
188, 200, 209; breaking cycle of
negative self-talk and, 216–23;
getting in touch with person
beneath, 190; in girls vs. boys,
109–10; harm done by, 110,
216–17; writing-to-heal and,
218–22

S

Sacks, Oliver, 32
sadness, feelings of, 234
safety, sense of, 72–73, 144; adversities
today's children face and, 13–17;
girl's brain changed by lack of,
104–11; in interactions with
parents, 131–33; nervous system
and, 139–41; in parent's own
childhood, 134; positive
experiences with women outside
family and, 178–79, 184; sex
differences in, 101–4
Scharmer, Otto, 227
school and mass shootings, 3, 5, 13, 14,
31, 39, 56, 67, 86, 163, 174

school mental health programs, 201–3
self, sense of, 204–23; breaking cycle of
    negative self-talk and, 216–23;
    disturbances in brain's default
    mode network and, 107–9; mastery
    and (finding a purpose or passion),
    205–9; voice of resistance and,
    209–15
self-blame, lessening likelihood of,
    209–10, 212–13, 215, 220
self-esteem, time spent on social media
    and, 26, 30–31, 236
self-harm behaviors, 29, 61, 74–76,
    206
self-narrative, 107, 124, 126, 205, 206;
    narrative writing-to-heal and, 123,
    128, 218–22
self-talk, negative. See ruminating
Seney, Marianne, 105–6, 111
sex, use of term, 9n
sexism, 43, 72, 98, 161, 179, 209–10;
    changing culture of, 228–29. See
    also gendered and sexist messaging
sexist remarks, responding to, 213–15
sexual assault, 56, 103, 210–11, 236;
    rape and, 95–96, 97, 98, 126, 236
sexual coercion, 96, 98, 126, 212–13,
    236. See also rape
sexual harassment, 31–32, 33–34, 67,
    103, 210–11, 236
sexualization imposed from outside,
    38–39, 92, 126, 133, 162–63
shared parenting, 184–87. See also
    avatars
shootings. See school and mass
    shootings
Slavich, George, 64, 65–66, 68, 69, 119,
    120, 176, 196, 216–17
Smith, Paxton, 97
social engagement system, 140–41
social media, 4–5, 18, 79, 103, 236;
    body image and, 4–5, 21, 25–26,
    28, 30, 33, 55–56, 236; chronic
    stress and, 13–15; emotional
    suffering in young people due to,
    171, 172–73; family life and,

167–73; fear and anxiety magnified
    by, 170; gendered and sexist
    messaging in, 25, 28, 30, 33, 55–56,
    161, 163; neurobiological
    responses to, 109, 170; self-esteem
    and time spent on, 26, 30–31, 236;
    setting limits for, 163–65, 167–73;
    toxic to teen girls' mental health,
    25–35, 38–39
Social Safety Theory, 64, 72, 100–101,
    110, 188
social stressors, 13–14
social threat response, 62–73, 108–9,
    188; inflammation and depression
    linked to, 66, 69–71; origins of, in
    hunter-gatherer times, 17–18,
    62–65, 71–72, 86, 109, 188;
    ruminating and, 68–69, 110
societal values, extrinsic vs. intrinsic,
    171, 209
somatic energy, 127
SPACE (Supportive Parenting for
    Anxious Childhood Emotions),
    154–55
Spears, Britney, 35
spirituality, 190, 191–92, 279n
starling effect, 40–43, 184
Starrs, Bronagh, 180
Still Face Experiment, 117–18, 120
Stixrud, William, 155
stress, 48–58, 235; autoimmune
    diseases and, 235; chronic,
    depression and, 84, 89, 104–7, 120;
    epigenetics and, 17, 49–52, 56–57,
    72–73, 78, 81n, 84, 105–6, 124–25,
    199, 217; four domains of, 12–14;
    healthy vs. toxic, 157; sex
    differences in response to, 104–11
stress response. See fight, flight, or
    freeze; social threat response
suicidal ideation, 76, 107, 137, 236,
    261n
suicide rate: in Black children, 66–67,
    234; rising among girls, 32; sex
    differences in, 10, 234, 249–50n
synaptic pruning, 55n, 104–7

T

talk therapy, 128, 193–98, 279n
Tannen, Deborah, 188–89
teacher, as avatar, 183
testosterone, 53, 258n
therapy, 128, 193–203; epigenetic
    effects of, 196, 199; mind-body
    techniques and, 198–200; need for
    greater accessibility to, 197;
    recognizing need for, 197–98, 201;
    school programs and, 201–3;
    talking to daughter about, 196–97;
    talk therapy and, 128, 193–98,
    279n
Traister, Rebecca, 97
transgender people, 9n, 81n, 284n
trauma story of parent, 155; biologic
    and epigenetic changes and,
    124–25; healing, 124–28, 133, 149;
    recognizing and understanding,
    120–23, 124, 125, 128, 144
Tronick, Ed, 117–18, 121–22
Twenge, Jean, 26–27, 172, 252n, 254n
Twitter, 27, 30, 31–32, 194, 202, 215

U

unattractiveness, feelings of, 25–26,
    236
uncertainty, sense of, 13–14, 15, 129

V

vagus nerve, 139–41, 149, 199
validating daughter's emotions, 145,
    146
values, intrinsic vs. extrinsic, 171, 209
VanElzakker, Michael, 102–3

W

West, Lindy, 212
Whitaker, Bob, 99–100, 101, 161, 163,
    272n
wobbles, leaving room for, 153–58
wondering aloud together, 158–61
worries, of child: about being
    evaluated, 188–89; importance of
    listening to, 274n
writing-to-heal, 218–23; narratives
    and, 123n, 128, 218–22; poetry
    and, 222–23; reframing and,
    220–22

X

X and Y chromosomes, 50–51, 257n

Y

Yehuda, Rachel, 124–25, 186, 196,
    221–22
yoga, 198–99

ABOUT THE AUTHOR

Donna Jackson Nakazawa is the author of four books exploring the intersection of neuroscience, immunology, and emotion, including *The Angel and the Assassin*, named one of the best books of 2020 by *Wired* magazine. Jackson Nakazawa's other books include *Childhood Disrupted*, which was a finalist for the Books for a Better Life award. For her writing on health and science, she received the AESKU life contribution award and the National Health Information Award. Jackson Nakazawa is also the creator and founder of the narrative writing-to-heal program, Your Healing Narrative, which uses a process called Neural Re-Narrating™ to help participants recognize and override their brain's old thought patterns and internalized stories, and create a new, more powerful, inner healing narrative that calms the body, brain, and nervous system. Her work has appeared in *Wired, Stat, The Boston Globe, The Washington Post, Health Affairs, Aeon, Parenting, AARP Magazine*, and *Glamour* and has been featured on the cover of *Parade* as well as in *Time*; she has also appeared on the *Today* show, NPR, NBC News, and ABC News. She is a regular speaker at universities, including the 2020 Harvard Division of Science Library Series, Johns Hopkins University, and the University of Arizona. She lives with her family in Maryland.